# FAMILY FARE

a Mugnolo Family cookbook

## KATHLEEN MUGNOLO

**ARPress**
ILLUMINATING IDEAS,
EMPOWERING VOICES

**ARPress**
45 Dan Road Suite 5
Canton MA 02021
Hotline: 1(888) 821-0229
Fax:      1(508) 545-7580

Ordering Information:
Quantity sales. Special discounts are available on quantity purchases by corporations, associations, and others. For details, contact the publisher at the address above.

Printed in the United States of America.

| ISBN-13: | Softcover | 979-8-89330-296-7 |
|----------|-----------|-------------------|
|          | eBook     | 979-8-89330-295-0 |

Library of Congress Control Number:    2024901600

# Dedication

I dedicate this cookbook first and foremost to my loving husband, Jim, who has been so supportive and believing over the years that I would, in fact, bring this cookbook to completion.

And next to our children Carl Joseph, Tara Lisa, and Michael Todd—by whom I am privileged to be called Mother. They are my reason this book came into being. They are my gifts from God, and this is my gift to them, my legacy.

And to my mother, Anna, and Jim's mother, Josephine (known as Dolly), who have now passed away, their memory lingers forever in my heart, and I am forever grateful to them for the wonderful role models they were for me. And to my father, Joseph and Jim's father, Carl (now deceased), for their labors of love in always being there for me when I needed them.

And to my grandchildren—Mason, Aaron, Jennifer, and Anna. They too are my legacy! And to all future generations in whose hands this cookbook may pass, I hope this cookbook

will bring you much joy in your kitchen and in your families. While I am only to pass this way once, I am glad it is in this family.

God bless you all.

My sister-in-law, Loretta Sturgill, loves this old Italian quote:

"Italians don't measure seasonings.
We just sprinkle and shake until the spirits of our ancestors
whisper 'enough my child."

# *Introduction*

Welcome!

In these pages I invite you to come along and enjoy with me the foods I love, recipes I have acquired over the years from family and friends.

Every Italian family love to boast that their sauce is the best. Of course, that holds true for this family too! In my opinion, however, a recipe is only as good as the cook's ability to prepare it.

The recipes you'll find here are those my family loves the most of all the foods I have prepared over the years. I don't claim to be a connoisseur or chef, just a mom who loves to cook. I was fortunate to have the influence of two very special women in my life, my mother, and my mother-in-law, who both were excellent cooks. Their memory lingers forever in the hearts of us family members who lovingly remember so well the wonderful aroma of their kitchens and how they pampered us in so many ways.

Life is all about making memories, and what better way but through sharing good food and good fellowship! Come with me now, explore, prepare, taste, share, and enjoy.

*Buon Appetito!*

*Kathy*

Kathy Mugnolo

# We Are Family

Since before any of us were born, God planned for us to share our lives with each other. He knew exactly how our strengths and weaknesses would balance one another, and the depth of love, understanding, and commitment we would learn to feel.

He knew that the richness of our separate characters would be developed through the hard times, and that the mutual trust and respect would be born as a result of overcoming the trials together.

He knew that we would laugh together and cry together. He knew we needed each other to hug, to help, to teach, to share, to love.

G. Copeland

# Appetizers
## Appetizers

## Appetizers

# Antipasto

Serves 4

*What comes before the pasta or main course.*

Several leaves of lettuce
(Romaine, green leaf, and red leaf are nice)
1 recipe of marinated artichokes*
1 recipe of marinated mushrooms*
1 recipe of tomatoes in oil*
1 recipe of roasted red peppers*
1 recipe of garlic olives*
1 recipe of melon and prosciutto*
Salami, sliced thin
Capicola, sliced thin
Mozzarella cheese, sliced thin, or
provolone cheese, sliced thin
Hard -cooked eggs
Whole pepperoni peppers
Fish (optional): anchovies, tuna, sardines
Italian dressing*
*See recipe in this book.

A rrange lettuce leaves on attractive platter.
Arrange the listed antipasto ingredients attractively
from left to right on top of lettuce on platter.
Drizzle Italian dressing lightly overall. Serve as a first
course before dinner or as an appetizer.

*Buon Appetito!*

# Shriveled Black Olives, Italian-Style

*A standard on our family table just about every day! These olives are not picked but ripen and shrivel on the tree wrinkling naturally. Nets are placed under the trees and the olives fall off when fully ripe. They can be eaten directly from the tree but are dry cured for commercial use— sold for eating and not for making olive oil.*

1 or 2 jars of black wrinkled Greek olives
⅛ - ¼ cup extra-virgin olive oil
2-3 cloves minced garlic
Oregano (dry leaves crushed)
Crushed red pepper flakes

Place olives in a container with lid. (I have a special pottery olive jar)
Pour extra-virgin olive oil over olives
Add minced garlic, oregano, and crushed red pepper flakes. Stir.
Put lid on jar.
Leave to marinade a few hours or overnight.
Serve alongside just about anything and enjoy!

# Kathy's Artichoke Dip

*Serves 4- 6 people*

*This dip is the hit of every party! Say you don't like artichokes?? This just may change your mind!*

1 can artichoke hearts, quartered (14-oz size)
1 cup Romano cheese, grated fine
1 cup mayonnaise
Dash of Worcestershire sauce
2 tbsp. onion, chopped fine
Garlic powder, to taste
1 long French baguette bread

Drain artichoke hearts.
Place in bowl and mash with fork.
Add remaining ingredients.
Spoon into an attractive, buttered baking dish.
Bake in preheated 350 degrees oven for approximately 30-40 minutes until bubbly and golden.
Serve hot with thin slices of the French/Italian baguette bread.

# Artichokes in Lemon Juice

*Serves 4*

*Great addition to antipasto tray!*

2 (13 oz.) cans artichoke hearts
¼ cup lemon juice
¼ cup olive oil
2 cloves garlic, chopped fine
½ tsp. salt
¼ tsp. black pepper

Drain artichoke hearts and place in refrigerator to chill.
Combine remaining ingredients
Add artichoke hearts.
Chill until ready to serve.
When ready to serve, stir and serve as a separate appetizer or as part of antipasto.

# Artichokes Squares

*Serves 4 – 6*

*Great addition to a party!*

2 (6 oz.) jars marinated artichoke hearts
1 small onion
1 clove garlic, minced
5 eggs
⅓ cup dry Italian breadcrumbs
¼ tsp. salt
¼ tsp. pepper
¼ tsp. oregano
¼ tsp. Tabasco
¼ lb. sharp cheese, grated
1 tbsp. chopped parsley leaves
1 tbsp. Romano cheese, grated

Drain the marinade from one jar artichokes only into frying pan. Drain off remaining jar of artichokes.

Chop all artichokes into pieces. Sauté chopped artichokes, onion, and garlic in marinade until limp.

Beat eggs with fork, and add breadcrumbs, salt, pepper, oregano, Tabasco, sharp cheddar cheese, and parsley. Add sautéed artichoke mixture to egg mixture.

Pour into slightly buttered 8-by-11 baking pan. Sprinkle top with grated Romano cheese.

Bake in preheated 350 degrees oven for 30 minutes. Remove from oven, let sit 5 minutes, and cut into 1- ½ -inch squares.

*Note: These can be served hot or cold*

# Baked Brie

*Easy to make and makes a nice impression!*

1 4 - to 5-inch round brie cheese
3 tbsp. raspberry jelly
2 tbsp. almond slivers, toasted

Remove rind from brie. Place brie in an attractive round baking dish. Heat jelly on after stovetop or in microwave until just pouring consistency. Pour over brie.

Sprinkle with coasted slivered almonds.
Bake at 350 degrees for 5 minutes or so to melt the brie.
Serve with your choice of crackers. Yummy!

# Barbecued Shrimp

*Yields approximately 40-50 hors d'oeuvres*
*Quick, easy, delicious, and very popular at parties.*

1 lb. raw fresh or raw frozen shrimp
10-12 slices bacon, cut into thirds Barbecue sauce, your choice, bought or homemade

Thaw shrimp if frozen; then rinse with cold water.
Remove vein down back of shrimp.
Wrap each shrimp with a piece of bacon, securing with a toothpick.

Spray baking sheet or broiler pan with nonstick cooking spray. Place shrimp on baking sheet / broiler pan. Baste each shrimp with barbecue sauce.

Broil about 4 inches from broiler for 8 to 10 minutes till bacon is crisp. Turn over and broil additional 4 to 5 minutes longer.

# *Blue Cheese Tapanade on Grilled Bread*

*Yields 8*

*Forsythe Family recipe shared by our niece, Heather (Mugnolo) Forsythe, and nephew, Bryan Forsythe.*

4 thick slices of crusty Italian bread, cut in half.
Olive oil
Salt / black pepper
Red and/or yellow pepper strips
Sugar
Balsamic vinegar
Thick slice of onion, Vidalia good
Cream cheese
Kalamata olives
Dried parsley
Crushed red pepper
One clove of raw garlic
Basil, green or purple leaf

Cut bread slices in half. Place olive oil on plate with salt. Dip bread in oil. Grill bread slices oil side down until lightly charred. Place thin strips of red and yellow pepper (8) on a baking pan. Cover peppers in olive oil, salt, black pepper, sugar, and balsamic vinegar mixture.
Broil peppers in the oven, skin side down until soft. Flip peppers over and turn broiler off.
Let peppers rest in hot oven for 5 minutes.
Broil a thick slice of onion with olive oil, salt, and black pepper on the same broiler pan.

In food processor put equal parts cream cheese (2 tbsp. each), 16 black kalamata olives (pitted), pinch of dried parsley, pinch of crushed red pepper, 1 or 2 tbsp. olive oil, one clove raw garlic, roasted onion slice from above. Process until combined.

Place a green or purple basil leaf on each grilled bread slice. Top with cream cheese tapanade and garnish with roasted pepper. Serve.

*Buon Appetito!*

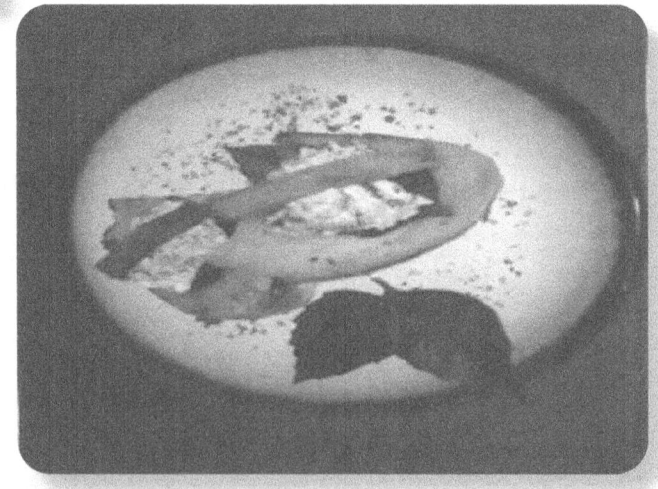

# Brie Cheese and Garlic/Shallot Spread

*Yields 1 cup*

*Easy make ahead spread to have on hand.*

6 cloves of garlic, unpeeled
2 shallots, unpeeled
6 tbsp. olive oil
7 oz. brie cheese, rind removed
2 tbsp. basil, chopped fine
Salt
Fresh cracked pepper
Baguette bread

Toss garlic cloves and shallots with 2 tbsp. of the olive oil. Bake wrapped in foil at 350 degrees Fahrenheit for approximately 35-40 minutes or until soft. Let cool completely, then squeeze the garlic and shallots from their skins and reserve.

Cut cheese in chunks and place it, remaining olive oil, garlic, and shallots in bowl of a food processor. Puree until smooth. Stir in chopped basil. Adjust seasoning with salt and fresh cracked pepper. Serve with garlic/buttered roasted slices of baguette bread. Enjoy!

# Broccoli Fondue

*Serve 6-8 people*

*Nice served in fondue pot.*

1 small onion, chopped
1 stick butter
1 pkg. chopped frozen broccoli
1 can cream of mushroom soup
1 small can mushrooms, chopped
1 pkg. boursin cheese (garlic/herb cheese)
3 shakes Tabasco
¼ tsp. black pepper
½ cup slivered almonds
Crackers, toast squares, or Melba rounds

Sauté onions in butter.

Drain broccoli.

Add to pan with onions and all other ingredients.

Simmer until thickened.

Serve in fondue pot with crackers, toast squares, or Melba rounds.

# *Broiled Chicken Wings*

*Serves 6-8 people*

*Everybody loves chicken wings, and these are no exception!*

2 lb. chicken wings*
6 tbsp. soy sauce
6 tbsp. lemon juice
¼ onion powder
2 tbsp. honey
2 tbsp. ketchup
Salt and pepper

*Drumettes are available in some grocery stores, which are only the half of the wing that resembles a chicken leg, which I like better.

Divide each wing into 2 parts at the joint.

Put in bowl.

Mix soy sauce, lemon juice, and onion powder, and pour over chicken.

Cover loosely and marinate in refrigerator several hours or overnight.

When ready to cook, arrange on foil-lined broiler pan.
Mix honey and ketchup with 2 tbsp. marinade, and brush half on wings.

Sprinkle with salt and pepper. Broil about 12 minutes.
Turn and brush with remaining basting sauce. Broil about 12 minutes more.

Serve as a finger-food appetizer.

# Broiled Stuffed Dates

*An unusual, delicious appetizers. Definitely that's something different*
*you might be looking for your next party!*

Dates (seeds removed)
Chopped nuts
Cream cheese
Sherry
Bacon

Soak dried dates in sherry at least 24 hours.

Split and fill dates with nuts or cream cheese or a combination of both.

Wrap ⅓ slice bacon around each tightly to seal in filling.

Secure with toothpick.

Broil or bake until bacon is crisp.

# Bruschetta

*Serves 8 people*

*I adapted this from a Mexican recipe for shrimp cocktail. Very popular as an appetizer at patio parties.*
*It is basically a Mexican salsa served Italian style on French baguette bread!*

¼ cup ketchup
¼ cup lime juice
1 to 2 tsp. Tabasco (hot pepper sauce)
1 lb. shrimp, fresh or frozen, peeled,
deveined, and cooked
2 cups chopped fresh tomato
¼ cup chopped onion
1 tsp. to 1 tbsp. snipped fresh cilantro
(your preference how much)
1 ripe avocado

In large bowl, stir together lime juice, ketchup, and hot pepper sauce.

Add shrimp, tomato, onion, and cilantro. Toss to coat.

Cover and chill for 2-4 hours. Just before serving, chop fine the pulp of avocado and add to salsa.

Serve with garlic toasted rounds of French baguette bread.

# Hot Cheese and Spinach Puffs

*Makes about 80 or more*
*Can be made ahead, frozen and reheated just before serving!*

1 10-oz. pkg. frozen, chopped spinach
½ cup chopped onion
2 slightly beaten eggs
½ cup grated Romano cheese
¼ cup shredded white Cheddar cheese
¼ cup butter or margarine, melted
⅛ tsp. garlic powder
1 cup herb stuffing mix (Pepperidge Farm)

Cook and drain spinach. Squeeze out liquid.
Combine with all remaining ingredients in bowl.
Chill mixture for 2 hours. Shape into balls.
Place on greased cookie sheet.
Bake at 350 degrees for 12 to 15 minutes.
Remove to paper towels. Cool. Freeze if desired.
When ready to serve, reheat on cookie sheet.
Must be served hot to be at their best.

# Cheese Log

*Yields 1 nice-sized log*
*Nice for the holidays.*

2 pkg. (3 oz.) cream cheese, softened
1 cup blue cheese, crumbled
3 tbsp. chili sauce
2 tbsp. onion, finely diced
1 tbsp. Dijon mustard
1 tsp. Worcestershire sauce
3 cups (12 oz.) cheddar cheese, shredded
¼ cup chopped green pepper
Pretzels. coarsely crushed

Beat first 6 ingredients together until smooth.

Stir in cheddar cheese and green pepper.

Shape into log.

Wrap in plastic wrap and chill several hours.

Just before serving, roll in crushed pretzels and garnish,

if desired

Serve with crackers or garlic-/butter-toasted baguette

bread slices.

# Cheese Ball

*A favorite at so many of our parties and family gatherings.*

2 8-oz. pkg. cheddar cheese
1 5-oz. pkg. blue cheese
2 8-oz. pkg. cream cheese
Dash garlic salt
Wine vinegar (2- 3 tbsp.)
Nuts, your choice, crushed

Blend all ingredients together. Refrigerate approximately 1 hour, then mold into ball.

Roll in crushed nuts.

Chill until serving time. Serve with your choice of crackers.

Note: Freezes nicely for future use.

# Cheese Fondue

*Serves 4-6 people*

*Nice treat to enjoy casually sitting around with family or friends.*

1 can cheddar cheese soup
1 cup French onion dip
4 oz. sharp cheddar cheese, shredded
Dash of crushed red pepper
1/2 tsp. dry mustard
French bread

Combine all ingredients in saucepan, and heat on low until cheese is melted. (The cheddar cheese melts quicker if grated first.)

Place in fondue pot. Light flame under pot. Stir often. Serve with chunks of French bread for dipping.

Enjoy!

# Chicken Drumettes (Italian Style)

*Serve 6-8 people*

*These are done basically just like my Italian Chicken in the Oven and are oh-so-good!*
*Great finger food. We served them often when boating on the Chesapeake Bay.*

3lb. chicken wings*
Cooking oil
3 cloves garlic
Salt, pepper
Parsley, chopped fine
Oregano
Red pepper flakes (optional)
Butter

*I cut off the excess fat before roasting

Cut wings at joint using only the drumstick end (or buy just the mini drumsticks at your grocery store to avoid waste).

Place enough cooking oil in bottom of open roast pan to coat lightly.

Place drumettes in pan. Sprinkle with garlic (chopped fine), salt, Pepper, parsley, oregano, and crushed red pepper if using to taste.

Dot with butter. Roast at 375 degrees for approximately 1 hour, turning occasionally.

Drain on paper towel and serve. Watch them disappear!

*Jim and me at Annapolis Inner Harbor*

# Crab Dabs

*Makes 30 hors d'oeuvres*
*A quick, easy, and delicious appetizer.*

18 oz. crabmeat, fresh or frozen
1/3 cup fine, soft breadcrumbs
1 tsp. dry mustard
1 tsp. chopped chives
2 tbsp. dry sherry or white wine
1/4 tsp. salt
10 to 12 slices bacon, cut in thirds

Drain crabmeat or thaw if frozen, then drain. Remove any cartilage.

Chop the crabmeat.
Combine all remaining ingredients except, the bacon.

Mix well. Chill for 25- 30 minutes.
Portion out crabmeat mixture by tablespoon.
Shape into small rolls about 1 1/2 inch each.

Wrap pieces of bacon around crab rolls and secure with a toothpick. Spray baking sheet with nonstick spray.
Place crab rolls on baking sheet, and broil about 4 inches from broiler for 8 to 10 minutes till bacon is crisp.

Turn rolls carefully and broil 4-5 minutes longer.

# Crab Dip

*Yields 1 cup*

*A favorite at so many of our family gatherings! My sister Mary has somehow inherited the task of making this for our family during the holidays and other special times.*

6 oz. fresh crabmeat
1 3-oz. pkg. cream cheese
1/4-cup mayonnaise
2 tbsp. minced onion
1 tbsp. ketchup

Pick crabmeat for cartilage and remove.
Combine remaining ingredients in bowl until fluffy.
Fold in crabmeat.
Chill until serving time. Serve with your choice of crackers.

Note: I at least double this recipe because it doesn't last long!

# Crab Boboli Appetizer

*Yields 8-10 wedges per Boboli*

*Boboli is a pizza-type round bread crust that can be purchased at most supermarkets.*

½ cup mayonnaise
1 tsp. lemon juice
¼ tsp. salt
1 6-oz. pkg. crabmeat
1 cup shredded Swiss cheese
1 11- inch Boboli crust (prebaked cheese crust)
1 tbs p. chopped green onions

Combine first 4 ingredients in medium bowl.
Add cheese. (This mixture can be prepared 8 hours ahead, covered and refrigerated until ready to use.)

Preheat oven to 450 degrees. Grease large baking sheet. Place crust on baking sheet. Spread crab mixture over. Sprinkle with green onions.

Bake until topping is puffed and brown, about 10 minutes. Cut into small wedges and serve immediately.

# Cucumber Dip

*Yields 3 cups*

*A nice, refreshing dip.*

3 8-oz. pkg. crem cheese
3 spring onions, grated
1 cucumber grated
1/2-pint sour cream
Sale, pepper, vinegar
Dash of red pepper
Assorted raw vegetables for dipping or your choice of crackers.

Mix all ingredients well. Season to taste.

Serve with your choice of crackers,
Melba rounds, assorted raw vegetables.

# Hot Pepper and Cheese Dip

*Yields 3cups*

1 1/2 pounds ground beef
1 large block of Velveeta cheese
2 cans Hormel brand of chili, without beans
1 jar of salsa, any brand
Garlic powder, to taste
Green chili peppers, chopped (optional)

Chop tomatoes and peppers.
Melt cheese in microwave or saucepan on low heat, being careful not to burn.
Combine with tomatoes, peppers, and onion.
Simmer for 1/2 hour on low. Stir occasionally.

Serve with your choice of crackers or tortilla chips.

# Deep Fried Mushrooms

*Serves 4-6*

*Serve these as is or great with a tangy ranch or blue cheese dressing!*

1 lb. mushrooms, clean and dry
1/4 cup flour
1 tsp. salt
1/16 tsp. black pepper
2 eggs, beaten
3/4 cup fine dry breadcrumbs
(Progresso Italian-style gives best flavor)

Trim mushrooms, leaving seems attached.
Dip each mushroom into flour mixed with salt and pepper, then into eggs.

Roll in breadcrumbs.
Fry in deep fat (about 1 to 2 inches deep fat) until golden. Drain on paper towels.

Serve as an hors d'oeuvre or accompaniment to meat.

# Hamburger Cheese Dip

*Serves a crowd*

*A specialty for our son, Carl. Adults and kids alike love this dip!*

2- lb. block Velveeta cheese
1 large can whole tomatoes, drained
1 large onion, chopped fine
1 can jalapeno peppers
Crackers or tortilla chips

Note: This is a great Super Bowl Dip!

Same the ground beef in a large skillet.

Add remaining ingredients.
Stir constantly until cheese melts and all ingredients are nicely blended.

Serve hot with your favorite brand of tortilla chips.

# Deviled Eggs

*Yields 24 halves*
*Simple and the way my family likes 'em!*

12 eggs, hard-boiled
Prepared mustard
Mayonnaise
Salt/ pepper
Paprika

Hard-boil the dozen eggs. Cool. Peel. Cut each egg in half. Carefully scoop out the hard-boiled egg yolk from inside each egg. Chop or mince very fine.

Place egg yolks in a bowl with desired amount of mustard, mayonnaise, salt, and pepper until the right taste and consistency.

Spoon filling back into egg halves.
Sprinkle with a little paprika, and chill until serving time. Enjoy!

# Deviled Eggs No.2

*Yields 24 halves*

*Another version, which is little different and very tasty.*

12 eggs, hard-boiled
1 tbsp. chives, fresh or dried is okay
2-3 tbsp. sour cream
Salt/pepper to taste
3 tbsp. butter
Seasoned breadcrumbs

(we use Italian seasoned, of course)

Hard-boil the dozen eggs and leave in the shell.
Take a sharp knife. Hold each egg on a nonslip surface. Proceed to cut each egg in half lengthwise carefully so as not to crush the shell.

Carefully scoop out the hard-boiled egg from the inside of each shell. Chop or mince egg very fine. Place in a bowl with the chives, sour cream, and a little salt and pepper. (You may add more of each if needed to blend.)

Spoon enough mixture back into each shell. Pat with spoon to level filling. Pour some breadcrumbs onto a plate. Invert each over breadcrumbs and press until coated. Melt butter in skillet. Brown each filled side in the butter until golden. Serve and enjoy!

# *Hot Mexican Bean Dip*

*Serves 4- 6 people*

*This dip has been a favorite of my kids, since they were little. Similar to the bean dip served at Anita's Mexican Restaurant in our area, but truly out of my head!*
*You may want to double the recipe. One just doesn't seem enough!*

1 can of refried beans
1 can chopped green chilies
Small can Hot Taco Sauce*
3 tbsp. cooking oil
Salt/pepper to taste
Garlic powder to taste
Monterey jack and/or sharp cheddar
Cheese, shredded
Tortilla chips

*Or maybe mild or medium, to taste.

Cover bottom of saucepan with cooking oil.
Add refried beans and heat slowly, stirring, while adding green chilies and Taco Sauce.

Taste, and add salt/pepper and garlic powder to suit your taste. Add 1/2 of the shredded cheese. Stir until melted, attending constantly to avoid burning.

Top with additional cheese just before serving, placing under broiler just until melted.

Serve hot with tortilla chips.

Note: You may do entire process in microwave oven, if desired. Heat on high 2 minutes at a time, stirring each time, till desired consistency, then top with more cheese and heat once more till melted. I serve this along with my version of tacos and Mexican rice (see recipes in this book).

# Italian Sausage Balls

*Serves a crowd*

*Very popular with the men at parties!*

4 lbs. Italian sausage
(hot or mild)
1 cup ketchup
1 cup wine vinegar
1 cup brown sugar
2 tbsp. soy sauce
1 tsp. ground ginger

Remove sausage meat from casings.
Form meat into walnut-size balls.
Fry in nonstick skillet till golden. *
Drain and marinate 4 hours to overnight in remaining ingredients.

Heat entire mixture in chafing dish and serve hot with toothpicks.

Double or triple recipe for parties as they do come back for more!

*Note: If not using a nonstick skillet, spray first with cooking spray

# Lobster Stuffed Mushrooms

*Makes 24 hors d'oeuvres*

*Very good!*

24 fresh mushrooms. about 1 1 /2
inches in diameter
1/2 lb. cooked lobster meat, fresh or frozen
2 tbsp. Italian breadcrumbs
1/4 cup cream of mushroom soup
2 tbsp. mayonnaise
Dash black pepper
1/4 tsp. Worcestershire sauce
1/8 tsp. hot sauce
Grated Romano cheese

Thaw lobster meal if frozen. Drain. Remove any cartilage or remaining shell. Chop meat.

Rinse mushrooms, pat dry, and remove stems.
Combine the soup, breadcrumbs, mayonnaise, pepper, Worcestershire sauce, hot sauce, and lobster.

Stuff each mushroom cap with a tablespoonful of mixture. Sprinkle with the grated Romano cheese. Bake in a wellgreased baking pan in a 400 degrees oven for 10 to 15 minutes or until lightly browned.

# *Layered Mexican Bean Dip*

*Serves a crowd*

*Great party dish.*

3 medium-size ripe avocados
2 tbs p. lemon juice
1/2 tsp. salt
1/4 tsp. black pepper
1 cup sour cream
1/2 cup mayonnaise
1 pkg. taco seasoning mix
2 cans refried beans
1 large bunch green onions with tops, chopped
3 medium tomatoes, cored, halved and diced
2 cans pitted ripe olives (3 1/2 oz.)
1 pkg. sharp cheddar cheese, shredded, large size
1 pkg. tortilla chips, large size

Peel, pit, and mash avocados with lemon juice salt and pepper.

Combine sour cream, mayonnaise, and taco seasoning mix in bowl.

Assemble in layers in a 9-by-13-inch glass Pyrex dish in following order:

Refried beans
Avocado mix
Sour cream, mayo, taco seasoning mix
Chopped onions
Tomatoes
Olives
Shredded cheese

Make top layer shredded cheddar.
Chill.

Very nice displayed in a colorful straw liner.
Serve, with tortilla chips.

# Marinated Mushrooms and Artichoke Hearts

*Serves 4*

*A long-time favorite of my husband, Jim, and our children, Carl, Tara,*

*and Michael. Great appetizer or addition to an antipasto tray!*

2 cans artichoke hearts
2 pkg. small fresh mushrooms*
1 cup white or red wine
vinegar, your choice
1/2 cup salad oil
1 clove garlic, crushed
1 1/2 tbsp. salt
1/2 tsp. black pepper
1/2 tsp. dried oregano leaves
1/2 tsp. chopped parsley leaves

* Or canned whole mushrooms.

Clean mushrooms by wiping with a clean, damp cloth.
Cut off tips of stems. Slice mushrooms in half and combine with halves of artichoke hearts.

Combine remaining ingredients.
Add to artichoke hearts and mushrooms. Pack into jars.

Marinate in refrigerator a minimum of 1 hour or overnight.
When ready to serve, stir and serve as a separate appetizer or as part of antipasto.

# Melon and Prosciutto

*Serves 8 people*

*This is exactly served the way Jim and I had it served to us at a restaurant in Rome, Italy. Buon Appetito!*

1 cantaloupe, chilled

8 thin slices prosciutto (Italian ham) Mint leaves

Wash and cut cantaloupe in half.

Remove seeds and skin and cut each half into four wedges.

Lay a slice or two prosciuttos on top of each wedge of cantaloupe.

Serve as an appetizer. Garnish with mint leaves

# Vegetable Dip

*Serves 4-6 people*

*Good old standby!*

1 10-oz. pkg. spinach, thawed and drained
1 can water chestnuts
1 pkg. dry vegetable soup mix
2 cups mayonnaise
1 cup sour cream

Mix all ingredients.

Chill in refrigerator until ready to use.

Serve with your choice of crackers and/or breads.

# Mom Mugnolo's Chicken Wings (Polynesian-Style)

*Serve 6-8 people*

*Jim's mom liked to branch out and try new things. This was definitely one of her best new things!*

3 lb. chicken wings
1/2 cup melted butter
1 tsp. salt
1/2 tsp. black pepper

**Sauce**

1/2 cup orange juice
1/2 cup creamed sherry or wine
1/2 cup soy sauce
1/2 cup sugar
1/8 tsp. garlic powder
1 tsp. ginger

Pour melted butter, salt, and black pepper mixture over chicken wings.
Stir to coat.

Bake in pan for 30 minutes at 325 degrees.
Next, put sauce ingredients in a saucepan.
Boil mixture together in saucepan for a short time and pour over wings.

Bake again at 325 degrees for 1-1 1/2 hours.

Turn wings occasionally.

Great for party dish or family gatherings!

# Parsleyed Cheese and Ham Pâté

*Serves a crowd!*

*A delicious, different spread well worth the effort. Garnish with a lemon slice and sprig of parsley.*

2 pkg. (8 oz.) cream cheese
1 cup Swiss cheese, grated
1 jar (4 3/4 oz.) stuffed olives, undrained
1/4 tsp. black pepper
1 tsp. dried basil leaves, or herb of your choice
2 envelopes unflavored gelatin
1 pkg. (8 oz.) boiled ham slices (thin)
1 can (10 3/4 oz.) condensed chicken broth, undiluted
1/2 cup dry white wine
1/4 cup chopped parsley
1 tbsp. each white-wine and tarragon vinegar

**Glaze**

Soften the other envelope of gelatin in 1/2 cup water. Heat slightly until gelatin dissolves. Combine with chicken broth, wine, parsley, and vinegars. Chill until consistency for spooning. Refrigerate entire pate just until glaze sets.

Lightly grease an 8 1/2 by 4 1/2 by 2 5/8-inch loaf pan.

Soften cream cheese and beat until smooth.

Chop olives. Stir in Swiss cheese, olives and juice, pepper, and basil.

In small bowl, sprinkle 1 envelope gelatin over 1/4 cup water. Let stand 5 minutes to soften. Heat just till gelatin dissolves. Cool slightly and stir into cheese mixture.

Arrange several ham slices in bottom of prepared pan. Spoon 1/3 of cheese mixture into pan. Top with half of remaining ham slices.

Continue layering, ending with cheese mixture.

Refrigerate 6 hours or overnight.

To serve, unmold onto nice serving tray. Spoon glaze over (see recipe) and serve at room temperature with small rye bread rounds or crackers.

# *Party Puffs*

*Makes about 36 small puffs*

*This recipe is for those industrious few! Actually, easy to make and makes a nice impression!*

1 cup water
1/2 cup margarine
1/2 tsp. salt
1 1/4 cups sifted flour
4 eggs
Filling, as desired

Bring water, margarine, and salt to full boil in saucepan.

Add flour all at once and bear rapidly over low heat until mixture leaves sides of pan and forms a smooth, compact ball.

Remove from heat.

Add unbeaten eggs, one at a time, beating well after each addition.

Mixture should be thick.

Drop by rounded teaspoonful onto ungreased cookie sheet, about 1 1/2 inches apart.

Bake at 375 degrees for 35 minutes. Cool on wire rack. Cut small opening in puffs and fill just before serving.

Suggestions: Chicken salad, tuna salad, ham salad, shrimp salad, etc.

# Pepperoni Roll

*Yields 2- 3 Rolls*

*This is a recipe given to me by a dear deceased friend years ago. It was her mother's recipe, and it is delicious and non-fail. It has become our family's favorite!*

## Bread Dough

1 pkg. dry yeast
1 cup warm water
3 cups all-purpose or bread flour
3 tbsp. cooking oil
1 tsp. salt

## Filling

8 oz. pepperoni, sliced thin
8 oz. mozzarella cheese, shredded
8 oz. provolone, sliced thin

Dissolve yeast in warm water. Add 1 cup flour. Stir well. Add the oil and salt. Stir well.

Add remaining flour and knead for 10 minutes. Place dough in oiled or greased bowl and cover with towel. Allow to rise until doubled. Punch down and use as directed.

Divide dough in half. Roll each half into approximately 9-by-12-inch rectangle. Divide pepperoni and cheeses evenly among the rectangles layering. Roll away from you tucking under the ends. Wrap up in aluminum foil. Label and store until you want to bake them. Freeze up to 2 months. Okay in refrigerator if you bake within two days. Thaw partially before baking.

Bake on the foil in preheated 400-425 degrees oven for 30-40 minutes till golden. Filling sometimes oozes out during baking, so roll up the edges of the foil. Remove from oven.
Let rest a few minutes. Slice and serve warm or room temperature.

*Buon Appetito!*

**Kathy**

# Raw Vegetables with Creamy Garlic Herb Dressing

*Makes approximately 1 ½ cups dressing*

*Crowd pleaser!*

1/4 cup milk
1 /2 cup mayonnaise
1/2 sour cream
2 cloves garlic, minced
1 tbsp. chopped parsley
1/2 tsp. fresh chopped basil
Salt/pepper to taste

## Raw Vegetable of Choice

Broccoli flowerets
Red and green pepper strips
Radishes
Celery strips
Cucumber slices
Carrot sticks

Crowd pleaser!

Combine milk, mayonnaise, sour cream, garlic cloves,
parsley and basil in blender. Cover and whirl until smooth.
Add salt/pepper to taste.

Chill in refrigerator until ready to use.
Serve with your choice of vegetables, crackers, and/or breads.
Also, good tOsscd over salad greens!

# Shrimp Pâté

*Serve 6-8*

*Looks nice on a bed of curly-leaf
lettuce*

1 lb. fresh cooked or frozen cooked shrimp
1/4 cup minced onion
1/2 cup butter
3 tbsp. lemon juice
1 tsp. horseradish
2/3 cup mayonnaise
1 tsp. salt
1/4 tsp. white pepper

Chop cooked shrimp very fine. Add minced onlon.
Melt butter. Pour over shrimp, mixing well.
Add lemon juice, horseradish, mayonnaise, salt, and pepper.
Pack into a 3-cup mold.
Chill in refrigerator 4 to 5 hours or overnight if possible.

Turn out onto serving plate.
Serve with crackers of your choice or Melba toast.

# Roasted Garlic

*This appetizer is very popular today and has climbed*
*to the top of the list of "best appetizers!"*

2 – full heads of garlic
Extra-Virgin olive oil*
Coarse sea salt or kosher salt
Fresh ground black pepper
Garlic baker
Paprika (optional) – just a sprinkle

*Extra-Virgin Olive Oil with Basil is very good too

Preheat oven to 275 degrees.
Cut the tops off the heads of garlic.
Put garlic heads in garlic baker or any deep dish with a lid to hold number of garlic heads desired.
Drizzle them with 1 – 2 Tbsp. extra-virgin olive oil.
Sprinkle with coarse sea/kosher salt and ground pepper. Cover and bake for 1 hour.
Uncover and baste with existing oil. Cover and bake approx. 1 hour longer until garlic is tender
When done, separate cloves. Squeeze baked garlic onto thin slices of Italian or French bread for a delicious appetizer or addition to your dinner.

# Salami Wedges

*Such an easy appetizer that goes over big!*

1 (3 oz.) pkg. cream cheese
9 slices Genoa or other salami

Soften cream cheese; spread over each of the 9 slices of salami.

Stack spread slices of salami one on top of the other, ending with a plain slice of salami without spread.

Cover and chill. Before serving, slice stack into 12 wedges. Double, triple recipe for more.

# Savory Potato Skins

*Makes 16 potato skins.*
*Company coming? Whip these up in a jiff!*

4 Idaho potatoes, baked
3 tbsp. butter, melted
Salt, garlic powder,
paprika to taste
Cheddar cheese (optional)
Sour cream

Bake potatoes in regular oven or microwave them until soft (leave skins on).

Halve each baked potato.
Scoop out inside and serve as mashed potatoes, leaving ¼ inch of potato in the shell.

Brush potato shells with melted butter.
Sprinkle lightly with salt, garlic powder and paprika.
Broil till golden, about 5 min.
Serve as is with sour cream or sprinkle with grated cheddar cheese before broiling, then serve with

sour cream
Yummy!

# *Shrimp Tree*

*"Festive" appetizer! Nice table centerpiece. My son, Michael, brought me a picture card home from school years ago, when he was in elementary school, something his teacher gave them for a treat for their moms. I made it that Christmas and have made these for many a party or holiday table ever since and they add so much to a buffet.*

If shrimp are fresh, steam until done (pink in color).
If frozen and cooked, thaw under running water a few minutes, drain and pat dry. Remove dark vein running down back of shrimp.

Chill in refrigerator until ready to make tree.

Then: With fancy toothpicks (frilly ended), fasten endive to Styrofoam cone in a spiral pattern to resemble a Christmas tree once covered top to bottom.

3 or 4 lbs. fresh or frozen shrimp, cooked
Fancy lettuce (escarole-curly)
Cocktail sauce
1 Styrofoam cone, approximately 18 inches frilly (fancy) toothpicks (the ones with the colored saran frills on one end)

With more toothpicks, fasten cooked shrimp to tree in same spiral pattern, fitting as many shrimps around tree as you can.
(Arrange extra shrimp around bottom of tree on plate.)
Serve with cocktail sauce. Tastes as good as it looks!

Note: Don't cut corners by placing shrimp and greenery on tree with same toothpick as greenery will fall off tree when shrimp are removed from tree leaving white cone visible!

# Spinach Squares

*Serves 6 people*

1 cup flour
2 eggs
1 pkg. frozen chopped spinach, thawed and squeezed dry
½ tsp. salt
1 tsp. baking powder
1 medium onion, chopped
1 cup milk
1 cup each, grated Monterey Jack and cheddar cheese
¼ cup grated Romano cheese

Mix all ingredients together.
Spread in greased 8 x 11 baking dish.

Bake in preheated 350 degrees oven for 25 to 30 minutes.

Remove from oven.
Cool.

Slice into squares and serve.

# Spinach Spread

*Serves 6 people*
*Easy as can be and so delicious!*

1 pkg. frozen, chopped spinach
1 cup mayonnaise
3 tbsp. minced green onions
½ lb. bacon, cooked crisp and
Crumbled crackers or party bread rounds

Thaw spinach and squeeze water out.

Mix all ingredients together

Chill.

Serve with crackers or party bread rounds.

# Stuffed Whole Artichokes

*Serves 4*

*These are nice served before a meal as an appetizer.*

*Often served on Christmas Eve at the St. Joseph's table.*

4 whole Artichokes, washed*
2 garlic cloves, chopped fine
½ cup grated Romano Cheese
1 tbsp. chopped parsley**
1 ½ cup Italian-style breadcrumbs
1 tsp. salt
¾ tsp. pepper
1 cup olive oil, divided in recipe
2 tbsp. water
2 tbsp. olive oil for each artichoke

*Pull center leaves out to expose the fuzzy choke. Scoop out choke and discard it.

*Fresh parsley is best.

Cut the stems off the artichokes to sit flat.
Cut the pointy tips off each leaf on each artichoke with sharp knife.
Spread leaves semi-open.

Mix chopped garlic, the grated cheese, parsley, breadcrumbs, salt and pepper together.
Moisten mixture with the 1/8 cup of olive oil and 2 tbsp. water.
Separate leaves slightly.
Fill each leaf with a tiny bit of mixture and fill the center of each artichoke as well.

Place the artichokes heads up in a deep pot in which you put 1 ½ cup water, ¼ cup oil.
Sprinkle each with the 2-tbsp. olive oil.

Simmer, covered, about 45-50 minutes or until leaves are tender.
Pour water off & serve immediately.
To eat, you break the leaves away from artichoke one at a time and scrape the cooked artichoke pulp and stuffing off with your teeth. Enjoy!

# Stuffed Mushrooms with Crabmeat & Garlic Cream Cheese

*Serves 4 - 6*

*Another great recipe!*

1 lb. long-stemmed mushrooms
½ lb. crabmeat, cartilage removed
½ lb. cream cheese, softened
½ cup garlic croutons, crushed fine
3 tbsp. grated Romano cheese
Dash of paprika

Grease cookie sheet. Clean mushrooms**and remove stems.
Place caps open side up on cookie sheet.

Mix together the crabmeat, cream cheese and garlic croutons till blended.

Mound mixture into mushroom caps.
Sprinkle tops generously with grated cheese and lightly with the paprika.

Broil until piping hot and cheese melted.
**Wipe mushrooms with a clean, damp cloth.

*Note: Either discard stems or chop them and sauté in butter
till golden and add them to the filling.*

# Spiced Nuts

*My friend, Lori, now deceased, gave us this*
*recipe in Gourmet Club. Everyone seems to love them!*
*Nice given at Christmas as a holiday treat.*

1 egg white
1 tbsp. water
1 cup sugar
1 tsp. cinnamon
1 tsp. salt
1 lb. pecan halves

Whip egg white with water until foamy.

Mix sugar, cinnamon and salt and set aside.
Add pecan halves to whipped egg white and toss to coat.

Add sugar/cinnamon/salt mixture. Totally coat pecans.

Put pecans on a greased cookie sheet and bake 1 hour at 250 degrees, stirring every 15 minutes, till nuts are fairly dry. Cool and store.

# Yummy Cheese Rolls

*Makes 2 or 3 rolls*
*These keep for weeks refrigerated.*

1 8 oz. cream cheese block
1 block Velveeta Cheese (2 lb.)
1 cup pecans, chopped
3 or 4 cloves garlic, minced Paprika
Crackers, your choice

Let cream cheese sit out to soften.
Grate Velveeta cheese. Mix cheeses and remaining ingredients together well in bowl.
Mix with hands to form any size rolls you want.

Roll lightly in paprika or finely chopped pecans.
Refrigerate until serving time.
Serve with crackers of your choice.

# Zesty Chicken Wings

*Makes about 2 dozen*
*So easy and so good!*

2 lbs. chicken wings
½ cup Miracle Whip
1 envelope Good Seasons
Zesty Italian Dressing Mix
2 tbsp. Tabasco

Mix Miracle Whip, salad dressing mix, and tabasco together until well blended.
Place chicken wings in shallow baking pan.
Preheat oven to 425 degrees.

Brush wings with half of the dressing mixture.
Bake 15 minutes. Turn. Brush remaining salad dressing mixture on wings.

Bake additional 15 minutes until browned.
Serve as an appetizer.

# Buffalo Chicken Wings

*Makes 8 servings*

24 chicken wings
2 tbsp. butter or margarine
4 – 5 tbsp. hot sauce*
2 tsp. apple cider vinegar

*I like Louisiana brand hot sauce

Preheat oven to 450 degrees. Cut each wing into two pieces.

Arrange wings on a flat rack in a roasting pan.

In small bowl combine butter, hot sauce and vinegar.
Brush half the sauce on wings. Roast 25 minutes.
Brush remaining sauce on wings. Roast 20 minutes longer.

Serve with celery sticks and Blue Cheese Dressing/Dip.
Enjoy!

# Spanakopita

*Makes a bunch*

*When we lived in Vienna, Virginia we would have the neighbors and family over on
Christmas Eve and these were always a big hit of all the food we had on the dining room table!*

2 (10 oz.) pkg. chopped spinach, thawed & drained
1 1/2 c. butter
¼ c. olive oil
3 scallions (green onion), chopped fine
1 sm. onion, finely chopped
½ c. fresh, finely chopped parsley
½ c. shredded mozzarella cheese
1 container (15 oz.) ricotta cheese
½ lb. feta cheese
4 oz. cream cheese
½ c. grated Romano cheese
3 eggs, beaten
I envelope Good Seasons Italian salad dressing mix
¼ tsp. nutmeg, optional
½ tsp. salt
½ tsp. pepper
1 (16 oz.) pkg. phyllo pastry dough

Thaw and drain spinach well. Melt 2 Tbsps. butter with the olive oil in skillet. Sauté onions, scallions, parsley, salt and pepper until golden. Set aside to cool.

Beat eggs with nutmeg and salad dressing mix in large bowl. Stir in cheeses, spinach and sautéed mixture in combining well.

Melt remaining butter in pan. Unfold phyllo pastry sheets very carefully. Lay out two sheets horizontally on clean, flat surface and cut into about six strips. Brush the top of the strips with the melted butter.

Place a spoonful of spinach mixture at one end of each strip. Fold the strips diagonally like a flag back and forth to form a triangle. Brush top of each pastry with more melted butter.

Place triangles on an ungreased cookie sheet.
Bake at 375 degrees for 15 – 20 minutes or until golden brown.

Serve warm.

*Note: Cut the dough into larger strips if larger appetizers are desired. Keep dough covered while working
with it with wax paper and a damp towel to prevent drying out.*

# Beverages

*Beverages*

# Italian Coffee

*Nice served "at the table" after dinner.*

For each cup:
5 oz. fresh brewed coffee
1 oz. Amaretto
1 oz. Brandy
Whipped cream
Cinnamon

For each cup:

Pour brewed coffee of your choice in cup.
Add the Amaretto and brandy.

Top with a dollop of whipped cream and
a sprinkle of cinnamon.
Enjoy!

# Jim's Morning Coffee

*A recipe (and habit) Jim acquired from his grandmother, Nellie Rossi many years*
*ago and one that remains a favorite – both in memory and taste!*

Brewed coffee
An egg
Milk
Sugar

Break one egg into your cup to start.
Add desired amount of milk and sugar.
Beat until frothy with fork.

Add desired amount of hot brewed coffee to cup,
continuing to beat with the fork to blend together.
It's different and unique. Breakfast in a cup!
Try it – you just might like it!

# Champagne Punch

*Serves 25*

*Delicious!*

2 cups water
1 ½ cups sugar
1 (6 oz.) can frozen lemonade, undiluted
1 (18 oz.) can pineapple juice
1 (12 oz.) can frozen orange juice, undiluted
2 quarts ginger ale
1 bottle of your favorite champagne

Dissolve water and sugar by boiling for approximately 3 min. Add orange juice, lemonade and pineapple juice. Chill.

Just before serving – add chilled ginger ale and champagne Garnish with cherries and orange slices, if desired.

*Note: Freeze part of the punch in a ring mold before adding the ginger ale to float atop the punch to keep it cold when serving.*

# Coffee Mocha Punch

*Serves 10 - 12*

*Delicious!*

2 – 3 cups milk
1 cup strong chilled coffee
½ tsp. amaretto (or almond extract)
Dash of salt
¼ cup sugar
1 quart chocolate ice cream, softened
1 cup heavy whipping cream
1 cup dark rum, optional

Combine milk, coffee, amaretto, salt and sugar in a punch bowl.

Spoon in half the softened chocolate ice cream. Stir until slightly melted.

Whip the heavy cream and fold in with remaining ice cream. Serve immediately

# Festive Eggnog

*Serves 6-8*

*I have served this at Christmas Open Houses or other holiday*
*functions over the years. Absolutely delicious and festive!*

1 cup granulated sugar
6 eggs, separated
1-pint heavy cream, whipped
1 pint milk
1 pint Bourbon whiskey
Nutmeg

Beat egg yolks. Add Bourbon. *Add sugar and milk.

Beat egg whites and fold in. Beat cream and fold in.
Chill minimum of 3 hours. Serve Individually or displayed
in attractive bowl.

*Note: Brandy and/or rum may be substituted for part or all
of the bourbon.

# Fruit Smoothies

*Yields Little over 1 cup*

*A healthy alternative to the milkshake!*

¼ cup fresh fruit, i.e., strawberries, bananas,
pineapples, mango, kiwi, etc. cut up
½ cup thickener, i.e., yogurt, frozen fruit juice, etc.
¼ cup liquid, i.e., milk, water, fruit juice, etc.
Additional flavoring, optional, i.e.
cinnamon, vanilla, etc.
Cracked ice, if desired.

Put all ingredients in blender. Blend until smooth.
Serve immediately or refrigerate.

*Note: Nice served in a chilled glass. These*
*measurements are not set in stone. The great thing*
*about smoothies is you can experiment to get exactly*
*what you want.*

*Enjoy!*

# Malted Milkshakes

3 tbsp. cold milk
1 tbsp. malted milk powder
2 large scoops ice cream*
Whipped cream for garnish
Maraschino cherry for garnish

* Vanilla, chocolate or strawberry.

Put all the ingredients, except the whipped cream
And cherry in a blender. Blend until smooth. Pour into
milkshake glass.
Top with whipped cream and a cherry.

Note: For an added treat, add a few malted milk balls at time
of blending when making a chocolate malt. Or in place of the
malted milk balls, add your favorite chocolate bar.

# Irish Coffee

*Nice served at the table after dinner.*

1 cup fresh-brewed coffee per person
1 oz. Irish Whiskey per person
1 pint heavy cream, whipped with
1 tsp. vanilla and
3 tbsp. confectioner's sugar

Whip the heavy cream adding the confectioner's sugar and
vanilla once cream begins to thicken. Pour each person a
cup of black fresh-brewed coffee 2/3 full, from a nice
serving pot. Add 1 oz. whiskey. Top coffee with a couple
nice dollops of the sweetened whipped cream.

Serve as is. Do not stir. Enjoy!

# Jim's Hot Rum Toddy

*Jim likes me to make this for him either when he has a cold, or*
*on those cold, wintry nights!*

For each Serving
1 cup milk
1 pat butter
1 shot of rum
Sugar, to taste

In a pot on stove – heat all ingredients together stirring until the butter melts and mixture is hot but comfortable to drink

Remove from stove and serve. A nice toddy that will also relax you after a hard day and help you sleep.

# Piña Coladas

*Popular at patio parties or rafting out on our Motor Yacht*
*on the Chesapeake Bay with friends!*

2 cans (14 ½ oz.) CoCo Lopez
2 cans (46 oz.) pineapple juice
2 cans (14 ½ oz.) rum*
Pineapple slices

*Just as good made with a combination of rum, gin and vodka you might have on hand to equal the 2 cans rum.

Mix all ingredients together.

Chill and serve with crushed ice and enjoy!
Finish off with a slice of pineapple in the glass or hanging on the side.

(Best made a day ahead. Beat with electric mixer or blend before serving if you notice white chunks of CoCo Lopez have formed.)

# Open House Punch

*Serves 32*

1 fifth of Southern Comfort
3 quarts 7-Up
6 oz. fresh lemon juice
1 (6 oz.) can frozen lemonade
1 (6 oz.) can frozen orange juice
Orange and lemon slices
Optional: drops of food coloring

Chill all ingredients.
Mix in punch bowl, adding 7-Up last.

Add drops of food coloring if desired.

Stir. Float block of ice or punch mixture.
Add orange and/or lemon slices.
Serve.

*Note: You can prepare this punch ahead of time. Just add the 7-Up and the ice mixture ring just before serving,*

# Cranberry Punch

2 cups Cranberry juice
1 ½ cups white wine
1 ½ cups club soda, chilled

Mix all ingredients together.
Chill before serving in punch bowl.
Float block of ice or punch mixture.
Serve.

*(As in the above recipe, you can prepare this ahead of time—just add the club soda and ice or punch ring just before serving.)*

# Sangria

*Serves 6-8*

*Great summertime drink served cold over ice!*

24 oz. Rose or White wine
¼ cup superfine sugar
3 oz. Cranberry juice
3 oz. Tequila
3 oz. Grapefruit juice
Assorted grapes

Freeze individual grapes (not touching) overnight on a baking sheet.

Combine remaining ingredients in a 3-quart pitcher.

Add frozen grapes and serve.

# Hot Mulled Wine

*Serves 18*

*Delightful aroma and mellow taste!*

4 cups sugar
1 tbsp. cinnamon or 6 sticks
1 tsp. ground cloves
2 cups boiling water
3 oranges, sliced thin
1 lemon, sliced thin
1 gallon dry red wine

Combine sugar, cinnamon, cloves and water in an 8-quart pot.

Add orange and lemon slices. Add wine. Heat on high. Boil 5 minutes, stir occasionally.

Ladle into individual heat safe glasses or cups and serve. Enjoy!

# *Mojito*

*Yields 1 serving*

*I first had one of these in Key West while Jim and I
were on a vacation with our boating friends.
So cool and refreshing!*

Ice
6 ounces light rum
12 mint sprigs, or spearmint
6 tablespoons fresh lime juice
4 tablespoons sugar
Club soda
4 slices lime

Place ice in shaker. Add rum

Break up 8 sprigs of mint and add with the lime juice and sugar. Shake well.

Serve over cracked ice in a high ball glass. Top off with a splash of club soda. Garnish with slice of lime and a sprig of mint. Enjoy'

# Snowflake Martini

*Serves 6-8*

*Fun for winter, the holidays or anytime!*

Ice
2 oz. Charbay Meyer Lemon Vodka
2 oz. White Grape Juice
1 Fresh Lemon
Sugar

Fill a cocktail shaker halfway with ice.
Add the 2 oz. Charbay Meyer Lemon Vodka.
Add 2 oz. white grape juice. Shake vigorously.

Moisten rim of martini glass with lemon and dip in sugar.
Strain into martini glass. Top with splash of cold ginger ale and garnish with a beautiful lemon twist and enjoy!

*Note: For a non-alcoholic version, skip the Vodka and use 4 oz. of sparkling white grape Juice.*

# Spiced (Mulled) Cider

*Serves 10 -12*

*Nice served during the holidays and smells so good heating on the stove!*

2 quarts apple cider
¼ cup packed brown sugar
1/8 tsp. ground ginger
1 orange (unpeeled)
2 cinnamon sticks
1 tsp. whole cloves
Brandy, optional

Combine cider, sugar and orange in a large pot on top of stove.

Tie the cinnamon sticks and cloves in a small cheesecloth bag. Add to pot.

Bring to a simmer, cover and cook on LOW 2 hours. The entire house will smell great! Remove the bag of spices. Serve.

*Note: If using the brandy – put a shot of brandy in a mug, then fill with the hot mulled cider. You can also make this in a crockpot. In crockpot, cook covered on low 2 – 4 hours.*

# Arnold Palmer (Iced Tea)

*My Jim's favorite summer cooler!*

Iced tea
Lemonade

Pour ½ iced tea and ½ prepared lemonade over cracked ice in glass.

Garnish with slice of lemon if desired. Stir and enjoy!

# Sun (Solar) Tea

*Delicious and clear tea!*

½ gallon clear glass jar
½ gallon cold water
5 – 6 tea bags

Fill jar with water.
Insert tea bags, with strings hanging out of jar.
Screw jar tight.

Place in sun for minimum of 4 hours.

Remove tea bags and store tea in or out of refrigerator.
Sweeten as you please.
Enjoy!

# Fresh Lemonade

*There is nothing like it and it is so easy!*

10 lemons
3 cups water
2 cups white sugar
4 cups crushed ice

Cut ½ of one lemon into thin slices and set aside.

Juice the remaining lemons and pour into a glass pitcher. Stir in the water and sugar until dissolved. Pour in the crushed ice and float the lemon slices on top. Enjoy!

# Breads

# Banana Bread

*Yields 1 (9 x 5 x 3 inch) loaf*
*Makes good use of those leftover bananas!*

1 ¾ cup all-purpose flour*
2 tsp. baking powder
1 ¼ tsp. baking soda
½ tsp. salt
3 soft bananas
1/3 cup shortening or cooking oil
2/3 cup sugar**
2 eggs
Walnuts or pecans, chopped (optional)

*½ whole wheat flour works ok for diabetic diets and the like.
*Also substitute Splenda for ½ of the sugar

Pour all ingredients into a mixing bowl except the flour and nuts if using. Mix till blended.

Add the flour (and nuts if using) and beat again until smooth.

Pour into prepared loaf pan (greased and floured. *

Bake in preheated 350 degrees oven for 1 hour or until toothpick inserted in center comes out clean.

Cool briefly, turn pan over and remove cake to cooling rack. I serve slices of this buttered or plain.

Tip: I line just the bottom of the greased pan with a piece of aluminum foil just enough to cover the bottom and grease the foil too. Cake removes so much easier once baked!

# Focaccia Bread Squares

*Yields about 2 dozen*

*Worth the Effort!*

Dough
3cups all-purpose flour
1 tsp. salt
1 cup warm water
1 1/2 tsp. olive oil
2 tsp. dried oregano
1 1/2 tsp. yeast
Topping
3 tbsp. olive or vegetable oil
1 clove garlic, minced fine
1/2 cup grated Romano cheese
2 tsp. minced fresh Parsley*

*Or rosemary.

Dissolve yeast in warm water.

Add salt, olive oil, oregano, and flour (1 cup at a time).
Knead in enough flour for a non-sticky dough.

Oil a 10 by-15-by -1-inch jelly roll pan.
Place dough in pan and gently stretch it with your hands to fit evenly in the pan.

Cover and let rise in warm place until double (about 45 to 60 minutes). Preheat oven to 400 degrees.

With two fingers, poke holes all over the dough.
Drizzle over top mixture of the oil and garlic.
Sprinkle with the cheese and parsley or rosemary.
Sprinkle a little kosher salt over sparingly.

Bake for 25- 30 minutes till golden brown.
Cool on wire rack and cut into squares or thin rectangles and serve warm.

# Garlic Bread

*Yields 1 loaf*

*It's the extra ingredient of "Romano Cheese"*
*that makes this version so good!*

1 long loaf unsliced Italian bread
½ cup butter or margarine, softened
1 clove garlic, crushed (or you may use desired amount of garlic powder)
3 tbsp. grated Romano Cheese
¼ tsp. pepper
Dash of crushed red pepper

Slice bread into 1-inch slices.
Combine remaining ingredients, stirring well.

Spread butter mixture between bread slices.

Place loaf on ungreased baking sheet.

Sprinkle bread with a few drops of water.

Bake at 350 degrees for 10 min. or until thoroughly heated and golden brown on top. *

Serve warm.

*\*As an alternative – spread butter mixture on thick slices of Italian Bread and broil 2 – 3 inches from heat in oven until golden. Or spread butter mixture on unsliced loaf, bake or broil, then slice and serve.*

# Heirloom Bread

*Yields 2 loaves*

*A nice, moist, sweet coffee bread.*

1 cup softened butter
2 cups granulated sugar
4 eggs
1 tsp. lemon extract
1 tsp. vanilla
2 cups applesauce
4 cups sifted flour
2 tsp. baking powder
2 tsp. cinnamon
2 tsp. salt
1 ½ tsp. baking soda
½ tsp. cloves
½ tsp. nutmeg
2/3 cup chopped pecans
½ cup currants

Cream butter. Add sugar. Cream again.
Beat in eggs, one at a time.
Add extracts and apple sauce.

Blend in sifted dry ingredients.
Mix well.

Stir in pecans and currants.

Pour into two greased 9 in. by 5 in. by 3
inch loaf pans.

Bake at 350 degrees for 55 to 60 minutes.

Remove from pans. Cool on rack.
Let stand 4 hours before slicing.

# *Italian Bread*

*Makes 2 loaves*

*Bread making is a true art and my mother baked all her own bread.*
*Her kitchen had such a nice "aroma" on the days she baked – but I can't help wondering*
*if this isn't fast becoming a lost art! Give it a try and keep tradition going!*

1 pkg. dry yeast or
1 cake soft yeast
2 cups warm water
1 tbsp. salt
3 to 5 cups all-purpose flour

Soften yeast in ¼ cup warm water. Set aside.
Meanwhile: Put 1 ¾ cups warm water and the salt in a large bowl. Blend in 3 cups flour. Stir the softened yeast and add to flour/water mixture. Mix well. Add another cup of flour to yeast mixture and beat until very smooth. Turn onto lightly floured surface. Mix in enough flour to form a nice soft dough. Allow to rest 5 to 10 minutes.

Note: To prepare pan for baking, grease pan and sprinkle lightly with cornmeal

Shape dough into smooth ball and place in greased bowl. Turn to bring greased surface to top. Cover bowl with waxed paper and towel and let stand in warm place until dough has doubled (1 ½ to 2 hours).

Optional: You may "twist" the two loaves together and bake as one if you would like!

Punch down with fist. Knead on lightly floured surface about 2 mins. Divide into 2 balls. Let stand covered 10 min. Roll each ball into a 14 x 8 in. rectangle. Roll up tightly into a long, slender loaf. Pinch ends to seal.

Place loaves on a prepared baking sheet, cover loosely with a towel and rise until doubled. Bake at 425 degrees 10 min. Reduce heat to 350 degrees and bake 1 hr. or till golden brown. To increase crustiness, place a flat pan of boiling water on bottom of oven at beginning of baking period. Enjoy!

# *Italian Bread Sticks*

*Yields about 4 dozen bread sticks*

*Worth the effort!*

Dough
Follow recipe for "Italian Bread"
in this cookbook, decreasing salt to 2 tsp.
1 egg
1 tbsp. milk
Coarse salt

Grease 3 or 4 baking sheets.
Roll dough out on floured board before rising To approx. 8-inch-wide rectangle. Cut dough crosswise with a floured knife into strips approx. 1 inch wide.

Use palm of hand to roll strips to pencil thickness,
keeping to about 7 – 8-inch lengths.
Place strips 2 inches apart on baking sheets.
Brush lightly with a mixture of egg, slightly beaten and 1 tbsp. milk.

Let rise in warm place until doubled, about 1 hr.
Again, brush with egg mixture and sprinkle with coarse salt.

Bake at 400 degrees for 18 to 20 min. or until breadsticks are lightly browned and crisp all the way through. Enjoy!

# *Italian Easter Bread*

*Yields 1 braided ring or oblong loaf*

*Jim's mother lovingly made each of our families one of these loaves every Easter and called them "Easter Dolls" – a Mugnolo family tradition we keep going! "Happy Easter!"*

4 eggs, uncooked
4 pkgs. dry yeast (or cake yeast)
½ cup very warm water
½ cup warm water
1 ½ cups all-purpose or bread flour
¾ cup shortening or soft butter
2 tbsp. lemon juice
1 tbsp. grated lemon rind
1 cup sugar
1 tsp. salt
3 eggs, well-beaten
4 cups all-purpose or bread flour
1 egg yolk
1 tbsp. milk
Raisins, amount desired

Dye 4 uncooked eggs and set aside.
Dissolve yeast in ½ cup very warm water. Add sugar to yeast.

Meanwhile: Pour other ½ cup warm water into a large bowl. Blend in 1 ½ cups flour. Stir softened yeast mixture into flour mixture. Beat until smooth. Cover bowl with waxed paper and let rise in warm place until double (1 ½ to 2 hours). Cream shortening, lemon juice and lemon rind. Add salt. Beat the 3 eggs. Add eggs and shortening mixture to yeast mixture. At this point you may add 1 or 2 cups raisins and one-half remaining flour.

Knead on floured surface to a nice dough. Rise in greased bowl until double as above. Divide dough into 2 parts, Roll into rolls and form into a loosely braided ring or oblong loaf. Insert eggs, spacing (2 for loaf; 3 or 4 for ring). Bake on greased sheet at 350 degrees for 40-45 minutes. Brush last 5 mins. baking time with egg yolk/milk mixture. Eggs will hard cook. Bread is very good served sliced and buttered or buttered then toasted in oven under the broiler.

# Lemon Bread

*Yields 1 loaf*

*A most delicious bread to serve with tea!*

1 cup sugar
6 tbsp. shortening
1 tbsp. grated lemon rind
2 eggs
1 ½ cups sifted all-purpose flour*
½ tsp. salt
1 tsp. baking powder
½ cup milk
½ cup nuts, chopped
¼ cup sugar
Juice of 1 lemon (3 tbsp.)
*Or use Wondra flour, which is fine.

Cream the sugar in a medium bowl with the shortening. Add lemon rind. Beat in eggs. Sift dry ingredients together and add alternately with the milk, beginning and ending with flour mixture. Stir in chopped nuts. Pour into greased 9 x 5 x 3- inch loaf pan.

Bake in preheated 325 degrees oven for 35 – 45 minutes. Cake is done when toothpick inserted in center comes out clean.

In small saucepan, heat the ¼ cup sugar with lemon juice, stirring until dissolved. Pour over hot bread. Allow to cool in pan. When cold remove from pan, slice, and serve (with unsalted sweet butter optional) accompanied by your favorite tea.

Enjoy!

*Tip: I put a piece of aluminum foil in the bottom of the greased pan just enough to cover bottom and grease the foil too. Cake removes so much easier once baked!*

# Persimmon Bread

*Yields 1 (9 x 5 x 3 inch) loaf*

*Our neighbors at our place on Lake Anna, Virginia, Tom (Doc) and Betty Jane Owens,
had a persimmon tree and used to let me pick the ripe persimmons for my bread.*

2 cups flour
1 tsp. baking soda
1 cup granulated sugar
1 ½ sticks margarine or butter
2 eggs
1 cup persimmon pulp
½ cup chopped nuts

Sift flour and baking soda together.
Cream sugar and margarine/butter together in separate bowl and add eggs, well-beaten.

Add flour/baking soda mixture, persimmon pulp and chopped nuts. Stir to a stiff batter. Grease and flour a loaf pan. I also put a piece of aluminum foil in the bottom of the greased pan and grease it to cover the bottom. Bread removes much easier once baked.

Bake at 325 degrees F. for 1 hour or until toothpick inserted in center of bread comes out clean. Remove from pan and cool. Freezes well.

# Popovers

*Yields 8 to 10 popovers*

*A little "extra special" treat nice served with dinner!*

1 cup flour
1 cup milk
3 tbsp. cooking oil
½ tsp. salt
3 eggs

Preheat oven to 400 degrees.
Put all ingredients in blender. Blend well.
Place greased muffin tins in oven for 10 minutes to heat.
Pour batter into hot tins, filling 2/3 full.

Reduce heat to 350 degrees and continue baking for 30 minutes. Do not open oven door until cooking time is finished or popovers will fall.

Serve and enjoy!

# Picadilly Lane Bread

*Yield depends on size of flowerpot(s)*

*Delicious herb bread...also known as "Flowerpot Bread!"*
*I initially made this to sale at our Garden Club's Holiday Show*
*when we lived in Lake Vale in Vienna, Virginia. It was so*
*good I would occasionally make it and serve it as a*
*"special" treat for my family!*

2 cups all-purpose flour

2 tbsp. sugar

1 tsp. salt

1 tbsp. minced onion

2 tsp. dill weed, fresh if you have it or dill seed is okay

¼ tsp. baking soda

1 pkg. dry yeast

1 tbsp. margarine or butter, softened

¼ cup hot tap water

1 cup creamed cottage cheese, at room temperature

1 egg, at room temperature

Small clay flowerpots for Individual loaves*

*Freeze well also to be given later as a gift adorned with bow.

(Can also be baked in bread pans, well-greased and dusted with either flour or cornmeal.)

Combine ¼ cup of the flour, the sugar, salt, onion, dill, baking soda and undissolved yeast. Add softened butter or margarine.

Add hot tap water. Beat 2 min. at medium speed. Add cottage cheese, egg, ½ cup flour. Beat again at high speed for 2 min. Stir in enough remaining flour to make a stiff batter. Cover. Let rise until double (about 1 ¼ hours).

Punch down. Place dough in well-greased, foil-lined clean clay flowerpots (grease both the pot and the foil well). Bake at 350 degrees for approx. 30 min. Remove from pot with foil and set aside to cool. Serve in pot at each place setting freshly lined with new foil.

# *Pumpkin Bread*

*Yields 2 loaves*

3 1/3 cups sifted all-purpose flour*
2 tsp. baking soda
1 ½ tsp. salt
1 tsp. cinnamon
1 tsp. nutmeg
3 cups sugar
1 cup chopped pecans
4 eggs
1 ½ cup canned pumpkin
1 cup cooking oil
2/3 cup water

*Or use Wondra flour which is fine

Mix and sift dry ingredients together. Add chopped nuts.

Combine slightly beaten eggs with remaining ingredients.

Pour all at once into dry ingredients and mix lightly.

Bake in 2 greased loaf pans (10 ¼" x 3 5/8" x 2 5/8") in a preheated 350 degrees oven for 1 hour. Cool slightly and remove from pan.

*Tip: I line just the bottom of the greased pan with a piece of aluminum foil just enough to cover the bottom and grease the foil too. Cake removes so much easier once baked!*

# Refrigerator Bran Muffins

*Yields approximately 24 muffins*

*This batter will keep up to 5 weeks in refrigerator.*

1 ½ cup sugar
½ cup solid shortening
2 eggs
2 ½ cups flour
2 ½ tsp. soda
½ tsp. salt
2 cups buttermilk*
1 cup boiling water
1 cup 100% Bran ready to eat cereal
¾ cup seedless raisins
2 cups All Bran ready to eat cereal

*Sour your own milk by adding lemon juice or vinegar to the milk in a cup until curdled

Thoroughly cream together sugar and shortening.
Add eggs. Mix well after each addition.
Add flour, soda, salt and buttermilk, mixing until smooth.

Meanwhile: Pour boiling water over 100% Bran.
Let stand until cereal has absorbed water and has cooled slightly.

Blend this mixture into batter.
Add raisins and All Bran. Mix thoroughly.

Refrigerate batter, covered. Will keep up to 5 weeks.

When ready to use: Dip batter from container (do not stir) into greased muffin tins. (Make the number of muffins you need and return rest of batter to refrigerator for another time.)

Bake at 400 degrees about 20 min. or till done.
Recipe doubles well.

# Roquefort Biscuits

*Yields 1 dozen biscuits*

*Different and delicious!*

2 cups sifted all-purpose flour
1 tsp. salt
3 tsp. baking powder
1 ½ oz. Roquefort cheese
¼ cup butter
2/3 cup milk

Sift together flour, salt and baking powder.

Crumble in Roquefort cheese.
Cut in butter with pastry blender until mixture is consistency of course cornmeal.
Add milk, slowly, and mix lightly.

Turn onto floured board, knead a little and roll to ½ inch thick. Cut with a floured biscuit cutter and place on greased baking sheet. Bake at 425 degrees for 12 minutes or until golden.

# Wheat Germ Muffins

*Yields 1 ½ dozen*

*Wholesome goodness!*

1 cup sifted all-purpose flour
½ tsp. salt
4 tsp. baking powder
1 cup wheat germ
1 egg
1/3 cup sugar
1 ¼ cup milk
1/3 cup butter or margarine, melted

Mix sifted flour with salt and baking powder
Stir in wheat germ.
Beat egg; add sugar, milk and melted butter

Combine with flour mixture.
Grease muffin tin or use muffin paper cups in tins
(fill 2/3 full). Bake 425 degrees for approximately 20 minutes.

Enjoy.

# Spoon Bread

*I first had this at Evan's Farm Inn- a well-known inn/restaurant in McLean, Virginia when we moved to Virginia. The women, dressed in their colonial attire, served it from table to table, spooned from a wooden bowl they cradled in their arms! A real "Southern" treat!*

1 cup cornmeal, water ground
2 cups milk
2 eggs, separated*
1 tbsp. butter
1 tsp. salt
*Beat egg whites till soft peaks form

Scald the milk. Add cornmeal, egg yolks, butter and salt. Continue to cook on low until smooth and thick. Remove from heat. Stir in beaten egg whites. Bake in a well-greased casserole for 45 minutes at 350 degrees. Serve hot, "spooning" at the table from casserole or wooden bowl, if desired. Enjoy!

# Spinach Spoon Bread

*Makes 8 servings*

*A slightly different twist to an old-fashioned Southern favorite!*

1 9 or 10 oz. pkg. frozen onions in cream sauce
1 10 oz. pkg. frozen chopped spinach
2 slightly beaten eggs
1 cup dairy sour cream
½ cup butter or margarine, melted
¼ tsp. salt
1 8 ½ oz. pkg. corn muffin mix
½ cup (2 oz.) shredded Swiss cheese

Prepare onions in cream sauce according to pkg. Set aside. Cook spinach according to pkg. Drain well.

In large mixing bowl, combine cooked onions in cream sauce, spinach, eggs, sour cream, butter or margarine, and salt. Stir in corn muffin mix. Pour mixture into greased 1 ½ quart casserole.

Bake in 350 degrees oven for 30-35 minutes or until wooden toothpick inserted in center comes out clean.

Sprinkle top of cornbread with shredded Swiss cheese. Bake about 2 minutes more or until cheese melts. Serve warm.

# Yeast Bread

*Yields 1 – 2 loaves*

*This is a tried-and-true recipe of an old friend and it's oh so good!*

2 pkgs. dry yeast
Pinch of sugar
½ cup lukewarm water
½ cup Crisco shortening
½ cup sugar
1 tbsp. salt
2 eggs
2 ½ cups lukewarm water
Flour

Mix dry yeast, pinch of sugar, and ½ cup lukewarm water. Let sit.

Cream shortening, ½ cup sugar.
Add salt, eggs, and 2 ½ cups lukewarm water. Mix thoroughly. Add yeast mixture.

Add enough flour (3 – 4 cups) to make a nice, soft dough.

Turn onto floured surface and knead until smooth. Put in greased bowl to rise until double

Punch down and make into 1 - 2 loaves or individual rolls. Place in greased pans, turn dough over to grease top. Cover with waxed paper and rise again until double (about 1 hour).

Bake in 400 degrees oven uncovered for 30 minutes. Enjoy!

# Zucchini Bread

*Yields two (9 x 5 x 3 inch) loaves*

*A delicious bread and so nutritious too!*

2 -3 cups zucchini, grated – skin on
1 tsp. baking soda
2 tsps. baking powder
1 tsp. cinnamon
1 tsp. salt
2 cups sugar
4 eggs
1 cup cooking oil
2 tsp. vanilla
3 cups flour
1 cup chopped nuts (walnuts, pecans, almonds, etc.)
½ tsp. grated lemon rind, optional

Cream Cheese Frosting:
1 (3 oz.) pkg. cream cheese room temp.
4 tbsp. margarine, softened
2 cups confectioner's sugar
1 tsp. vanilla
Little milk

Beat all ingredients together until nice icing consistency. Use more sugar, margarine or milk as needed.

Drain grated zucchini well.

Pour all ingredients into a mixing bowl except the flour, baking powder, baking soda and nuts.
Mix till blended.

Sift dry ingredients and add. Stir in nuts and grated rind.

Pour into 2 prepared 9 x 5 x 3-inch loaf pans (greased and floured. *)

Bake in preheated 350 degrees oven for 1 hour or until toothpick inserted in center comes out clean.

Cool briefly, turn pan over and remove cake to cooling rack. Slice and serve or freezes well for later. Serve slices buttered or Ice the top of each loaf with a cream cheese frosting once cool.

*Tip: I put a piece of aluminum foil in the bottom of the greased pan just enough to cover bottom and grease the foil too. Cake removes so much easier once baked!*

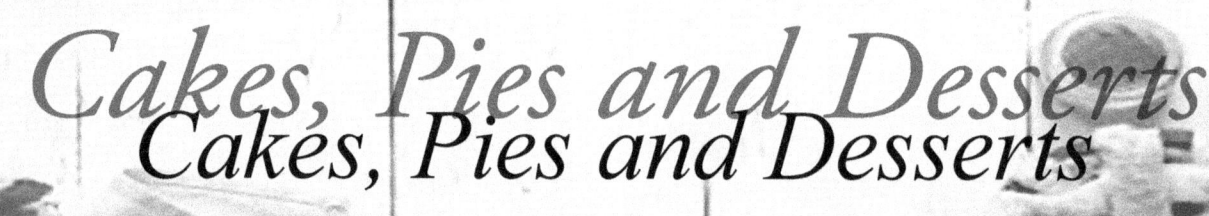

# Cakes, Pies and Desserts

# Anisette Sponge Cake

*Serves 10 – 12 people*

*Couldn't be easier and so-o-o-o good!*

2 pkgs. Anisette Sponge cookies*
1 large box instant chocolate pudding
1 large box instant vanilla pudding
5 cups cold milk
2 pkgs. Dream Whip topping mix
1 8 oz. container Cool Whip
or 8 oz. of fresh whipped cream
Almonds (salted) for garnish

* I like Stella Dora

¼ cup Kahlua or amaretto sprinkled on the cookies before pudding goes on, optional

In a deep springform pan, place a layer of half the cookies on bottom. If using the liquor – at this time sprinkle it over the cookies.

Prepare Dream Whip:
Put all of the Dream Whip in a deep mixing bowl. Add 2 tsps. vanilla extract and 1 cup very cold milk. Beat on medium, then high until stiff peaks form. Set aside in cool place.

Prepare puddings:
Put the instant vanilla and instant chocolate dry pudding mixes in separate bowls.
Add 2 cups cold milk to each. Beat vanilla first with electric mixer until it thickens.
Fold ½ of the whipped Dream Whip into the vanilla pudding.
Set aside in a cool place.

Beat chocolate pudding next just as you did the vanilla pudding. Fold the remaining ½ of the whipped Dream Whip into the chocolate pudding.

Pour chocolate pudding mixture over the first layer of cookies in pan. Place another layer of cookies over the pudding. Pour vanilla pudding mixture over second layer of cookies.

Top with a generous layer of Cool Whip. Sprinkle with chopped almonds. (I like the contrasting taste of "salted" almonds.) Chill until serving time. Enjoy!

# *Apple Dumplings*

*Yields 6 dumplings*

*I made these for my family when they were growing up. A family favorite!*

## Pastry:

2/3 cup shortening
2 - 3cups all-purpose flour
1 tsp. salt
4 – 6 tbsps. cold water

## Filling:

6 baking apples (Granny Smith or Macintosh are good)
½ cup butter
¾ cup brown sugar, packed
1 tsp. cinnamon
½ tsp. nutmeg
3 cups water
2 cups white sugar
1 tsp. vanilla extract

## Pastry

Cut shortening into flour and salt until pea-size particles form. Sprinkle in water, 1 tbsp. at a time, tossing with fork until all flour is moistened and pastry almost comes away from side of bowl. Add 1 – 2 Tbsp. more water if necessary.

Roll pastry to a large rectangle on a lightly floured surface. Cut into 6 squares large enough to wrap around size of apple.

Peel and core apples. Place each on a square. Cut butter into 8 pieces. Place 1 piece in each apple.
Reserve other 2 for sauce.

Pour brown sugar in and around each apple on square.
Sprinkle with cinnamon and nutmeg.
Wet fingertips and bring each point of dough to top of apple, pinching the dough to seal apple shut. Place in greased dish. Combine water, white sugar, vanilla extract and reserved butter in saucepan. Boil 5 min. Pour over dumplings in prepared dish.

Bake in preheated 400 degrees oven approx. 50-60minutes. Serve in bowl with sauce and vanilla ice cream. Enjoy!

# Aunt Esther's Apple Squares

*Makes 1 (9 x 13 inch) pan*

*My mother's sister gave me this recipe and she was excellent
cook too. Always, if you went to visit, she had something
yummy baked and waiting for you!*

5 cups flour
3 cups shortening (Crisco)
1 ½ tsp. salt
2 eggs
Milk
½ cup corn flakes*
8 apples, peeled and sliced just before using
1 cup sugar
Confectioner's sugar
Vanilla extract

Icing: (if desired)

Confectioner's sugar
Milk
Vanilla extract

In bowl, stir 1 – 2cups confectioner's sugar with
enough milk and a little vanilla extract to make a
white icing thin enough to spread over top crust.

Separate eggs. Set whites aside. In a small bowl, mix yolks with
enough milk to make 1 cup total.
Cut shortening into flour, add salt and then add milk mixture.

Form dough and spread ½ of the dough out in an oblong (9 x
13 inch) baking dish. Reserve other half.

Crush the cornflakes and spread over bottom of dough. Peel
and slice apples and place over cornflakes. Sprinkle apples with
1 cup sugar. Roll out rest of dough. Moisten bottom dough's
edges with water and place top dough on, crimping or fluting
edges.

Bake at 400 degrees for approx. 1 hour or until your crust is
crisp and golden. Cool first if icing. Delicious and – yes – this
one has real apples.

(My aunt used the cornflakes because she said they help to
keep the bottom crust from becoming soggy.)

# Mary's Pound Cake

*Makes 1 large "tube pan" cake.*

*Delicious, easy pound cake my sister makes so well!*

1 cup margarine
1 ½ cup sugar
3 cups flour
4 eggs – separated
¼ tsp. salt
3 tsps. baking powder
1 cup milk
1 tsp. vanilla

Cream margarine and sugar together.
Add egg yolks one at a time, beating after each.
Sift dry ingredients together.
Add alternately with milk and vanilla, beating after each addition.

Beat egg whites till stiff.
Fold into batter. Pour into greased and floured tube pan (10 inch).
Bake at 350 degrees for 1 hour or till toothpick comes out clean. Cool in pan before removing.

# Aunt Esther's Pound Cake

*Makes 1 large "tube pan" cake.*

*My aunt, now deceased, was one of the best cooks in our family and her cakes were her specialty.*

3 cups flour
3 cups sugar
½ cup Crisco
2 sticks margarine
6 eggs
1 cup milk
2 tsp. lemon flavoring
1 tsp. vanilla flavoring

Cream Crisco, margarine and sugar.
Then beat good.
Add ½ of the flour and ½ of the milk.
Blend each egg at a time with the remaining flour, milk and flavoring.

Bake at 350 degrees for 45 to 50 minutes.
Test with a toothpick – cake is done when toothpick comes out clean.

# "Best Ever" Chocolate Icing

*A "toss up" with Brown Beauty Icing!*
*I really don't know which one I like best!!*

½ cup confectioner's sugar
1/3 cup evaporated "skim" milk
2 tbsp. margarine
½ tsp. vanilla extract
6 tbsp. cocoa

More confectioner's sugar

Combine first 5 ingredients in mixing bowl.
Beat till smooth.

Add enough additional confectioner's sugar to
beat to a light, fluffy, "light chocolate" icing.

Truly delicious!

# "Brown Beauty Icing"

*This too is a "delicious" icing. I most often make it for my Black Midnight*
*Cake but it is a "gourmet compliment" to any cake!*

1 1/3 cups confectioner's sugar
¼ cup shortening
¼ cup milk
3 pkgs. pre-melted, unsweetened baking chocolate
1 tsp. pure vanilla extract
1 egg

In deep mixing bowl, beat together the confectioner's sugar,
shortening, milk, chocolate and vanilla extract.

Add egg. Beat just until smooth

Chill slightly to thicken, if necessary.
You can add a little more confectioner's sugar too if desired, but
keep in mind you want this icing smooth and creamy.

# Black Midnight Cake

*Serves 12*

*This is a delicious torte!*

2/3 cup soft shortening
1 2/3 cups sugar
3 eggs
2 ¼ cups cake flour*
2/3 cup cocoa
¼ tsp. baking powder
1 ¼ tsp. baking soda
1 tsp. salt
1 1/3 cups water
1 tsp. vanilla extract

*For a light cake flour: add 2 to 3 tbsp. cornstarch to the flour called for. Sift through 3 times before using and see if your cakes don't come out much lighter.

Sweetened Whipped Cream:
Beat 2 cups chilled whipping cream with ¼ cup confectioner's sugar and ½ tsp. vanilla until stiff peaks form

Preheat oven to 350 degrees F.

Grease and flour two 9 x 1 ½ inch cake pans. Cream shortening, sugar and eggs until fluffy. Beat for 5 minutes at high speed on mixer.

Blend flour, cocoa, baking powder, baking soda and salt. Add alternately to creamed mixture with the water and vanilla extract, using low speed on electric mixer.

Pour into pans. Bake at 350 degrees for approx. 35 minutes. Cool.
Cut each layer in half, placing smooth side up for ease in icing. Fill between each layer with sweetened whipped cream.

Frost with Brown Beauty Icing (see recipe in this book).
Refrigerate cake until serving.
Will keep refrigerated for 2 to 3 days.

# *Butter Tarts*

*Yields 2 dozen*

*Absolutely delicious! Recipe given to me by a good friend
in Canada. It has been said that these are the "best
butter tarts in Canada!" Her secret is in the vinegar!*

2 eggs
1 cup brown sugar
½ cup corn syrup
1 tbsp. vinegar
2 tsp. vanilla
½ cup real butter
½ cup raisins or sultanas
½ cup chopped nuts, optional

Tart-size pie shells, home-baked using your favorite
pie dough recipe, or bought are ok too.

Combine all ingredients.

Bake in tart-sized pie shells at 425 degrees for about 15
minutes. Best if not over baked.

Cool slightly before serving. Freeze well for later use.

Great served along or extra good with a dollop of whipped
cream or ice cream!!

*We used to vacation the first 2 weeks in August at Kahshe Lake Resort before we bought our own lake place in Virginia.
Jim went Muskie fishing there. Everyone – kids and adults alike – had a ball together. Great corn roasts "on the beach"
at night. Casual dinners – potluck – and dances in the "hall" – again adults and kids alike. Great memories! Like the
night the kids put a gigantic bull frog in my bed!!!*

# *Carrot Cake*

*A real family favorite!*

Cake:
2 cups sifted flour
2 tsp. cinnamon
1 tsp. ginger
1 tsp. baking soda
1 tsp. baking powder
¼ tsp. salt
2 cups granulated sugar
4 eggs, unbeaten
1 ½ cups vegetable oil
1 tsp. vanilla
2 cups carrots, grated**
½ cup chopped nuts (walnuts, pecans) *

*Optional,
** As an alternative -you may also cook, cool and mash the carrots instead.

Icing:
1 (8 oz.) pkg. cream cheese, softened
½ cup butter or margarine, softened
1 tsp. vanilla extract
1 box confectioner's sugar
1 cup pecans, chopped (optional)

Cream together the softened cream cheese and butter or margarine. Add vanilla extract and enough confectioner's sugar to beat to a nice spreading consistency. Frost cake and sprinkle with chopped pecans. (I like to use salted nuts as I think the little bit of salt compliments the sweetness of the sugar.)

Preheat oven to 375 degrees.

**Cake**
Combine dry ingredients.
Blend together eggs and vegetable oil.

Add grated carrots and dry ingredients.

Bake in two 8 or 9 inch greased and floured cake pans
*for approximately 35 to 40 minutes.

Cool, remove from pans and ice.

*If you want a lighter, torte-like cake, use three cake pans.

# Carrot Cake Supreme

*Clara's way in 3 layers like a torte!*

1 cup white all-purpose flour
1 cup whole wheat flour
2 tsp. baking soda
2 tsp. ground cinnamon
½ tsp. salt
½ tsp. ground nutmeg
¼ tsp. ground ginger
1 cup white granulated sugar
1 cup dark brown sugar
1 cup buttermilk
¾ cup vegetable oil
5 eggs
1 ½ tsp. vanilla extract
1 lb. carrots, grated
8 oz. crushed pineapple
1 cup black walnuts, chopped*
½ cup flaked coconut, optional
½ cup raisins, optional
1 tsp. grated orange rind/zest, optional

* English Walnuts fine too.

Icing
1 (8 oz.) pkg. cream cheese, softened
½ cup butter or margarine, softened
1 tsp. vanilla extract
1 box confectioner's sugar
1 cup pecans, chopped (optional)

Cream together the softened cream cheese and butter or margarine. Add vanilla extract and enough confectioner's sugar to beat to a nice spreading consistency. Frost cake and sprinkle with chopped pecans. (I like to use salted nuts as I think the little bit of salt compliments the sweetness of the sugar.)

Preheat oven to 350 degrees.
Combine dry ingredients.
Add buttermilk, vegetable oil, eggs, and vanilla extract.

Add carrots, crushed pineapple, chopped walnuts, and remaining ingredients if using.

Bake in three 8 or 9 inch greased and floured cake pans* for approximately 25 to 30 minutes or until toothpick inserted in center of layer comes out clean (dry).

Cool slightly, remove from pans and ice with cream cheese frosting recipe in this book.

# Cheesecake

*A real favorite of Jim's and our family.*
*Better prepared a day before serving.*

4 beaten eggs
8 (3 oz.) pkgs. cream cheese, softened
1 cup sugar
2 tsp. lemon juice
1 tsp. salt
3 cups sour cream
4 tbsp. sugar
1 tsp. vanilla
1/8 tsp. salt

Make a graham cracker crust to line the bottom of a 9-inch spring form pan. *

Mix well the eggs, softened cream cheese, 1 cup sugar, lemon juice and 1 tsp. salt.

Pour into pan lined with graham cracker mixture.
Bake in 375 degrees oven for 40 minutes.

Remove cake from oven.

Reset oven to 425 degrees. Let cake cool to room temperature. Mix well and pour over the cake the sour cream, 4 tbsp. sugar, 1 tsp. vanilla and 1/8 tsp. salt.

Cook in hot oven for 5 minutes. Remove from oven.
Cool. Refrigerate until ready to serve.

* Recipe can be found in this book

# Chewy Wheat Germ Brownies

*Yields Approximately 24*
*A delicious, healthy brownie my kids loved!*

4 squares unsweetened chocolate
¾ cup margarine
1 ¼ cups all-purpose flour
2 tsp. baking powder
1 tsp. salt
1 cup wheat germ
2 cups granulated sugar
3 eggs, well beaten
1 tsp. vanilla flavoring
1 cup coarsely chopped walnuts

Melt chocolate in small pan with the margarine.
Set aside.

In large bowl, combine the next five ingredients.
Mix well.

Stir in melted chocolate mixture, eggs and vanilla.
Mix well. Fold in nuts and spread in greased
9 x 13 x 2-inch pan.

Bake in preheated 350 degrees oven about 30 minutes.
Cool and cut in squares. Sprinkle with confectioner's sugar and store in airtight container.

Freeze well. Good for lunch boxes and nutritious!

# Chocolate Almond Biscotti

*Makes 2 ½ dozen cookies*

*A decadent delight!*

1 pkg. Moist Deluxe Dark
Chocolate Cake Mix
1 cup all-purpose flour
½ cup (1 stick) butter, melted
2 eggs
1 tsp. almond extract
½ cup chopped almonds
White chocolate, melted (optional to dip biscotti*)
Combine

Combine cake mix, flour, butter, eggs and almond extract in large bowl.
Beat at low speed with electric mixer until well
Blended. Stir in nuts.
Divide dough in half.
Shape each half into a 12 x 2-inch log.
Place logs on prepared baking sheets.

Bake at 350 degrees 30 to 35 minutes or until toothpick in center comes out clean. Remove logs from oven; cool on baking sheets 15 minutes. Using serrated knife, cut logs into ½ inch slices.
Arrange slices on baking sheets.

Bake biscotti 10 minutes. Remove to cooling rack.
Cool completely.

Dip one end of each biscotti in melted white chocolate, if desired. Allow white chocolate to set at room temperature before storing in airtight container.

*Tip: To melt white chocolate in microwave, place 4 to 6 unwrapped 1-ounce squares of chocolate or 1 cup of chopped chocolate in small microwavable bowl. Microwave at high1to 1½ minutes.*

*Stir after 1 minute and at 30-second intervals after first minute.*

# *Chocolate-Covered Strawberries*

*Not as hard to do as you would think!*

8 oz. quality chocolate*
12 to 14 large, very fresh strawberries

* White chocolate is fine too

In a glass bowl, melt chocolate in the microwave for approximately 30 seconds. Do not overheat it.
The glass bowl will retain heat and even if you still see lumps, the heat will melt the chocolate.

Be sure your strawberries are completely dry.
Even a little water will break down the chocolate.

Dip the fresh strawberries in the melted chocolate three quarters of the way. Put the berries on a sheet of waxed paper to cool.

Let set until the chocolate hardens. You can place them in the refrigerator for a few minutes to hasten the chocolate to harden.

Serve on a plate or in small paper candy cups for a nice presentation or gift giving.

# Chocolate Cream Pie

*Serves 8*

*This is delicious, and so easy. Little kids and "big"
kids love it!*

1 baked piecrust (see "My Own Pie Crust" recipe in this cookbook) or buy a ready-made crust at the store and bake accordingly

Chocolate filling:
1 small box Instant Chocolate Pudding mix
1 envelope Dream Whip topping
2 cups cold milk

Meringue topping:
3 - 4 egg whites
1 tbsp. granulated sugar per egg
¼ tsp. cream of tartar

Prepare piecrust. Cool.
Combine pudding mix in a bowl with 1 ½cups cold milk.
Blend with electric mixer until it thickens. Set aside.

Combine Dream Whip topping in a bowl with ½ cup cold milk and 1 tsp. vanilla extract. Beat with mixer until stiff peaks form.

Fold Dream Whip topping into the chocolate pudding lightly until a light chocolate color. Pour into cooled pie shell.

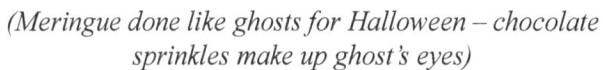

*(Meringue done like ghosts for Halloween – chocolate
sprinkles make up ghost's eyes)*

Make Meringue: Turn broiler on in oven. Beat egg whites with cream of tartar at high speed of electric mixer until they just begin to hold their shape. Gradually beat in the granulated sugar at high speed until stiff and shiny. Spoon meringue over pie filling in pie shell, being careful to spread the meringue to connect with the pie crust around the pie. Put in oven about 2 inches under broiler. Watch closely; turn pie so meringue will brown evenly to golden. Do not burn. Cool slightly; refrigerate until serving time.

# Chocolate "Merlot" Cake

*Serves 12*

*Unusual and delicious!*

2 cups all-purpose flour
¾ cup cocoa
1 ¼ tsp. baking soda
½ tsp. salt
¾ cup butter
1 ¾ cup sugar
2 eggs
1 tsp. vanilla
1 ¼ cups red wine (Merlot)
Confectioner's sugar

Wine Jelly:
½ cup Concord grape jelly
2 to 3 tbsps. red wine

Heat oven to 350 degrees.
Butter cake pans and line each with a round of parchment paper, brush again with butter. Sprinkle pans with flour.

Sift flour with cocoa, baking soda & salt in bowl.
Cream butter in electric mixer; beat in sugar and beat 3 to 5 min. till light and fluffy. Add eggs and vanilla and continue beating 1 to 2 min. Sift 1/3 of the flour mixture over butter mixture.

Fold in 1/3 of the wine. Add remaining flour and wine alternatively in two batches.

Spread batter in pans. Bake at 350 degrees for 30-35 min. till toothpick inserted in center comes out clean. Cool in pans 10 min. then turn out on rack to cool.

Meanwhile: Make the wine jelly: Melt the grape jelly with the wine over low heat, stirring gently until combined.
Let cool.

Shortly before serving: Sandwich the cake with the cooled jelly. Sprinkle top with confectioner's sugar and place on cake plate to serve. Serve with a dollop of whipped cream.

# Cloud Top Cherry Pie

*Serves 6 – 8*

*I started making this for Jim when he was in the Navy stationed at Mayport Naval Base in Florida.
It soon became one of his favorites. So much so that we grow our own sour cherry tree!*

½ cup sugar*
2 tbsp. cornstarch
1 can tart pitted cherries**
1 tsp. lemon juice
Few drops red food coloring (optional)
1 (3 oz.) pkg. cream cheese
2 tbsp. lemon juice
9-inch baked pie crust***
2/3 cup Pet evaporated milk, chilled in ice tray in freezer
¼ cup sugar*
½ tsp. almond extract
Slivered or sliced almonds (toasted)

*If diabetic, use ½ amount of sugar called for and ½ Splenda for the other half sugar called for. Works well.

**We now have our own tart cherry tree and use fresh

***See recipe in this cookbook.

Combine ½ cup sugar (or ¼ cup sugar – ¼ cup Splenda) and cornstarch in saucepan. Drain cherries reserving juice.

Add water to make 1 cup. Stir gradually into sugar mixture and stir over medium heat until boiling.
Stir and boil for 1 minute. Remove from heat.

Stir in cherries, 1 tsp. lemon juice and food coloring if using. Cool. Spread into baked piecrust.

Mix until smooth softened cream cheese with 2 tbsp. lemon juice. Chill 2/3 cup evaporated milk in ice tray until almost frozen at edges. Put ice cold milk, ¼ cup sugar (or 1/8 cup sugar – 1/8 cup Splenda) and almond extract into a cold bowl.

Using cold beaters, whip with electric mixer until stiff. Beat in the cream cheese mixture at medium speed. Spoon over cherries.

Chill 3 hours. Top with toasted slivered or sliced almonds if desired.

# Cranberry Cheesecake

*Serves 8*

*Especially nice during the Christmas holidays.*

2 pkgs. (8 oz. each) Cream Cheese
½ cup sugar
½ tsp. grated orange peel
½ tsp. vanilla
2 eggs
¾ cup chopped dried cranberries, divided
1 already made graham cracker crust
(9-inch pie dish)

Mix cream cheese, sugar, peel, and vanilla with electric mixer on medium speed till well blended.

Add eggs; mix until blended. Stir in ½ cup of the cranberries. Pour into Graham Cracker crust. Sprinkle with remaining ¼ cup cranberries.

Bake at 350 degrees for 40 minutes or until center is almost set. Cool. Refrigerate 3 hours min. or overnight. Garnish with additional cranberries, mint leaves or spiraled orange peel.

# Crema Di Limone

*Serves 6*

*Such a light, "delightful" dessert!*

½ pint heavy whipping cream
¼ cup sugar
1 lemon
1/3 cup light rum

Whip the cream until almost stiff, then start beating in sugar a little at a time.

Add grated lemon rind and juice of ½ lemon.

Last, whip in the rum.

Fill 6 dessert cups and chill thoroughly in freezer one hour, no longer. Enjoy!

# Cream Cheese Braid

*Yields 3 large rolls*

*An old friend gave this recipe to me
one Christmas and it, too, has become a family
favorite – especially of my sister, Mary, who likes to make this
at Christmas and bring it to family gatherings to share.*

Dough
2 pkgs. yeast
6 tbsp. sugar
½ lb. butter
3 eggs
1 cup sour cream
5 cups flour
Filling
4 large pkgs. cream cheese
4 egg yolks
10 tbsp. sugar
4 tsp. vanilla
Icing
Confectioner's sugar
Milk
Vanilla extract

In bowl, stir 1 – 2 cups confectioner's sugar with enough milk and a little vanilla extract to make a white icing thin enough to drizzle over

**For dough**
Dissolve yeast in small amount of water.
Cream the sugar, butter, eggs and sour cream.
Add flour and yeast. Mix well. Refrigerate overnight.

Next day, divide dough into 6 parts. Roll each into Rectangles 9 x 12 inches. Leaving a 3-inch strip in the middle, cut 1-inch strips into the middle.

**Filling**
Beat well the cream cheese, egg yolks, sugar and vanilla. Divide filling in thirds allowing filling for each roll. Place filling down middle of dough.

Braid by alternately crossing dough strips. Cover. Let rise till double (about 1 hour). Bake at 350 degrees for 20 – 25 minutes till golden. Cool and decorate top with icing drizzled over top and 1 – 3 maraschino cherries placed on top with something green to mimic holly.

# Cream Cheese Frosting

*Very easy, non-fail frosting.*

1 (8 oz.) pkg. cream cheese, softened
½ cup butter or margarine, softened
1 tsp. vanilla extract
1 box confectioner's sugar
Milk, if needed to thin frosting
1 cup pecans, chopped
(optional)

Cream together the softened cream cheese and butter or margarine.
Add vanilla extract and enough confectioner's sugar to beat to a nice spreading consistency.

Frost cake and sprinkle with chopped pecans, if using.
(I like to use salted nuts as I think the little bit of salt compensates the sweetness of the sugar.)

# Fast Frosting

*So easy if you don't like making frosting, and so good!*

1 pkg. Dream Whip
1 pkg. (3.4 oz.) instant pudding
(any flavor)
1 – 1 ¾ cup milk

Combine all ingredients in mixing bowl.

Beat with electric mixer until a firm, spreading consistency.

Note: Cakes iced with this frosting do need to be refrigerated.

# Jim's Favorite Crumb Cake

*Serves 6 – 8*

*Jim loves this cake and likes it served warm with a cup of tea.*

1 ½ cups Bisquick mix
½ cup sugar*
½ cup milk or water
2 tbsp. butter or margarine
1 tsp. vanilla
1 egg

My very own topping:

¼ cup brown sugar
¼ cup confectioner's sugar
1/8 cup all-purpose flour
3 tbsp. butter or margarine, softened
1 to 2 tbsp. milk

Combine and sprinkle over cake before baking.

*You can substitute half the sugar with half Splenda. Works fine.

Preheat oven to 350 degrees.

Grease and flour an 8-to-9-inch cake pan.

Combine all ingredients except topping in a bowl and beat on low speed briefly, scraping sides of bowl as you go.

Beat on medium speed approx. 4 – 5 min. Continue to scrape sides of bowl.

Pour into prepared pan. Sprinkle topping mixture over cake.

Bake for approx. 30 minutes or until cake tests done (toothpick inserted in center comes out clean).

Cool slightly. Sprinkle with a little more confectioner's sugar and serve now or later.

# Death By Chocolate

*Serves 8-10*

*Popular at so many neighborhood parties!*
*A soon to become favorite for those chocolate lovers in your life!*
*Very similar to English Trifle. Wonderful during the holidays!*

1 devil's food cake made from mix
Kahlua, ½ cup
2 pkgs. chocolate mousse mix
2 "Skor" candy bars*
1 medium-sized Cool Whip

*Heath bars work well if you can't find Skor candy bars.

Make cake from mix. Cool slightly.
Put holes in cake.
Pour Kahlua over. Let sit.

Prepare the 2 pkgs. mousse according to directions on box. Crush candy bars.

Divide cake. Cut up and put in layers in deep glass trifle-type bowl with the mousse, crushed candy bars and Cool Whip. Repeat layers, sprinkling last of crushed candy bars on top.

Chill till serving time. Dip out and serve.
Yum! yum!

# *Dessert Delight*

*Serves 12*

*Absolutely delicious!*

1 ½ cups graham cracker crumbs
¼ cup sugar*
1/3 cup melted butter or margarine
1 pkg. (8 oz.) cream cheese, softened
¼ cup sugar*
2 tbsp. milk
1 container (8oz.) Cool Whip whipped topping, thawed
2 pkgs. (4 serving size) Jell-O Instant pudding & pie filling, any flavor**
3 ½ cups cold milk

*Half sugar/half Splenda works if you are watching your sugar intake
**I use chocolate.

Combine graham cracker crumbs, ¼ cup sugar (or half sugar/half Splenda), and melted butter.

Press firmly into bottom of a 13 x 9-inch pan.

Beat cream cheese with next ¼ cup sugar and 2 tbsp. milk until smooth.

Fold in half the whipped topping.
Spread over crust. Prepare pudding as directed on package using the 3 ½ cups milk.

Pour over cream cheese layer. Chill several Hours or overnight. Spread with remaining whipped topping over pudding. Garnish with grated/shaved chocolate and/or chopped nuts.

*Note: I like to use "salted" almonds chopped fine as a garnish. That bit of salt compliments the sweetness and I consider this "my signature" to this dessert and similar other desserts I make!*

# Easy Ice Cream Roll

*Yields 6-8 servings*

*I made this a lot for my family as they were growing up.*
*It's really very easy and very special!*

1 jelly roll baking pan
(cookie sheet with sides works well)
1 cake mix, your choice
Ice cream, your choice of flavor

(I prefer chocolate cake with vanilla ice cream)

Follow box directions for cake mixture.
Mix and spread cake mixture onto jelly roll cake pan which you first line with waxed paper you have greased.

Bake in preheated 375 degrees oven for approximately 15 – 20 minutes. Test for doneness. Should spring back when touched and toothpick come out clean when inserted in center.

Remove cake from oven. Loosen from pan and dump onto a clean dish towel dusted with confectioner's sugar. Roll cake and towel up while cake is still hot. Cool completely in towel.

Unroll carefully and spread with softened ice cream.
Re-roll only the cake and ice cream and freeze wrapped in plastic wrap. To serve: remove from freezer about 15 – 20 min. before serving time to allow cake to soften but not the ice cream. Enjoy!

# Easy Lemon Meringue Pie

*Serves 8*

*This is a delicious, short version that is truly
one of Jim's favorite desserts!*

1 baked piecrust
(see "My Own Pie Crust" recipe in this cookbook)
or buy a ready-made crust at the store and bake
accordingly

Lemon filling:

Buy either 1 or 2 cans lemon pie filling (if you can
find it) or a box of Jell-O lemon filling you cook and
follow directions on the box

Meringue topping:
3 - 4 egg whites
1 tbsp. granulated sugar per egg
¼ tsp. cream of tartar

Prepare piecrust. Cool slightly.
Cook lemon pie filling according to directions on box. Pour into pie shell.

Make meringue:
Put broiler on in oven.
Beat egg whites with cream of tartar at high speed of electric mixer until they just begin to hold their shape. Gradually beat in the granulated sugar at high speed until stiff and shiny.

Spoon meringue over pie filling in pie shell, being careful to spread the meringue to connect with the pie crust all around the pie.

Put in oven about 2 inches under broiler. Watch closely, turning pie to allow meringue to cook evenly to a gold tone – do not burn.

Cool slightly, then refrigerate until serving time.

# Elegant Lemon Torte

*For the "lemon lovers" in your life! Scrumptious!*

Lemon filling: *
2 large egg yolks
1/3 cup granulated sugar
¼ cup fresh lemon juice
2 tbsp. unsalted butter, softened
Pinch of salt
1 tsp. finely grated lemon zest
½ cup heavy cream

Cake batter:
2 cups all-purpose flour
1 tbsp. baking powder
½ tsp. salt
1 ½ cups sugar
¾ cup shortening (I use Crisco)
2 tsp. vanilla extract
1 cup milk
4 egg whites

Frosting:
3 cups confectioner's sugar
2/3 cup shortening
2 tbsp. milk
1 tsp. vanilla
Flaked coconut

Beat all but coconut to a nice spreading consistency. Frost cake. Coat sides with the flaked coconut.

*You may use lemon pudding in the box you buy and cook in lieu this filling

Preheat oven to 350 degrees. Make lemon filling – in medium saucepan – whisk together the yolks and sugar. Whisk in lemon juice, butter, salt. Cook over medium-low heat (stir constantly with wooden spoon) 5 to 6 min. until mixture turns opaque, thickens & coats the back of a spoon. Do not boil or it will curdle. Pour through mesh sieve into a medium bowl. Stir in lemon zest and heavy cream and place in refrigerator to cool.

Meanwhile for cake: Combine flour, baking powder and salt. In large bowl, beat sugar, shortening and vanilla until fluffy.

Add flour mixture alternately with milk beating well. Beat egg whites in a small bowl till stiff but not dry. Fold into batter.

Spread into two greased and floured 8- or 9-inch round cake pans. Bake for 25 minutes or until toothpick comes out clean. Cool 10 minutes. Remove from pans. Cool completely. Split each layer into two layers, making a torte.

Spread about ½ cup lemon filling between each layer and on top to within 1 inch of edge. Frost sides covering the edge. Coat sides of cake with flaked coconut. Store in refrigerator until serving.

# Best Scones

*A recipe shared with us by the owner of a Bed & Breakfast in Massachusetts and truly the best I have ever tasted! Melt in your mouth delicious – great for breakfast, brunch, as well as "afternoon tea!" She said she got this recipe from a man from Africa staying at her B & B who offered it to add to her collection. She has made these ever since, serves them every day at her B & B and claims they are "the best!"*

4 cups all-purpose flour
1 cup granulated sugar
½ tsp. salt
6 tsps. baking powder
1 cup of golden raisins or drie cranberries
2 sticks softened butter
2 eggs
¾ cup milk
1 tsp. vanilla, lemon or almond extract
(or other of your choice)

Egg Wash
Beat together an egg and a little milk in small bowl. Lightly brush on tops of scones before baking. Or…

If you prefer, rather than egg wash, brush tops with mixture of ½ cup powdered sugar and enough lemon juice stirred to an icing you can drizzle over scones before baking.

Heat oven to 380 degrees. (Yes - 380 degrees)

Whisk together flour, salt, sugar and baking powder. Gradually mix in dried fruit used.

Add softened butter to dry ingredients. Mix in with fingertips until evenly blended. (Will have a cornmeal texture.)

Whisk together eggs, milk, and extract. Gradually mix this into flour mixture with fork until nice dough forms. (Do not overwork mixture should be "doughy" overall like soft lumpy mashed potatoes.)

Pat dough on floured surface into a high round ring. Using round edge of measuring cup as a cookie cutter place each scone on a greased cookie sheet. *

Bake for about 18 – 19 minutes. (Top with an egg wash before baking, if you wish…see recipe to left.)

Note: If serving with afternoon tea, serve with clotted cream (buy it as to make it you need unhomogenized milk/cream) or use whipped cream for a little extra special touch! Enjoy!

# Foundation or Plain Cake

*Jim's grandmother, Nellie Rossi's recipe. No icing,*
*just a plain yellow cake. Yummy!*
*Another of Jim's favorites.*

1 ½ cups flour
2 tsp. baking powder
¼ tsp. salt
1/3 cup shortening
½ - ¾ cup sugar
6 egg yolks*
½ cup milk
1 tsp. vanilla

*You can use 3 eggs, but Grandma used only the yolks

Sift flour, baking powder and salt together.
Cream shortening. Add sugar and cream until fluffy.
Add egg yolks (or eggs), then dry ingredients alternately with milk and vanilla.

Beat. Pour into greased 8- or 9-inch cake pan.
Do not flour pan.
Bake in moderate (350 degrees) oven for approximately 25 minutes.
Good with coffee or tea as is.

# French Cream Tarts with Fruit

*Serves 6*

*Easy dessert!*

Filling

1 8 oz. pkg. cream cheese, softened
1 cup powdered sugar
½ pint whipping cream, whipped
1 tsp. vanilla extract
Fruit, such as strawberries, Blueberries,
Raspberries, Cherries
6 baked pastry shells, or make you own

Pastry shells
Make out of any pie dough recipe or try this dough:
1 (3 oz.) pkg. cream cheese
½ cup butter
1 cup sifted all-purpose flour

Soften the cream cheese and blend with softened butter. Stir in flour. Chill for 1 hour. Shape into 1 – 2-inch size balls. Place each ball in ungreased tart tins. Spread dough out in tins with finger to form the little tart shells. Bake at 325 degrees for 25 min. or till golden. Cool and fill.

Filling

Combine the softened cream cheese and powdered sugar. Beat until fluffy.

Fold in whipped cream and vanilla.
Spoon into pastry shells.
Top with various fruits, diced to fit shells.

Refrigerate until ready to serve.

Note: You may omit the pastry shells and spoon the cream cheese filling into dessert dishes and then top with the fruit if you so wish. When serving, top with a "dollop" of whipped cream for a nice presentation and finish off with a sprig of mint, if desired.

# Graham Cracker Crust

1 ½ cups graham cracker crumbs
(10 graham cracker sheets)
2 tbsp. sugar
1 tbsp. brown sugar, packed
7 tbsp. butter, melted

Crush graham crackers by rolling over them with a rolling pin or pulverize them in food processor.
Combine crumbs with sugar.
Add the melted butter. Blend well with a fork.

Spread mixture in bottom of pie dish. Press all around the pan to pack crumbs gently on bottom and up sides.

Bake in preheated 375 degrees oven for 7 – 10 minutes. Refrigerate before filling.

(If making the crust for a cheesecake, put the crumb mixture in the bottom of a springform pan, spreading over bottom and up sides as far as it goes. Pour in the cheesecake filling and bake according to your cheesecake recipe).

# Key Lime Pie

*Serves 8*

*Jim and I have been going to Captiva Island in Florida for years and love the Key Lime Pie they serve at the "Mucky Duck" there. If you've been there, you know what I mean! They serve it slightly frozen, and it is scrumptious! I think I have just about mastered it here. Enjoy!*

1 (8 oz.) can sweetened condensed milk
8 tbsp. Key Lime juice
4 egg whites
1 prepared 9-inch graham cracker piecrust*
Whipped cream

*See my recipe in this cookbook.

Combine the condensed milk and lime juice in a mixing bowl. In another bowl, whip the egg whites until stiff. Add them to condensed milk and lime juice mixture. Whisk together slowly so you don't deflate the egg whites. Pour mixture into prepared* piecrust and freeze. Serve slightly frozen slices topped with whipped cream!
Luscious!

*Note: Follow directions if using bought graham cracker crust. If you make your own and want to bake it first – cool completely before filling.*

# *Kway Lapis*

*(Multi-Layer Cake)*

*This recipe is from an old Chinese friend from the neighborhood we raised our children in who has long passed away. She served this most unusual cake at the patio luncheon after a neighborhood Garden Tour and everyone raved about it. Later, she had several of us women to her home and taught us how to make it, step-by-step. Long process but definitely worth it!*

12 eggs (12 yolks and 7 whites)
1 lb. butter
1 cup sugar
½ cup brandy, rum or cognac
½ cup condensed milk
Vanilla extract
1 cup flour

Whip butter, brandy, condensed milk and vanilla extract together until light and fluffy. In separate bowl: whip egg whites until stiff but not dry. Add sugar gradually, then yolks, one at a time, until light. Add butter mixture and fold in flour. In a greased, waxed paper-lined 10-inch spring form cake pan, pour ¾ cup of the mixture, spread evenly, and bake at 500 degrees until golden brown (about 2 – 3 minutes). Remove cake from oven. Now turn oven to broil. Spread ¾ cup of mixture evenly again in same manner and broil until golden brown (2 – 3 minutes). Repeat this procedure until all mixture is used. watch carefully or it will burn. (Should result in about 20 layers)

*Note: This cake will keep well refrigerated for at least 2 weeks or may be frozen in foil. It is most unusual and delicious!*

# Lemon Icebox Petit Fours

*Yields approximately 24*
*Very nice when you want just a light finger dessert*

1 pkg. cream cheese (8 oz.)
1 can condensed milk (14 oz.)
½ cup fresh lemon juice*
1 tbsp. lemon zest
1 tsp. pure vanilla extract
1 graham cracker crust, bought or
see recipe in this cookbook

*For an "Italian" flare, use the Italian liquor "Limoncello"

Combine cream cheese, condensed milk, lemon juice (or lemoncello), lemon zest and vanilla in bowl.

Mix on medium speed of mixer until smooth. Pour into graham cracker crust. Refrigerate overnight. Cut into small squares and serve as petit small paper pastry cups.

Note: This recipe can also be prepared and served as a pie. If planning to serve as squares, however, remember to prepare in a square pan.

# Mary Jane's Pie Crust

*Jim's mother wrote, "So fond to me are the memories of*
*Mary Jane's fresh-baked pies to greet us evenings in*
*Wisconsin when we went over to visit, chat and*
*watch the deer in their back yard overlooking*
*Pelican Lake!"*

4 cups flour + 2 tsp. baking powder
1 ¾ cups shortening (Crisco)
1 tbsp. sugar
2 tsp. salt
1 tbsp. vinegar ("cider" vinegar)
1 egg
½ cup water

Combine flour, baking powder, shortening, sugar and salt. Mix with a fork until of a crumb texture.
Beat vinegar, egg and water together and add to crumbed mixture. Chill at least 15 minutes.

Wrap ball-size dough in waxed paper or plastic wrap and freeze until needed. Or – roll immediately into crusts the size of your pie pans and freeze until needed.

# Light and Fluffy Cream Pies

*Serves 8*

*I was making this pie before they came out with the idea
commercially to add a whipped topping to pie fillings! Very light and delicious!*

8 – 9-inch baked pie crust*
1 box (3.9 oz.) preferred flavor of Instant Jell-O
   Pudding (i.e., vanilla, chocolate, coconut cream,
   banana cream)
1 ½ cups cold milk
1 pkg. Dream Whip prepared according to directions
   on package or container of Cool Whip Topping
   already prepared

*See recipe in this book

Meringue
(for one 8-9 inch pie)
3 – 4 egg whites
1/8 tsp. cream of tartar
3 – 4 tbsp. granulated sugar

Beat egg whites till frothy.
Add the cream of tartar, continuing beating.
Add the sugar a Tbsp. at a time while continuing
beating until stiff peaks form. Immediately spread
atop cool cream pie, being careful to spread to join
inner pie crust edge to seal. Place under broiler and
watch closely, turning pie to brown meringue just to
a nice golden color evenly. Remove immediately and
store in refrigerator until ready to serve.

*Okay to use bought pie crust / graham
cracker crust for a quick pie.

Prepare 1 envelope Dream Whip according to package
whipping until stiff and set aside - or have on hand in refrigerator
a container of Cool Whip Topping which is already prepared.
Keep cool.

In medium-large mixing bowl, beat the pudding mix and cold
milk with wire whisk or electric mixer until mixture begins to
thicken.

Fold the whipped topping into the pudding mixture. Pour into
cooled, pre-baked pie shell/graham cracker shell.

Top with either more Dream Whip topping, Cool Whip, or
meringue (see recipe). I top with meringue most of the time.
Refrigerate until serving time. Enjoy!

# Mandarin Orange Cake

*Serves 12*

*Also known as "Pineapple Delight" or "Pineapple Surprise!"*
*This cake is an absolute favorite at our parties and family gatherings –*
*especially Christmas! And it is definitely a favorite of mine!*

1 (18 oz.) pkg. yellow cake mix, without pudding
1 (11 oz.) can mandarin oranges, undrained
4 eggs
½ cup vegetable oil
1 (15 ¼ oz.) can crushed pineapple, undrained
1 large carton Cool Whip, thawed
1 (3 ¾ oz.) pkg. vanilla instant pudding

Combine cake mix, oranges, eggs, and oil.
Beat 2 minutes at highest speed of electric mixer. Reduce speed to low, beat 1 minute longer. Pour batter into 3 greased and floured 9-inch round cake pans.

Bake at 350 degrees F for 20-25 minutes.
Cool briefly in pans. Remove and cool completely.

Combine crushed pineapple, Cool Whip, and instant pudding. Beat 2 minutes at medium speed. Let stand 5 minutes or until mixture is spreading consistency.
Spread mixture between layers and on top and sides of cake. Chill at least 2 hours before serving. Store in refrigerator.

*Note: You might add sliced strawberries between layers also for an even more gourmet touch!*

# Mary's Chocolate Pecan Clusters

*So easy to make and so delicious!*
*My sister, Mary, makes these during the holidays.*

3 (6 oz. each) pkgs. shelled pecan halves
1 bag (11.5 oz.) Hershey's Milk Chocolate Chips
½ stick (1/4 cup) butter

Melt butter in bottom of oblong roast pan.
Stir pecan halves till coated with the melted butter.
Roast the pecans in the butter in a 300 degrees oven for approximately 30 min., stirring every 15 minutes.

Meanwhile, melt Hershey's Milk Chocolate Chips in a deep bowl in microwave oven, 30 seconds at a time on High until just melted.

Remove pecans from oven and stir into melted chocolate. Let stand for approx. 10 minutes to cool enough that mixture will spoon nicely onto waxed paper in clusters (3 or 4 pecans halves to one cluster). Cool well and store in tins.

# Mary's Fudge

*Our friend, Mary, always made this*
*for my Jim at Christmas and he so looked forward to it!*
*In his opinion, no one can make fudge like Mary!*

5 cups of white sugar
1 (13 oz) can evaporated milk
2 sticks oleo (margarine)
1 pkg. chocolate bits (large)
Desired amount of chopped nuts
1 tsp. vanilla

Combine sugar, evaporated milk and oleo. Bring to boil and stir constantly. When it starts to boil, stir for 5 more minutes.
Remove from heat and add the chocolate bits, nuts and vanilla.

Mix well. Pour into buttered pan. Cool and cut in squares.

# Fresh Strawberry Pie

*So easy to make and so delicious! Great for those hot summer evenings*
*when you want something quick and refreshing!*

8- or 9-inch baked pie shell
Fresh strawberries
Strawberry pie topping (sold in most grocery stores near the strawberries)
Whipped cream, canned or fresh
Sweetened whipped cream
(Or seedless strawberry jelly/jam)

To make, you'll need the following:
1 pint heaving whipping cream
1 tbsp. confectioners' sugar
Whip together at high speed until stiff peaks form.

Either make your pie shell, bake, and let cool, or buy one ready-made at the grocery store.

Cut up enough strawberries to fill pie shell, leaving the nicest halves for the top.

Pour strawberry pie topping over pie. Refrigerate until serving time. Serve with dollops of whipped cream. Enjoy!

(If using seedless strawberry jelly/jam for topping, heat it first, just enough for ease in pouring over the strawberries.)

# Baker's Frosting

*Light and fluffy frosting and so worth the effort!*

4 tbsp. flour
1 cup milk
Dash salt
½ cup butter
½ cup shortening (Crisco)
1 cup sugar, granulated
2 tsp. vanilla extract

Cook flour, milk and salt, stirring constantly until thick and creamy. Remove from stove and cool.

Beat together the butter, shortening, Granulated sugar and vanilla extract separately until creamy. Add the cooled flour mixture. Beat well until a nice spreading consistency.

# Michael's Delight

*Serves 12*

*My son Michael's favorite cake, which he says should really be called Better than Sex Cake!*

1 box 2-layer Marble cake mix, any brand
1 small box Jell-O Instant Chocolate Pudding Mix
1 small box Jell-O Instant Vanilla Pudding Mix
1 large container Cool Whip, regular or light works well too
Chopped salted, toasted almonds

Prepare cake according to box directions. Divide batter between three 8-inch round cake pans. Bake until done per box

Cool cake layer in pan for 15 minutes. Turn cake layers out of pans onto cooling racks. Cool completely. When cake is cool, prepare puddings in separate bowls.

Place first cake layer on serving plate. Top with the chocolate pudding.
Place second cake layer on and top with the vanilla pudding.
If any pudding is left, place on top of second layer.

Ice cake with the Cool Whip, being generous. Sprinkle top of cake with chopped salted almonds. ** Refrigerate until serving time.

This cake will bring rave reviews!

*\*\*My signature ingredient to enhance whipped toppings on cakes.*

# Mile-High Ice Cream Pie

*Serves 8*

*This pie is delicious and great for those summer gatherings. A conversation piece!*

1 prepared 9-inch graham cracker pie crust*
1 quart vanilla ice cream
1 quart chocolate ice cream
1 pint strawberry ice cream
1 banana
5 or 6 strawberries
1 cup pineapple chunks
1/8 cup salted almonds, chopped fine
Whipped cream
Maraschino cherries, optional

*See cookbook index for home baked recipe for graham cracker crust or just buy one.

Bake graham cracker pie crust. Cool completely.

Soften ice creams just enough to be able to spread them in piecrust.

Spread a 1-inch layer of vanilla ice cream in bottom of piecrust. Add layer of bananas slices. Cover with a layer of chocolate ice cream.

Add a layer of strawberry ice cream. Add a layer of sliced strawberries. Spread remainder of the strawberry ice cream over.

Spread remaining of the chocolate ice cream over.

Add a layer of pineapple chunks. Top with a good layer of vanilla ice cream, swirling it as you spread.

Sprinkle the finely chopped almonds over. Freeze until serving time.

*Note: Follow direction if using bought graham cracker crust. If you make your own, bake it first. Cool completely before filling. Also, method above is flexible, layer all as you wish, as high as you wish!*

# Miriam's Christmas Pudding

*Serves 12-16*

*Recipe of my lifelong "pen pal" and dear friend, Miriam Whitmore of Halesworth, Suffolk, England.*

4 oz. flour
2 oz. breadcrumbs
1 tsp. mixed spice
1 level tsp. cinnamon
1 level tsp. nutmeg
4 oz. shredded suet
4 oz. brown sugar
4 oz. grated apple
1 small carrot, grated
4 oz. mixed crystallized peel
4 oz. currants
8 oz. raisins
4 oz. sultanas
2 oz. prunes or dried apricots, chopped
4 oz. almonds, chopped
grated rind of ½ lemon juice
grated rind of ½ orange
1 tbsp. golden syrup
1/ 2 pint ale, beer, or milk
2 eggs

Brandy butter:
4 oz. butter
6 oz. icing sugar (confectioners)
2 tbsp. brandy

Mix ingredients and leave overnight, then stir again.
Put into the greased basin or basins (glass not metal), cover with foil, greaseproof paper (waxed paper/ parchment paper), or a cloth.

Grease both inside and outside of the paper to keep the pudding dry on top.

Steam for 2 – 3 hours, allowing longer time for one pudding. Remove the covers when cooked. Then, put on dry covers and re-steam for 2-3 hours when needed.

Beat or blend the butter and icing sugar together for the brandy butter. Beat in the brandy.

Serve with the pudding.

# Mom Mugnolo's Mock Apple Pie

*Serves 8-10*

*Jim's mom loved making this pie and trying to fool everyone! A friend of ours,
Jim Bequette, loved it and gave it his own name – "Apple Spinnelli!" Very rich.*

Pastry
4 ½ cups flour
1 tsp. baking powder
1 ½ tsp. salt
1 ½ cups vegetable shortening (Crisco)
2 eggs
½ cup milk (very cold)

Filling
6 cups water
3 cups sugar
6 heaping tsp. cream of tartar
Zest of 1 lemon (skin grated off lemon)
3 tbsp. lemon juice (from fresh lemon)
72 Ritz crackers (keep crackers whole)
2 tbsp. Butter
½ - 1 tsp. cinnamon

Icing (if desired – and Mom desired)
1 box Confectioner's sugar
Milk
Vanilla extract
In bowl, stir 1 – 2 cups confectioner's sugar with enough milk and a little vanilla extract to make a white icing thin enough to spread over top crust.

So there is not an apple in the pie

Preheat oven to 425 degrees. Sift together the flour, baking powder and salt. Cut vegetable shortening into flour mixture. Beat together eggs and the ½ cup milk. Add flour mixture slowly. Stir with a fork to blend, then use hands to knead to a nice dough.

Divide dough in two. Roll out on floured board. Grease a 9 x 13 glass dish with shortening. Line bottom of dish with first layer of dough.

**Filling**
Combine water, sugar and cream of tartar. Bring to a boil. Reduce heat and simmer for 15 min. Add the lemon zest and juice. Cool slightly. Crumble Ritz crackers slightly in a bowl. Pour syrup over crackers.

Pour filling into bottom crust. Dot with butter and sprinkle with cinnamon. Put on top pastry, moistening bottom crust edge with water to help seal. Cut slits in top of pie to allow steam to escape; crimp edges. Bake for 30 – 40 min. Frost while still warm.

So delicious and not an apple

*"Mock Apple Pie"*

# My Mom's Brownies

*Makes 1 (9 x 9 or 9 x 13 inch) pan*

*For the chocolate lovers in your life! Yummy!*

¾ cup shortening (part margarine if desired)
¾ cup cocoa powder
1 ½ cups brown sugar
1 ½ cups white granulated sugar
3 eggs
1 ½ cups all-purpose flour
1 ½ tsp. salt
1 cup chopped nuts

Grease baking pan and set aside.
Melt shortening/margarine and cool slightly.
Add the cocoa powder and stir to blend.

Blend in sugars and eggs and stir until smooth.
Add in the flour, salt and chopped nuts. Stir to blend.

Bake in 400 degrees oven approximately 20 minutes.
Remove from oven - they will look half-baked but they will harden as they cool. Cut in squares to serve. They resemble fudge in taste and appearance

# Mom's Donuts

*My Mom's very own recipe for the donuts she made for us. Yummy!*

2 cups flour
½ teaspoon salt
2 teaspoons baking powder
¼ cup sugar
½ cup milk
1 egg
½ teaspoon vanilla
1tbsp. melted shortening
Cooking oil for frying

Mix all ingredients together.
Roll dough out to ½ inch thick.
Cut with donut cutter or rim of glass for donut and bottle for hole.
Drop in hot lard (or cooking oil) and fry 3 minutes.

Remove from hot oil and sprinkle with granulated sugar; cool on brown paper. Enjoy!

# *My Cake Yeast Donuts*

*These donuts are made from a dough made for bread and they are light and delicious!*

1 cake of yeast
1 cup milk
3 ½ cups flour
¼ cup Crisco, soft
¼ cup sugar
1 tsp. salt
1 egg, beaten

If icing:
Confectioner's sugar
Milk
Vanilla flavoring

Dissolve cake of yeast in lukewarm milk.
Add 1 ½ cups flour and beat until smooth.
Cover and set aside in a warm place until it begins to rise.

Add the soft Crisco, sugar, salt and beaten egg.
Add remaining flour. Knead dough into a ball and set aside to rise again (on floured board or in greased bowl) till double.

Roll dough out on floured surface to about ½ inch thick. Cut with donut cutter or use the rims of two glasses, one smaller than the other. Allow to rise on floured surface.

Fry in deep fat till golden on both sides. Remove from hot oil and either roll in granulated sugar or ice with right consistency of an icing made of the confectioner's sugar, milk and vanilla flavoring and place on rack until icing stops running.

# My Mom's Sour Cherry Pie

*Serves 6 – 8*

*Absolutely delicious!*

1 can Red Sour Pitted Cherries

2 tbsp. flour

1 tbsp. butter

1 cup sugar

## Pastry dough

2 cups all-purpose flour

2 tbsp. granulated sugar

½ tsp. salt

1/3 cup shortening (Crisco) or butter or margarine
softened

Ice water

## Hint

I cover the rim of my pie before baking with a narrow border of aluminum foil to keep the outer crust from burning during baking. Remove it 5 or 10 min. before pie is done.

Make pastry dough.

Put flour and salt (sifting if desired) and sugar in bowl, blend in softened shortening, butter or margarine until mixture resembles cornmeal texture. (Use a pastry blender, fork and/or your hands.)

Add enough ice water sparingly at first to stir and blend into a dough that forms a nice ball that pulls away from the bowl. Not too dry. Divide dough into two balls. Roll the first ball out on a floured surface large enough to fit the bottom of your pie pan. Grease the pie pan and place the dough into pan.

Proceed with pie. Drain the cherries (reserve juice), cover with sugar and let stand 15 minutes. Add flour and butter to the cherry juice and cook until slightly thickened. Cool.

Fill pastry crust with the cherries and pour thickened juice over. Sprinkle with a little extra sugar. Roll out top pastry to fit over pie hanging over enough to crimp edges around top of pie. Make a vent hole In center of top* and prick top of pie here and there with a fork to allow steam to escape.

Bake at 425 degrees for approximately 30-45 min. until crust is golden.

*My signature to my pies is the "S" I carve in the center of the top crust before baking for the vent. The S stands for "Scetti", which was the nickname Jim's friends called him when I met him. Short for spaghetti! Memories are made of this!*

# My Own Pie Crust

*Yields 1 pie crust*
*Using "ice water" is a must for a good, flaky pie crust!*

1 ½ cups all-purpose flour
¼ tsp. salt
½ cup shortening
2 tbsp. sugar
4 – 5 tbsp. ice cold water

Put flour, salt and sugar in bowl. Cut shortening into flour until of a crumbly consistency. Add enough ice water to work with fork into a nice, soft dough– not sticky. If sticky, add a little more flour.

Roll out on floured cloth or board to a circle slightly larger than your pie pan. Press into greased pie pan.
Allow and overlap of dough at top, turn under and crimp edges with the tines of a fork or pinch with your finger to form a nicer edge. Prick bottom of crust with times of a fork to allow crust to bake flat.

Bake in preheated oven at 425 degrees approximately 10 -12 minutes until golden. *

Remove from oven, cool and fill with desired filling.

*Note: Double recipe for two piece crusts. Roll the first one out, put into greased pie pan (do not crimp edges), pour pie filling, roll out the second crust, and place on top of filled crust – but first wet the edges of the top crust with water before placing the top crust on, then press edges together to seal and then crimp or pinch in usual manner. Follow directions for your filled pie recipe from there.*

*(Granddaughter, Anna)*

# Nut Roll

*Yields 8 rolls*

*I make these mostly at Christmas and not only serve
them to family and guests on Christmas Day but often to
take home or as gifts. When I first gave one to a neighbor in Vienna,
Virginia, she remarked that it was just like her father used to make in his
bakery back home in Vienna, Austria when she was growing up!*

4 cups all-purpose flour, sifted
¾ tsp. baking soda
½ tsp. salt
1 pkg. dry yeast
½ lb. butter, softened
5 egg yolks
½ pint sour cream
Confectioner's sugar

Nut filling
1 lb. ground pecans or walnuts
5 egg whites, beaten stiff but not dry
1 cup granulated sugar

Combine flour, soda, salt and yeast.
Cut butter into flour mixture until it resembles coarse meal.
Add egg yolks and sour cream to mixture.
Blend well with hands. Cut dough into 4 parts. Wrap each in waxed paper and put in refrigerator 4 hours or overnight.

Next day: Sift confectioner's sugar on cloth or board.
Cut each piece of dough in half. Roll one piece of dough at a time till paper thin (approx. 15 by 12 inches). Spread with filling mixture. Roll up so roll is 15 inches long.

Place 2 rolls on well-greased cookie sheet and bake in preheated 375 degrees oven for 20 minutes until golden.
Sprinkle with sifted confectioner's sugar while still warm.
When rolls have cooled slightly, run knife under each roll for easy removal from cookie sheet. The nut rolls can be frozen for later up to 2 months, or they keep well in the refrigerator up to 4 weeks. Cut in ½ inch slices for serving.
Enjoy!

# Old-Fashioned Spice Cake

*Yields 2 loaf pans*

*Remember the good old days and the spice cake the A & P used to sell?*
*This is as close as you can get to the real thing! Moist and delicious!*

1 stick butter
1/4 cup shortening
2 large eggs, beaten
1 tsp. pure vanilla extract
1 1/2 cups sugar
1 cup chunky applesauce*
1 cup plump raisins**
2 ½ cups all-purpose flour
1 tsp. baking soda
½ tsp. salt
2 tsp. cinnamon
1 tsp. nutmeg (fresh grated if you can)
¼ tsp. ginger

*Homemade applesauce is best – see recipe for mine in this cookbook
** Plump raisins by soaking in warm water briefly.

Sift together the flour, baking soda, baking powder, salt, cinnamon, ginger and nutmeg. Set aside.

Cream the butter, shortening, and beaten eggs together.
Blend well. On low speed of mixer, add vanilla and applesauce. Add raisins. Keeping mixer on low speed, start adding dry ingredients. Mix only until the flour mixture is blended in – do not over mix.

Divide mixture between two loaf pans*. Bake in the middle of the oven for approximately 45 minutes or until cake tests done with toothpick inserted in middle.
Remove from pans and cool on rack. Frost first layer, put second cake layer on top of first layer, then frost just the top of the cake (with Cream Cheese Frosting, see recipe in this cookbook).

*Tip: I grease and flour pans but also put a strip of aluminum foil in bottom of each pan and grease it. Makes removal of the cake from the pan much easier.*

# *Petit Fours*

*Fancy little cakes I used to make for ladies' luncheons but very
nice for any special occasion or just because.*

Any cake (mix or from scratch)

Icing
6 cups of confectioners' sugar
5 tbsp. water
5 tbsp. corn syrup
1 tsp. vanilla
Few drops food coloring

Candied violets (see recipe in this cookbook
in Miscellaneous)

Grease and flour a jelly roll pan or cookie sheet with sides (15 ½ by 10 ½ by inch).

Make batter for a sheet cake from any cake recipe you have, or box mix following directions. Bake at 350 degrees for 20 to 25 minutes. When cool, cut cake into 1 ½ inch squares.

**Ice Squares**
Mix Confectioners' sugar, water corn syrup, vanilla and food coloring in top of double boiler. Heat just to pouring consistency.

Place cake squares on a metal rack on top of disposable paper or foil. Slowly pour icing over the squares, thus creating the petit fours. Let sit until icing hardens. Decorate as desired. (See candied violet recipe in cookbook.)*

*\*Any icing that drips through rack onto waxed paper can be reused. Simply scrape up and reheat.*

# *Pina Colada Cake*

*Serves 12*

*This was given to me by Jim's aunt Mary, now deceased, from Chicago.*
*A great cake as is or served as a torte with sweetened whipped cream and fresh strawberries.*

1 box (18 oz.) White Cake Mix
1 box (3 5/8 oz.) Coconut Cream
Instant Pudding Mix
4 eggs
½ cup water
1/3 cup light or dark rum
¼ cup cooking oil
Pina colada frosting (recipe below)
1 cup flaked coconut

Combine cake mix, 1 box pudding mix, ½ cup water, rum and cooking oil in large bowl of electric mixer.

Beat on medium speed about 4 minutes.

Pour into 2 greased and floured 9-inch layer cake pans (3 pans if doing making a torte).

Bake at 350 degrees for 25-30 minutes. Or until cake springs back when touched lightly.

Cool completely on rack. Fill and frost layers. Sprinkle with flaked coconut. Chill until serving time.

Frosting
1 can (8 oz.) crushed pineapple in juice
1 box. (3 5/8 oz.) Coconut Cream
Instant Pudding
1/3 cup light or dark rum
9 oz. container Cool Whip, thawed

Combine crushed pineapple with juice with pudding mix and rum till well blended. Fold in thawed Cool Whip. Yields approximately 2 ½ cups frosting. *

(For more frosting just add more Cool Whip keeping all other ingredients the same.

# Poppy Seed Cake

*Serves 16 people*

*Maybe not as good as Mom Mugnolo used to make, but nonetheless pretty darn good!*

1 cup softened butter
1 ½ cups granulated sugar
1 can poppy seed filling
4 eggs, separated
1 tsp. vanilla*
1 cup sour cream
2 ½ cups all-purposed flour
1 tsp. baking soda
1 tsp. salt
Confectioners' sugar
Lemon flavoring or lemon juice
(optional)

Preheat oven to 350 degrees Fahrenheit. Grease and flour a 12-cup Bundt pan or 10-inch tube pan and set aside.

Beat butter and sugar on large bowl with electric mixer until light and fluffy. Add poppy seed filling; beat until well blended.

Beat in egg yolks, 1 at a time. Beat well after each addition.

Add vanilla and sour cream and beat till blended.
Combine flour, baking soda and salt. Add to poppy seed mixture gradually, beating well after each addition.

Beat egg whites in separate bowl with electric mixer until stiff. Fold into batter evenly. Bake 60 minutes to 1 hour 15 minutes in prepared pan or until cake tester inserted in center comes out clean.

Cool in pan 10 minutes. Remove from pan and cool completely on wire rack. Dust with confectioners' sugar just before serving.

# *Poteca (Slovenian Nut Roll)*

*Yields One large roll*

*My Aunt Esther used to make this and it was often served at family weddings.*

Dough
2 tsp. active dry yeast
½ cup warm milk
1 tbsp. granulated sugar
1 ½ cups milk
¾ cup shortening
5 egg yolks
¾ granulated sugar
2 tsp. salt
1 tbsp. vanilla extract
1 tsp. nutmeg
7 cups all-purpose flour

Walnut Filling
1 cup milk
2 cups granulated sugar
½ cup (1 stick) butter
Grated peel of one lemon
½ cup honey
1 tbsp. vanilla extract
5 egg whites
Cinnamon
2 pounds walnuts, finely ground

Dissolve yeast and 1 tbsp. sugar in warm milk. Let stand 5 minutes to activate the yeast. Combine yeast mixture and the remainder of the dough ingredients (except half the flour). Mix well, then add enough remaining flour until the dough can be handled without sticking. Takes about 10 minutes of kneading by hand or 5 minutes on a mixer with dough hook.

Put dough into large greased bowl, cover with plastic wrap and set in warm place to rise until double.

## Filling
Combine softened butter, sugar, egg whites, honey, vanilla extract, grated lemon peel, cinnamon and ground nuts. Add just enough milk until mixture is of spreading consistency.
Set aside.

Punch down dough. Roll into a 30-by-20-inch rectangle. Spread filling within 1 inch of edges. Roll up from long side. Pinch seams and ends to seal. Shape into a right spiral on greased baking sheet. Cover and let rise till double, approximately 1 hour.

Bake at 350 degrees for 35 minutes or till golden brown. Cool on rack. If desired, brush with a glazed of confectioners' sugar and milk. Slice and enjoy!

# *Pumpkin Bars*

*Serves 10-12*

*A recipe our daughter, Tara, gave us. Very moist and delicious!*

4 eggs
1 2/3 cups granulated sugar
2 cups flour
1 cup cooking oil
16 oz. Pumpkin
2 tsp. baking powder
2 tsp. Cinnamon
1 tsp. Salt
1 tsp. baking soda

Frosting
8 oz. pkg. cream cheese
1 box confectioners' sugar
1 stick butter
1 tsp. vanilla
Little milk

In large bowl, mix together eggs, granulated sugar, flour, cooking oil, pumpkin, baking powder, baking soda, cinnamon, and salt.

Pour into prepared oblong 9-by-13 baking pan (greased and floured).

Bake in preheated 350 degrees oven for 25 minutes, check after 20 minutes. When toothpick comes out clean, cake is done.

Cool.

Prepare frosting. Beat cream cheese, confectioners' sugar, softened butter, vanilla and milk together to nice spreading consistency.

# *Ricotta Fritters*

*Another Italian recipe from a Texas friend.*

8 oz. ricotta cheese
1/3 cup all-purpose flour
Grated peel of 1 lemon
Vegetable oil for frying
2 eggs
1 ½ tbsp. softened butter
Salt
Honey

Put ricotta cheese in bowl and heat until rather creamy.

Put eggs in another bowl and beat lightly. Add to ricotta, beating with a whisk.

Put in the flour, a little at a time, using a whisk.

Add the butter, lemon peel and a pinch of salt. Mix well. Set the batter aside and let it rest at room temperature at least 2 hours but no longer than 3 hours.

Heat oil in frying pan until hot. Drop batter a tablespoon at a time. Should float to surface. Don't overcrowd. When golden brown on one side, turn and brown on other side. They should puff up while frying. If they don't, oil is too hot.

Drain on paper towels. Pour honey over them and serve while still hot. Often stacked and served as a tower at weddings!

*Buon Appetito!*

# *Rum Cake*

*Serves 8*

*My sons Carl's and Michael's favorite cake. I always make this at
Christmastime and try to make one just for them to take home.*

1 box butter recipe golden cake mix, double
  layer
1 pkg. vanilla instant pudding mix
  (3 ¾ o z. s ize)
½ cup light rum
½ cup water
½ cup all-vegetable cooking oil
(Crisco)
4 eggs
½ cup chopped pecans, optional (add to batter is
used)

Hot Rum Glaze
1 cup sugar ¼ cup light rum
1 stick margarine ¼ cup water

Place ingredients in small pan.
Boil 2-3 minutes.

Note:
To make a superb chocolate rum
cake, substitute a butter recipe
fudge cake mix in above recipe.

Grease and flour a bundt cake pan.
Place cake and pudding mix in large mixing bowl.

Add rum, water, oil, and eggs.
Mix with electric mixer for two minutes. (Add chopped pecans
here to batter if using.)

Pour batter into prepared cake pan.

Bake at 325 degrees for 50 to 60 minutes.

Remove cake from oven and immediately pour on Hot Rum
Glaze (see recipe). Hot glaze will cause cake to settle but don't
be alarmed. The cake will be yummy.

Cool cake in pan 30 minutes, then remove from pan to serving
plate.

*"Rum Cake"*

# Scandinavian Almond Cake

*Yields 1 half round cake*

*This is a delicious, different cake and so worth the effort! Baked in a half round cake pan.*
*Recipe given to me by a Scandinavian friend who lives in Michigan.*

1 ¼ cup sugar
1 egg
1 ½ tsp. pure almond extract
2/3 cup milk
1 ¼ cups flour
½ tsp. baking powder
1 stick margarine, melted

Spray pan with Pam with flour or another cooking spray, Beat well the sugar, egg, almond extract, and milk. Add the flour and baking powder. Add the melted margarine. Mix well.

Bake at 350 degrees for 40-50 minutes. Edges must be golden brown. Cool in pan before removing. Cake will break apart if removed too soon. Sprinkle with confectioners' sugar.

# Short Breads

*Recipe given me by my friend and daughter-in-law's mother,*
*Jeanette Smith, from Ontario, Canada. Melt in your mouth delicious!*

1 lb. butter
1 cup powdered sugar
1 cup rice flour
3 cups instant blend flour (Wondra)

Alternate ingredients you can use if you don't have above:
1 lb. butter
1 cup powdered sugar
2 cups sifted all-purpose flour
½ cup corn starch
½ tsp. salt

Put butter in bowl. Beat till creamy. Work in sugar by hand, then add flours a little at a time until blended and a little dry.

Roll out on floured surface. Cut into circles. Bake on greased and floured cookie sheets or double layer of brown paper in a 325 degrees oven for 15 to 20 minutes until lightly golden.

# Tartlett Pie Shells

*Yields 2-3 dozen tart shells*

*Good recipe for any tarlet recipe in this book.*

1 cup butter or margarine, softened
1 cup shredded cheese (suggest a mild cheese such as Gruyére)
2 cups flour
Dash salt

Tip:
Can be made ahead and frozen baked or unbaked.
Can fill unbaked shells and then bake.

Cream butter and shredded cheese together. Add flour and salt. Mix thoroughly. Shape dough into a ball and chill at least 3 hours.

Remove from refrigerator. Roll fairly thin. Cut into 3-inch rounds or squares. Place in individual tart tins, prick bottoms with fork, and bake in preheated 425 degrees oven until golden, approximately 8-10 minutes cool slightly. Tap out of tins.

Fill with cool fillings of your choice and serve. Or fill unbaked shells with fillings to be cooked and bake them 10 – 20 minutes.

# Mom's Sour Milk Cookies

*My father's absolute favorite cookie my mother used to make for him!*

1 cup Spry (Crisco today) and butter*
½ cup sour milk
1 ½ cups sugar
2 eggs, beat till fluffy
2 teaspoon baking powder
1 teaspoon baking soda
4 cups flour

*1 cup total of Crisco/butter

Preheat oven to 375-400 degrees. Combine Spry (Crisco), butter, sour milk and sugar together.

Beat eggs till fluffy. Add to mixture with the baking powder, baking soda and flour. Stir to blend.

Drop by tablespoons onto ungreased baking sheet. Bake for approximately 12 minutes or till slightly golden on top. Remove cookies to cool on rack.

# Seven-Minute Frosting

*Yields frosting for 2 8-inch layers*

*Another specialty of my mom's.*

**White Icing**

2 unbeaten egg whites

1 ½ cup granulated sugar

¼ tsp. cream of tartar

3 tbsp. cold water

1 tsp. vanilla extract flavoring

**For Chocolate**

Add to above 1 ½ oz. melted unsweetened chocolate 2 minutes before taking from stove.

**For Coffee**

Use cold brewed coffee in place of water.

Combine all ingredients except vanilla in the top of a double boiler pan. (Do not put this mixture on the stove yet.) Beat mixture on low speed for about 30 seconds.

Then place over boiling water and beat with beater or electric mixer for seven minutes or until stiff peaks form. Be careful not to let top pan touch the water.

Remove from heat. Add vanilla extract, continue beating*until cool, light, and fluffy and good spreading consistency. (Place over bowl of ice water if desired to speed cooling while beating.) Spread immediately on cake. Very light and fluffy icing. Enjoy!

*\*Some people say this stage takes longer that 7 minutes. Give it a try. It is worth the effort for the fluffy, light, melt-in-your mouth end result!*

# Spumone

*Yields 6-8 servings*

*I serve this at special times or when we have company. Very special and so worth the effort!*

1 cup milk
½ cup sugar
1/8 tsp. salt
3 egg yolks, slightly beaten
½ square chocolate (1/2 oz.)
1 cup heavy whipping cream
1 tbsp. sugar
1/8 pistachio extract
Green food coloring
Maraschino cherries, drained and chilled
½ cup chilled whipping cream
1 tbsp. sugar
6 almonds, chopped fine
¼ tsp. almond extract

*To scald milk, bring it nearly to a boil, stirring constantly, to keep from forming a skin on the surface. Meant to kill harmful bacteria in the old days! Now, with pasteurization. Just warming the milk is enough.

Chill a large mixing bowl and beaters in refrigerator.

Scald*the milk in top of double boiler.
Stir in ½ cup sugar and salt.

Stir 3 tbsp. of the hot mixture into 3 slightly beaten egg yolks. Immediately blend into entire mixture in top of double boiler. Cook over simmering water 5 minutes, stirring constantly, until mixture coats a silver spoon. Remove from heat and cool.

Meanwhile, melt square of chocolate and set aside. Stir into cooled egg mixture 1 cup heavy whipping cream. Divide mixture equally into two bowls. Add chocolate to one bowl, mixing thoroughly. Place in refrigerator.

Add ½ tsp. rum extract to remaining bowl, mixing well. Pour mixture into refrigerator tray.
Freeze until mushy.

# *SPUMONE continued*

*as this is the rest of the Spumone recipe method*

Turn rum mixture into chilled bowl and beat with chilled beater until mixture is smooth and creamy. Spoon into dessert and freeze until firm.

Next, beat ½ chilled whipping cream in bowl with chilled rotary beater until stiff peaks form when beater is slowly lifted upright. Beat 1 tbsp. sugar and 1/8 tsp. pistachio extract into the whipped cream till blended. Mix in a drop at a time of green food coloring to tint pistachio mixture as desired.

Spoon this mixture over rum layer in dishes and return to freezer.

When pistachio cream layer becomes firm, place 1 maraschino cherry in center and return to freezer.

Last layer, beat with chilled beaters ½ cup whipping cream again until it stands in stiff peaks. Fold or beat into this 1 tbsp. sugar, chopped almond and almond extract. Spoon this mixture over firm pistachio cream layer in dessert dishes. Return to freezer.

When almond layer is firm, pour chocolate mixture into refrigerator tray. Freeze until mushy. Beat in chilled bowl until smooth and creamy. Spoon mixture over firm pistachio layer and cherry. Cover each with waxed paper, freeze 6-8 hours or until spumoni is firm.

Enjoy!

# *Tortoni*

*Yields 8-10 servings*

*A very easy, delicious and special dessert! Homemade Italian ice cream. Very worth the effort!*

1 cup dry macaroon cookie crumbs
1 cup chilled whipping cream
1/3 cup sifted confectioner's sugar
1 egg white, stiffly beaten
1 tbsp. rum or sherry

Paper baking cups like you use for cupcakes, or use dessert dishes.

Chill small mixing bowl and beaters.

Grind up enough macaroons to make 1 cup crumbs (see recipe in cookbook index to make your own or bought are fine).

Set aside.

Beat whipping cream in chilled bowl until stiff peaks form when beater is slowly lifted upright.

Fold ½ cup of the macaroon crumbs into the whipping cream with the confectioners' sugar and stiffly beaten egg white and rum or sherry.

Pour mixture into paper cups or dessert dishes. Sprinkle each with remaining macaroon crumbs. Place in refrigerator.
Freeze about 3-4 hours or until firm. Serve and enjoy! Truly a delight!

# *Wacky Cake*

*Serves 8-10*

*An old-fashioned delight!*

## Cake Ingredients

3 cups flour
2 cups sugar
1 tsp. salt
6 tbsp. cocoa
1 ½ to 2 tsps. baking soda
¾ cup cooking oil
2 tsp. vanilla extract
2 tbsp. white vinegar
2 cups water

## Baker's Frosting

4 tbsp. flour
1 cup milk
Dash salt
½ cup butter
½ cup shortening
1 cup granulated sugar
2 tsp. vanilla extract

## Method

Put flour, milk and salt in pan. Cook mixture, stirring constantly until thick and creamy. Remove and let cool.
Beat together butter, shortening, sugar and vanilla till creamy. Add to flour mixture and beat well until nice spreading consistency.

In a deep bowl, stir together the flour, sugar, salt, baking soda, and cocoa. Make 4 indentations into dry mixture and into each hole pour one each of the following: the cooking oil in one-hole, vanilla extract in another, vinegar in another and water in another.

Stir just until blended. Bake in greased and floured 13-by-9-inch pan at 350 degrees for 20-30 minutes.
Cool. Leave in pan.

Frost with your favorite icing or Baker's Frosting
(see recipe at left).

Casseroles
*Casseroles*

# Cheese Soufflé

*Serves 4*

*This is a nice, light meal served with a salad of your choice!*

3 tbsp. butter
3 tbsp. flour
1 cup milk
4 beaten egg yolks
5 tbsp. grated Romano Cheese
2 tbsp. grated Gruyere Cheese
4 egg whites
Slices of Swiss Cheese, cut into fancy shapes
1 small onion, chopped fine (optional)

Melt butter over low heat in pan. Add flour and blend over low heat for about 3 to 5 minutes. Stir in milk (you may scald milk first if you wish but not necessary).

Cook this cream sauce and stir with wire whisk or wooden spoon until thickened and smooth. Remove from heat for a minute or so.

Add, stirring well, the egg yolks and grated cheeses. Beat egg whites until stiff but not dry. Fold into the cheese mixture. (If using onion, add it at this point.)

Pour into a 7 inch (or 4 individual) ungreased soufflé dish(es). * For a "top hat" that puffs in the oven, trace a circle through mixture with knife 1 inch from edge and 1 inch deep.

Top with fancy slices of Swiss cheese (optional) and bake at 350 degrees for approx. 25 to 30 minutes or until set or knife inserted off- center comes out clean.

Serve immediately as it will drop. Enjoy!

*\*Prepare dish(es) by greasing bottom and sides well with butter and coating with flour and grated cheese.*

# Cheese Strata

*Serves 6 – 8*

*Great for breakfast, brunch or lunch!*

8 slices buttered, cubed bread
2 ½ cups grated cheese
(Swiss, sharp cheddar, asiago, your choice)
3 eggs
2 ½ cups milk
1 tsp. salt
¼ tsp. white pepper
½ tsp. dry mustard

Grease a 9 x 13-inch glass casserole. Alternate layers of bread and cheese(s). Make the top layer cheese. Combine the eggs, milk and seasonings. Pour over the layers. Let stand at least one hour before baking or prepare the casserole the night before and refrigerate overnight.

Bake in preheated 350 degrees oven approximately 60 minutes until brown and fluffy. Strata is done if knife inserted in middle comes out clean.

*Note: Vary recipe. add cooked meat bacon or sausage and/or mushrooms, green pepper.*

# Clara's Chicken Casserole

*Serves 6 – 8*

*Clara and Sam are like family to us and they have spoiled us with delicious food like this casserole of Clara's.*

4 cups pre-cooked chicken pieces
cut into bite-sized pieces
1 can Cream of Mushroom Soup
1 can Cream of Chicken Soup
1 can Cream of Celery Soup
8 oz. can Carnation Evaporated Milk
1 large pkg. frozen broccoli pieces, unthawed
1 8 oz. pkg. egg noodles black pepper to taste
1 can dried onions (optional)

In a 9 x 13-inch oblong casserole dish place the pre-cooked chicken pieces. Add the soups, milk, broccoli pieces and egg noodles. Stir to blend.

Top with the dried onion (I recommend using them.) Bake at a 350 degrees approximately 45 minutes to 1 hour until bubbly and golden.

# Company Casserole

*Serves 8*

*Good standby for luncheon or parties.*

4 cups cooked, diced chicken
1 (8 ½ oz.) cans artichoke hearts, drained and
    quartered
1 cup butter or margarine
½ cup all-purpose flour
¼ tsp. cayenne pepper
1 tsp. salt
1 clove garlic, crushed
3 ½ cups milk
1 cup (4 oz.) shredded sharp
Cheddar cheese
1 (8 oz.) can mushroom buttons, drained and halves
1 cup crisp cereal crumbs cornflakes)
2 tbsp. butter, melted

Spread cooked chicken pieces in greased 3-quart baking dish. Top with artichoke hearts. Melt 1 cup butter in 2-quart saucepan; Add flour, cayenne, salt, garlic. Stir until smooth.

Cook 1 minute, stirring constantly. Gradually stir in milk; cook over medium heat until thick and smooth.
Add cheeses and stir until cheese melts. Add mushrooms.

Pour over chicken and artichokes. Combine cereal crumbs with the 2-tbsp. melted butter, sprinkle over cheese sauce. Bake at 350 degrees for 30 minutes. Serve with salad and nice, crusty bread.

# Macaroni and Cheese

*Serves 4 – 6*

*Another of Clara's specialties!*

8 oz. macaroni
2 tbsp. cooking oil
½ stick butter, melted
Salt, to taste
Pepper, to taste
1 8-oz. block cheddar cheese
½ pkg. saltine crackers
2 eggs
Little milk

Cook macaroni in enough boiling water to cover macaroni to which the cooking oil has been added until done al dente (just underdone).

Drain, Put macaroni in a bowl. Mix in the melted butter, salt, cheese (cubed or shredded), and saltine crackers crumbled.

Beat 2 eggs and pour into mixture above. Add ½ to 1 cup milk. Mix together.

Put mixture in a prepared oblong baking dish (lightly buttered or sprayed with cooking spray). Cover with aluminum foil and bake in 375 degrees oven approximately 20 minutes until milk is absorbed but still creamy.

Remove from oven. Too with more shredded cheese while hot. Serve.

# Goulash

*Serves 8*

*Good standby for dinner. My children even liked this cold or reheated.*

1 lb. ground beef
½ cup onion
¼ cup chopped green pepper
2 tbsp. butter or margarine
2 cups elbow macaroni
2 8-oz. cans tomato sauce
Salt/pepper to taste
1 garlic clove, minced

Melt butter or margarine in skillet. Add onion, green pepper and minced garlic and sauté till onion and garlic are golden. Remove from skillet and set aside in bowl. Add ground beef to skillet and brown well. Add onion/green pepper/minced garlic back to skillet with the meat. Set aside.

Cook macaroni in boiling water until al dente stage. Drain. Add to mixture in skillet with salt pepper to taste. Mix well and pour into buttered casserole. Add tomato sauce.

Cover and bake in preheated 350 degrees oven for approximately 45 minutes.

# Green Chile Casserole

*Every once in a while, this family likes a Mexican dish!*

3 (4 oz.) cans whole green chilies
1 cup half-and-half
3 eggs, beaten
1/3 cup flour
1 ½ lb. monterey jack cheese, grated
½ lb. cheddar, grated
1 8 oz. can tomato sauce

Split chilies lengthwise, rinse out seeds and drain. Combine half-and-half, eggs, and flour. In another bowl, mix cheeses. Reserve ½ cup.

Butter a 1 – ½ quart casserole. Layer egg mixture, chilies and cheeses.

Spread tomato sauce on top and sprinkle with reserved cheese. Bake 1 hour at 350 degrees. Serve.

# Italian-Style Salami and Cheese Strata

*Serves 6 – 8*

*Another great dish for breakfast, brunch or lunch!*

10 slices buttered, cubed bread (day old is best)
½ lb. Genoa or other Salami, cubed 3 cups
grated cheese (Asiago and/or Monterrey Jack or your choice)
5 eggs
2 ½ cups milk
1/3 cup white wine
1 tsp. salt
¼ tsp. crushed red pepper
¼ tsp. cracked black pepper
1 tsp. dry mustard
¼ cup scallions, sliced

Grease a 9-by-13-inch glass casserole.
Alternate layers of bread, meat and cheese.
Make the top layer cheese.
Combine the eggs, milk wine and seasonings and scallions. Pour over the layers.
Let stand at least one hour before baking or prepare the casserole the night before and refrigerate overnight.
Bake in preheated 350 degrees oven approximately 60 minutes until brown and fluffy. Strata is done if knife inserted in middle comes out clean.
Serve with a nice side salad of mixed greens.

# Pot Pies

*Serves 4*

*These I make from either leftover beef, chicken or turkey. Another of my family's favorites!*

½ cup minced onion
2 tbsp. fat/shortening
2 cups leftover beef, chicken, turkey cut
　　into bite-sized pieces
1 cup cooked potatoes, diced
1 cup cooked carrots, diced
½ cup frozen peas
1 tbsp. Worcestershire sauce
1 tsp. salt
1/8 tsp. black pepper
2-2 ½ leftover gravy*
Flaky pastry**

*If none leftover, use package gravy from store (beef or chicken as appropriate).

**Either make your own pastry or buy boxed pastry mix and prepare according to directions on box; the stores also have wonderful pre-made pastry sheets sold in rectangular boxes – 2 rounds in each box. Ready to put in prepared plate! Find in section with crack-open biscuits or the like.

Sauté onion in fat over low heat until golden and tender. Add remaining ingredients (except pastry). Stir to blend.

Divide mixture among 4 greased individual foil pie pans or one deep 8-inch casserole.

Roll pastry 1/8 inch thick. (Either one piece to fit the 8-inch casserole or 4 individual pieces to fit the individual foil pie pans.) Fit on top of the meat/vegetable mixture. (No dough on bottom.)

Brush lightly with egg white or ice water. Bake for 20 minutes in hot 450 degrees oven till crust is golden. Serve hot.

Note: We flip the pies out onto a dinner plate so that the pastry is on the bottom and the filling on top when we eat them, but you may serve them right side up if you wish.

# Shepherd's Pie

*Serves 4 – 6*

*Another nice way to use up leftover meats and very delicious!*

2 cups cooked meat, cut in bite-sized pieces
2 cups mashed potatoes
2 eggs, separated
½ cup gravy or cream of mushroom or cream of
   chicken soup if no gravy*
½ cup chopped onion
½ cup other vegetable – mushrooms, carrots,
   celery, etc.
Butter
Grated cheese

*Add a little water to thin soups.

Beat egg yolks only into the mashed potatoes. Whip egg whites separately with a little salt until stiff but not dry. Fold into potatoes. Heat meat with gravy or soup mixture and vegetables.

Spread half the potato mixture in bottom of a greased baking dish. Pour hot meat mixture on top. Cover with remaining potato mixture. Dot with butter. Sprinkle with grated cheese. Bake in 400 degrees oven until browned – approximately 20 – 30 minutes. Serve in wedges like a pie.

# Spinach Soufflé

*Serves 12*

*A nice light lunch or dinner.*

2 pkg. frozen, chopped spinach
2 lb. cottage cheese, drained
1 lb. sharp cheddar cheese, coarsely grated
6 eggs, stirred to break yolks
¼ lb. butter or margarine*

*If you double this recipe, use less butter.

Cook spinach enough to loosen with fork.
Put all ingredients together and mix.
Place in a 2-quart buttered casserole.
Bake at 350 degrees for approximately 1 hour.
Serve immediately with nice hot rolls and salad of your choice.

Suggestion: Place casserole on round pizza-type pan while baking in case it cooks over.

# Spinach Casserole

*Serves 4 – 6*

*An absolutely delicious accompaniment to any dinner entrée!*

2 pkg. frozen spinach, chopped and drained
1 egg, beaten
1 cup herb stuffing mix
1 cup shredded cheddar cheese
1 can cream of chicken soup
¼ cup melted butter
1 tbsp. chopped onion
½ cup sliced mushrooms

Mix all ingredients, with reserving 1/3 cup stuffing. Put into buttered casserole dish.

Sprinkle remaining stuffing mix on top.

Bake at 350 degrees for 30 to 35 minutes. Serve alongside your choice of main entrée.

Note: Recipe doubles nicely.

# Herbed Spinach Casserole

*Serves 6*

*This is the recipe my kids loved growing up. I would cut it in sqares and send it in their school lunches
or keep it in the refrigerator as a snack between meals.
Great way to get your kids to eat their spinach!*

1 (10 oz.) pkg. chopped spinach
1 cup cooked rice
1 cup grated sharp cheese
¼ cup grated mozzarella cheese
2 eggs, slightly beaten
2 tbsp. melted butter
½ cup milk
2 tbsp. chopped onion
½ tsp. Worcestershire sauce
1 tsp. salt
¼ tsp. thyme

Cook and drain spinach. Cool. Mix with remaining ingredients. Place in greased shallow baking dish (10 by 6 by 1 1/2 inches).

Bake in 350 degrees oven for 25 – 30 minutes until just turning Golden at edges and top. Serve immediately or store in refrigerator and serve later as desired.

# Summer Squash Casserole

*Serves 4 – 6*

*An absolutely delicious accompaniment to any dinner entrée!*

3 lb. squash (yellow or zucchini, or combo)
½ cup chopped onion
½ cup breadcrumbs*
½ tsp. black pepper
2 eggs, beaten
1 tsp. salt
1 tbsp. sugar
1 cup cheddar cheese, grated**

*I use Italian-style breadcrumbs.
**I use white, sharp cheddar.

Wash and cut up squash into medium size chunks. Boil in water until tender.
Drain thoroughly. Mash.
Add all remaining ingredients, except ½ of the cheddar

Pour squash mixture into a buttered baking dish.
Top with remaining cheese.
Bake at 375 degrees for 1 hour or until cheese is melted and squash is bubbly and golden on sides.
Serve alongside your choice of entrée.

# Squash Casserole

*Serves 4 – 6*

*A nice accompaniment to any meal, and another of Clara's dishes we all love!*

4 yellow squash
4 zucchini squash
1 medium yellow onion
Salt
Pepper ½ stick butter, melted
2 eggs
½ cup milk
½ cup shredded cheese
(cheddar, parmesan, your choice)

Wash squash and cut up in cubes. Quarter and slice onion thin. Cook in boiling water until tender. Drain in colander.

Mix in bowl with salt, pepper. Beat 2 eggs and add with the melted butter. Place mixture in a prepared baking pan buttered or sprayed with cooking spray. Bake at 350 – 375 degrees for 25 to 30 minutes until liquid is cooked down.

Remove from oven.
Sprinkle with shredded cheese while casserole is still hot and serve.

# *Stuffed Bell Peppers*

*Serves 4 – 6*

*Good "old – fashioned" dish I raised my family on.*

6 green bell peppers
1 medium onion, diced
1 – ½ lb. ground beef
1 ½ cups long-grain white rice (Uncle Ben's)*
2 cans (1 lb. 13 oz. each) tomato sauce
Salt/pepper to taste

*Works well with brown rice too.

Slice tops off the peppers and remove seeds. Place pepper in dutch oven pot in about 3 inches of water. Bring to boil and simmer until the peppers turn dark. Immediately drain hot water and add cold water and set aside.

Meanwhile: Place rice and 3 cups water in a pot and cook covered for 20 minutes till fluffy. Remove from heat and set aside.

Sauté the onion and ground beef in a skillet. Add the cooked rice and stir to blend. Season with salt/ pepper to taste.

Place peppers in a deep oblong baking dish big enough to accommodate 6 peppers, ladling a little tomato sauce on bottom of dish first. Spoon rice/beef mixture into each pepper filling to top. Pour remaining tomato sauce overall.

Bake in preheated 350 degrees oven for approximately 45 minutes till done with a lid placed offside enough to allow a little opening so mixture does not cook over. Serve with your favorite bread and butter.
Enjoy!

# Stuffed Cabbage

*Serves 4 – 6*

*The way my mother made them for me when I was growing up, and I, in turn, raised my family on. Very similar to the way I make the stuffed bell peppers.*

1 large head of cabbage
1 medium onion, diced
1 – ½ lb. ground beef
1 cup long-grain white rice (Uncle Ben's)
2 cans (1 lb. 13 oz. each) tomato sauce
Salt/pepper to taste

Wash and partially core the head of cabbage. Place in dutch oven pot in about 3 inches of water. Bring to boil and simmer until cabbage softens. Immediately drain water set aside in the pot and keep covered.

Meanwhile: Place rice and 2 cups water in a pot and cook covered for 20 minutes till fluffy. Remove from heat and set aside. Sauté the onion and ground beef in a skillet. Add the cooked rice and stir to blend. Season with salt/pepper to taste.

Ladle a little tomato sauce on bottom of dish first. Pull cabbage leaves away from head carefully trying not to tear them. Trim off the hard membrane near the core (for easier rolling). Spoon about ¼ cup rice/beef mixture onto each leaf and roll up one end to the other, folding in the sides as you roll and tucking in the ends when done. Place in baking dish. Pour remaining tomato sauce overall.

Bake in preheated 350 degrees oven for approximately 35 minutes covered till done.

Serve with your favorite bread and butter. Enjoy!

Cookies

# Gingerbread House (Chalet)

*Figure 1: This is just one of the many Gingerbread Houses I have made over the years. This one is patterned after a cottage we had for 22 years on Lake Anna in Virginia, a modified A-Frame. The actual house had straight walls on the sides and upper balconies on either side of the cottage.*

To make the Gingerbread:

Take two pieces of 8 1/2 –by 11 copy paper. Fold one in half lengthwise. Then draw lines from the mid-point of the paper to the bottom corners (see Figure 1 below). Cut on dotes lines to form a triangle. This piece becomes the pattern for the front and back panels of the house. (Cut 2 from gingerbread rolled out on floured board.) The other piece of paper you leave whole. This one becomes the pattern for the side walls of the Gingerbread House (cut 2).

Bake gingerbread according to recipe for gingerbread in this book. Remove from baking sheet and let cool. Glue parts of house together with the following:

**Royal Icing**
3 egg whites, room temperature
1 lb. confectioners' sugar
½ tsp. cream of tartar
Combine ingredients beat at high speed for 7 – 10 minutes until stiff icing forms.

Royal icing is a hard drying icing. Please keep covered with a damp cloth. Humidity will greatly affect this icing. Grease will greatly affect this icing. Be sure to wash all utensils with a good dish soap. To glue house parts together, fill a knife with icing. Apply icing on edges of each part and hold together till bonded. Icing dries hard. Decorate with candies, etc. as you wish. Enjoy!

# Gingerbread Men

*Yields 3 – 4 dozen cookies*
*I baked these at Christmas for my children and often the neighborhood children. I would put their names*
*on the cookies and hang them on our tree for them to find on Christmas Day. One Christmas our*
*Collie, Dusty, ate any she could reach on the tree!*

6 cups all- purpose flour
1 tbsp. baking powder
1 tbsp. ground ginger
1 tsp. ground nutmeg
1 tsp. ground cloves
1 tsp. ground cinnamon
1 cup shortening, melted and cooled slightly
1 cup molasses
1 cup brown sugar
½ cup water
1 egg
1 tsp. vanilla extract

Sift the flour, baking powder, ginger, nutmeg, cloves and cinnamon together. Set aside. Mix together in a medium bowl the shortening, molasses, brown sugar, water, egg and vanilla until smooth.

Stir in dry ingredients until completely absorbed. Divide dough into 3 pieces, pat down to 1 ½ inch thickness, and refrigerate wrapped in plastic wrap for about 3 hours.

Preheat oven to 350 degrees Fahrenheit. Roll the dough out to ¼ inch thickness on floured board. Cut into gingerbread men with cookie cutter.

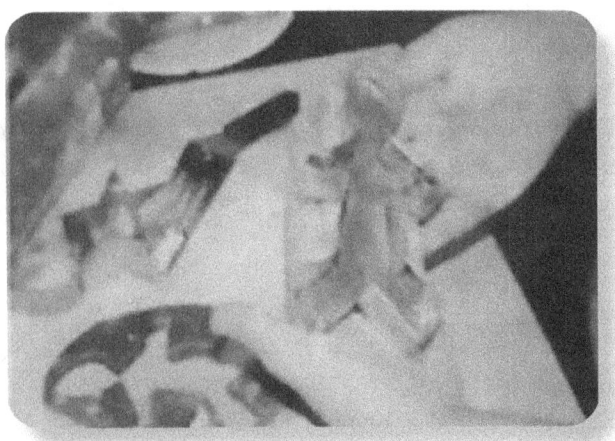

Bake 1 inch apart on ungreased cookie sheets for 10 – 12 minutes. Cookies will look dry but are still soft the touch. Remove from baking sheet to cool on wire rack. Decorate with frosting as desired.

# Bow Ties (Farfallette Dolci)

*Yields 1 1/2 -2 dozen*

*A treat Jim's mother made at special times of the year, like Christmas.*
*Another item you might find on the St. Joseph's Table on Christmas Eve.*

6 eggs
3 tbsp. granulated sugar
1 tsp. flavoring (vanilla, almond, etc.)
¼ tsp. salt
2 tbsp. butter
3 cups flour
3 cups peanut oil (for frying)
½ cup confectioners' sugar

Beat the eggs lightly and add the granulated sugar, salt, and flavoring. Blend thoroughly.

Place flour on board. Cut in butter. Add egg mixture.
Knead until a smooth ball is obtained. If dough is too soft, add some flour but not too much, Set aside to rest for 30 minutes.

Cut dough into 4 sections. Roll each out on a well-floured board until very thin. Cut into 6 inch by ¾ inch strips with pastry cutter. Tie each strip into a loose knot.

Fry in hot peanut oil about 3 minutes or until only light golden brown. Lift and drain on paper towels. Cool. Sprinkle with confectioner's sugar.

A real treat you'll sometimes see in good Italian restaurants. Enjoy!

# Pecan Tassies

*Yields 2 dozen*

*I've been making these since my children were small! Yummy!*

Pastry Shells
1 (3 oz.) pkg. cream cheese, Softened
½ cup butter, softened
1 cup sifted all-purpose flour
Filling
1 egg
¾ cup brown sugar
1 tbsp. softened butter
1 tsp. vanilla
Dash of salt
½ cup pecan pieces

Blend together softened cream cheese and softened butter. Stir in flour till a nice dough forms. Chill 1 hour. Place in ungreased mini muffin tins. Press dough against sides and bottom to form shells.

Filling: Beat together egg, brown sugar, 1 tbsp. softened butter, vanilla and salt just till smooth. Add pecan pieces and spoon into pastry shells. (Double filling if desired). Bake at 325 degrees for 25 minutes or till filling is set. Cool. Remove from pans.

# Chocolate Cherry Bourbon Balls

*Yields 54*

*These get better with age – keep well up to 1 month stored in tightly covered tin.*

6 oz. semi-sweet chocolate chips, melted
½ cup confectioners' sugar
¼ cup light corn syrup
1/3 cup bourbon
2 ½ cups fine vanilla wafer cookie crumbs
1 cup (4oz.) pecans, ground coarse ½ cup granulated sugar
For Decoration
Candied red or green cherry halves.

Mix chocolate, confectioners' sugar, corn syrup, and bourbon in a medium-sized bowl. Stir in cookie crumbs and nuts until blended. Roll rounded teaspoons of dough into 1-inch balls. (If mixture is too dry and crumbly to shape, add a little more bourbon or water.)

Roll in granulated sugar to coat. Arrange on prepared waxed paper lined cookie sheet or tray. Press a cherry halve into each. Let sit on tray for about 1 hour, then store in airtight tin up to one month.

# Cinnamon Pinwheel Pie Dough Cookies

*My mother was very economical and made these from leftover pie dough. Our family loves them, so I make extra dough when making pies just so I can make some! Our grandson, Mason, loves these cookies. I sent them to him when he was deployed to Afghanistan in the U.S. Army. They were a big hit!*

## Dough
1 cup flour
Dash of salt
¼ cup Crisco shortening
2 tbsp. sugar
Ice water

## Filling
½ stick butter, melted
Cinnamon
Granulated sugar

Put flour and salt in bowl. Cut shortening into flour until of a crumbly consistency. Add enough ice water to work into a nice, soft dough – not sticky. If sticky, add a little more flour. Roll out on floured cloth or board to a rectangle.

Drizzle the melted butter over the dough, staying away from edges. Sprinkle generous amount (your call) of sugar and cinnamon over the butter.

Roll the dough up into a cylinder. With a knife, cut into rounds of cookies about ½ inch wide. Place on lightly greased cookie sheets about 2 inches apart.

Bake at 400 degrees for about 10 – 12 minutes or until golden. Remove immediately from pan and cool on plates. Enjoy!

*Note: You may also line your cookie sheets with parchment paper and bake the cookies on the parchment. Still lightly grease the pan before lining with Parchment paper.*

# Chewy Brownie Cookies

*Yields approximately 2 – 3 dozen*
*From my niece, Heather, and nephew, Bryan Forsythe.*
*They say these are the best cookies they've ever tasted.*

2/3 cup shortening
1 ½ cups brown sugar, packed
1 tbsp. water
1 tbsp. vanilla extract
2 eggs
1 ½ cups all-purpose flour
1/3 cup baking cocoa
½ tsp. salt
¼ tsp. baking soda
2 cups semisweet chocolate chips
½ cup chopped walnuts or pecans

In a large mixing bowl, cream the shortening, sugar, water and vanilla.

Beat in eggs.

Combine flour, cocoa, salt and baking soda.
Gradually add to creamed mixture and beat just until blended.

Stir in chocolate chips and nuts.

Drop by rounded teaspoonfuls 2 inches apart on ungreased baking sheets.

Bake at 375 degrees for 7 – 9 minutes. Do not over bake. Cool 2 minutes before removing to wire racks.

# Coconut Macaroon Cookies

*Yields about a dozen cookies – depending on size*

*Very light cookie.*

2 egg whites
1/8 tsp. salt
½ cup sugar
½ tsp. vanilla flavoring
3 cups flaked coconut
¼ cup all-purpose flour

Grease and flour a baking sheet.

Beat egg whites and salt at high speed in small bowl until soft peaks form.

Sprinkle sugar in, 2 tbsp. at a time, beating well after each addition until sugar is completely dissolved. Whites should be in stiff peaks and glossy at this point.

Beat in vanilla flavoring. With rubber spatula, fold in coconut and flour.

Drop by teaspoonfuls the baking sheet about an inch apart. Bake at 350 degrees Fahrenheit for approximately 20 minutes, or until lightly browned. Carefully remove cookies to sack to cool. Store in tightly covered container for up to 3 days.

# Greek Cookies

*Yields approximately 3 – 4 dozen*

*Jim's mother, Dolly as she was called by family and friends, made tons of these delicious cookies and gave them to everyone. They literally melt in your mouth!*

1 lb. sweet butter, softened
2 tbsp. confectioners' sugar
1 tsp. vanilla
1 ½ tsp. baking powder
4 ½ cups Wondra flour
2 egg yolks
1 shot brandy of your choice

Mix softened butter with remaining ingredients. Roll dough into small balls. Place on cookie sheet (line with parchment paper if desired).

Press lightly in center of each cookie with index finger.

Bake at 350 degrees for 20 minutes or till slightly turning brown. Remove from oven. Roll in confectioners' sugar while hot and again when cool.

*Note: Sweet butter is unsalted butter. Wondra flour comes in a blue and white canister type container or box. If hard to find, all-purpose flour sifted three times works just as well.*

# Gullets (Pizzelles)

*Makes 4 – 5 dozen*

*A traditional holiday cookie, my mother's original recipe. She always called these Gullets all my growing up days. I later learned Italians call them pizzelles, and Belgians do call them as my mother did. However, their spelling is gaulettes.*

½ lb. butter
4 large or 5 small eggs
1 cup granulated sugar
Pinch of salt
1 tsp. vanilla extract
2 cups flour, all-purpose
1 cup flaked coconut

Note: The coconut was my mother's "signature ingredient" in these wonderful cookies.

Separate egg yolks and whites. Beat butter and sugar together in mixing bowl. Add egg yolks, salt, and vanilla extract.

Beat egg whites in separate bowl until frothy but not dry. Blend into above mixture alternately with the flour and coconut.

Bake on preheated pizzelle iron (electric or nonelectric) according to instruction for the particular iron you are using. (Be sure to grease your iron between cookies and expect to lose the first couple cookies until your iron is regulated.)

*(Today there are wonderful non-stick irons but do still at least spray on the iron with a cooking spray such as PAM.)*

# Jimmy's Knot Cookies

*Yields about 2 dozen cookies, depending on size.*

3 eggs
¼ cup cooking oil
1 ¼ tbsp. baking powder
¾ cup granulated sugar
1 ¼ tbsp. vanilla extract
1 tsp. lemon extract
4 cups flour
Milk, as needed

### Icing
1 ½ tsp. lemon extract
2 cups confectioners' sugar
Milk

Combine all ingredients in bowl.
Stir, adding enough milk sparingly to make an icing of medium consistency that will adhere to warm cookies.

Jim's mother taught me to make these cookies one day to send to him when he was stationed in the US Navy at boot camp in San Diego.
I made so many my knuckles were red from kneading the dough. I might add they were well-received, and Jim said they didn't last long once the box was opened! These are Jim's absolute "favorite" cookies!

Combine cooking oil, sugar, and eggs in mixing bowl.
Stir in vanilla, lemon extract and a little milk. Mix well, stirring in flour and baking powder gradually. Knead dough with hands until it forms a good ball, adding Flour as needed to keep dough from being too sticky.

Break off pieces of dough and roll to a 4-inch pencil shape, then tie loosely to form the knots. Bake in preheated 350 degrees oven for approximately 17 – 20 minutes on greased and floured pans. Dip each cookie, face down, while still warm into the icing.

Cool on racks or plates until icing is firm and store in airtight container. Jim likes to dunk his cookies in his cup of hot tea! Great with a glass of milk! Enjoy!

# Lemon-Coconut Meltaways

*Yields approximately 4 – 5 dozen*

*A light, delightful cookie whose flavor is enhanced by the coconut.*

1 cup unsalted butter, softened
½ cup sugar
1 ½ tbsp. freshly grated lemon zest
1 tsp. vanilla extract
¼ tsp. lemon extract
2 cups all-purpose flour
¼ tsp. kosher or sea salt
1 cup sweetened flaked coconut toasted and cooled.
Confectioners' sugar

## Toast Coconut

Spread coconut on a baking sheet in oven preheated to 325 degrees. The flakes will toast quickly (5 – 10 minutes). Stir for even color and remove when golden.

Note: F or a lighter cookie, use Wondra flour.

Cream butter with sugar until light and fluffy.
Beat in lemon zest and vanilla and lemon extract.

Add flour and salt and beat well. Stir in the coconut.

Divide the dough in half and place half on waxed paper. Form each into an 8-inch log.
Wrap each log in waked paper. Refrigerate 4 hours or overnight.

Heat oven to 300 degrees. Place rack in middle of oven. Cut logs into ¼-inch-thick slices with a sharp knife. Arrange 2 inches apart on a lightly buttered baking sheet.

Bake for 25 – 30 minutes or until pale golden.
Remove cookies to racks to cool sprinkling Generously with confectioners' sugar while warm and again when cool. Enjoy!

# Melting Moments

*Yields 3 – 3 ½ dozen*

*A light, delightful cookie that well earns its name!*

1 cup butter, softened
2 cups confectioners' sugar
1 ¼ cups all-purpose flour*
¾ cup cornstarch
3 tbsp. orange juice
Grated orange peel, optional

*Or use Wondra flour, which is lighter.

## Icing

Remaining 1 ½ cups confectioners' sugar

Little orange juice

Mix together in small bowl until just a nice dipping consistency.

Cream butter with ½ cup confectioners' sugar until light and fluffy.

Add flour and cornstarch, stirring until well mixed and orange juice and peel if using.

Refrigerate batter 2 hours.

Then roll into 1-inch balls. Place on ungreased baking sheet.

Bake in preheated 325 – 350 degrees oven for 8 to 10 minutes until firm and golden.

Cool on rack. Ice cookies by dipping each into the icing. Set aside on rack again until icing sets and dries totally. Store airtight. Enjoy!

# My Children's Favorite Chocolate Chip Cookies

*Yields approximately 4 – 6 dozen*

*This is the cookie my kids loved the most when they were growing up and still do!*

2 ½ to 3 cups all-purpose flour
1 tsp. baking soda
1 tsp. salt
1 cup softened butter or shortening
¾ cup granulated sugar
¾ cup firmly packed brown sugar
1 tsp. vanilla
½ tsp. water
2 eggs
1 pkg. semisweet chocolate chips
1 cup chopped walnut or pecan pieces (optional)
1 cup quick 1 minute oatmeal

Combine butter, sugars, vanilla, and water. Beat till creamy. Beat in eggs.

Combine 2 cups flour only, baking soda, salt and oatmeal. Add to butter mixture with the chopped nuts and chocolate chips. Mix well, add enough remaining flour to form firm balls by teaspoon.

Bake on greased cookie sheets at 375 degrees for 10 – 12 minutes till golden.

Let sit briefly on pans and then remove to cool on racks or plates. Enjoy!

# Mom's Sour Milk Cookies

*Yields 2 – 3 dozen*

*My father's absolute favorite cookie my mother used to make for him.*

1 cup half Spry (Crisco today) and half butter
½ cup sour milk
1 ½ cups sugar
2 eggs, beat till fluffy
2 tsp. baking powder
1 tsp. baking soda
4 cups flour

Preheat oven to 375 – 400 degrees Fahrenheit. Combine Spry (Crisco), butter, sour milk, and sugar together. Beat eggs till fluffy.

Add to mixture with the baking powder, baking soda and flour. Stir to blend.

Drop by tablespoons onto ungreased baking sheet, Bake for approximately 12 minutes or till slightly golden on top. Remove cookies to cool on rack.

*Note: My father liked a soft cookie, so my mom would be sure and not over bake these cookies just for him!*

# Potato Chip Cookies

*Yields approximately 8 – 10 dozen*

*Very yummy!*

1 lb. (4 sticks) butter, room temperature
3 cups all-purpose flour
1 cup sugar
2 tsps. Vanilla extract
2 cups crushed potato chips
½ cup chopped walnuts (optional)
Powdered (confectioners') sugar

Cream butter in medium bowl until light and fluffy with sugar. Add vanilla. Add alternately the potato chips with the flour. Add walnuts if using. Mix. Bake at 350 degrees Fahrenheit until golden brown. Sprinkle with powdered sugar when cool.
Enjoy!

# *Valentine Cookies*

*Yields about 2 dozen cookies, depending on size*

*Heart-shaped butter cookies for that special Valentine's Day treat! Package up in cellophane bags once dry tied with a ribbon for gift giving!*

½ cup butter
1 cup sugar
1 egg
¼ cup milk
½ tsp. vanilla
3 cups flour, approximately
2 tsp. baking powder

## Icing No. 1

1 ½ tsp. lemon extract
2 cups confectioners' sugar
Milk
Combine ingredients in bowl, stirring and adding enough milk sparingly to make an icing of medium consistency that will adhere to warm cookies.

## Icing No. 2

2 tbsp. egg whites
2 cups confectioners' sugar
Flavoring, optional

Whisk together the egg whites and sugar. Ice cookies as desired. If using sprinkles, add immediately upon icing so they adhere.

Cream the butter with the sugar. Add the egg and vanilla. Sift together 1 cup of the flour and the baking powder. Mix it into a batter.

Add some or all of the flour until the dough is easy to handle, turn in bowl with more flour as needed until no longer sticky.

Form into a ball, flatten slightly, and wrap in plastic wrap. Chill in refrigerator minimum of 2 hours.

Roll out on lightly floured surface about ¼ inch thick. Cut out heart shapes. Place on greased cookie sheet.

Bake in preheated 375 degrees oven for 8 to 10 minutes until a light golden brown. Remove from oven and let cool.

Ice cookies, adding sprinkles immediately, and place on metal racks to dry.

# *Italian Weddings Cookies*

*Yields approximately 2 – 3 dozen depending on size*

*A favorite of mine from long way back, before I met this Italian and married him! Delicious! Great Christmas cookie too!*

1 ½ stick butter (I use unsalted)
4 rounded tbsp. confectioners' sugar
1 tbsp. vanilla
2 cups all-purpose flour
1 tsp. water
1 cup chopped nuts (almonds, walnuts, or pecans)

Set butter out on counter to soften. Cream (beat) the butter till light and fluffy.

Add remaining ingredients. Mix well. Form into a ball of dough.

Break off walnut-sized pieces of dough and roll around in your hands to a nice ball.

Place on ungreased cookie sheet.

Bake in preheated 350 degrees oven approximately 15–20 minutes until still light – do not let brown.

Remove from oven. While still hot, roll each cookie in confectioners' sugar, then again when cool.

Recipe can be double or tripled, as desired. There are never enough of these delicious cookies!

# Meringue Crescents

*Makes about 5 – 6 dozen*

*One of the best cookies I have ever eaten! Good cookie for the holidays!*

## Dough
4 cups all-purpose flour
½ tsp. salt
1 pkg. yeast
1 ¼ cups butter
3 egg yolks, beaten
½ cup sour cream
1 tsp. vanilla
¾ cup chopped nuts

## Filling
3 egg whites, beaten
1 cup sugar
1 tsp. vanilla

## Frosting
1 cup confectioners' sugar
½ tsp. vanilla
1/3 cup milk

## Dough
Mix together flour, salt and yeast. Cut in butter. Mix together and add to flour mixture the beaten egg yolks, sour cream, vanilla and chopped nuts. Mix thoroughly with hands.

Divide into 10 portions. Roll into balls and refrigerate in waxed paper while doing filling.

## Filling (Meringue)
Beat egg whites, add 1 cup sugar ¼ cup at a time and the vanilla.

Heat oven to 350 degrees. Sift confectioners' sugar onto board. Roll each ball of dough out to a 7- or 8-inch circle. Spread some meringue over dough. Sprinkle with 1 tbsp. chopped nuts.

Cut each circle into 12 wedges. Begin at wide end and roll up loosely, placing point side down on ungreased pans

Bake 12-15 minutes till meringue is lightly browned. Frost with mixture of the confectioners' sugar, vanilla and milk by dipping and sprinkle with chopped nuts.

Happy Holidays!

# White Chocolate Macadamia Nut Cookies

*Yields approximately 2 dozen*

*Very yummy! I started making these after our first trip to Kona on the Big Island of Hawaii when we brought back lots of macadamia nuts.*

1 cup all-purpose flour
¾ tsp. baking powder
1/8 tsp. salt
1/8 tsp. baking soda
½ cup, plus 2 tbsp.
(1 ¼ sticks) unsalted butter
¾ cup packed brown sugar
1 tsp. vanilla extract
1 large egg
1 ½ cup white chocolate chips
¾ cup coarsely chopped macadamia nuts
¾ coarsely chopped pecans

Preheat oven to 350 degrees. Grease 2 cookie sheets.

Mix first 4 ingredients together.

Beat softened butter, sugar and vanilla in large bowl until fluffy.

Add egg. Stir in dry ingredients, then white chocolate chips and chopped nuts.

Drop by spoonful onto greased baking sheets.

Bake 15 minutes. Cool 5 minutes on baking sheets.

Remove from pans and store airtight when cool.

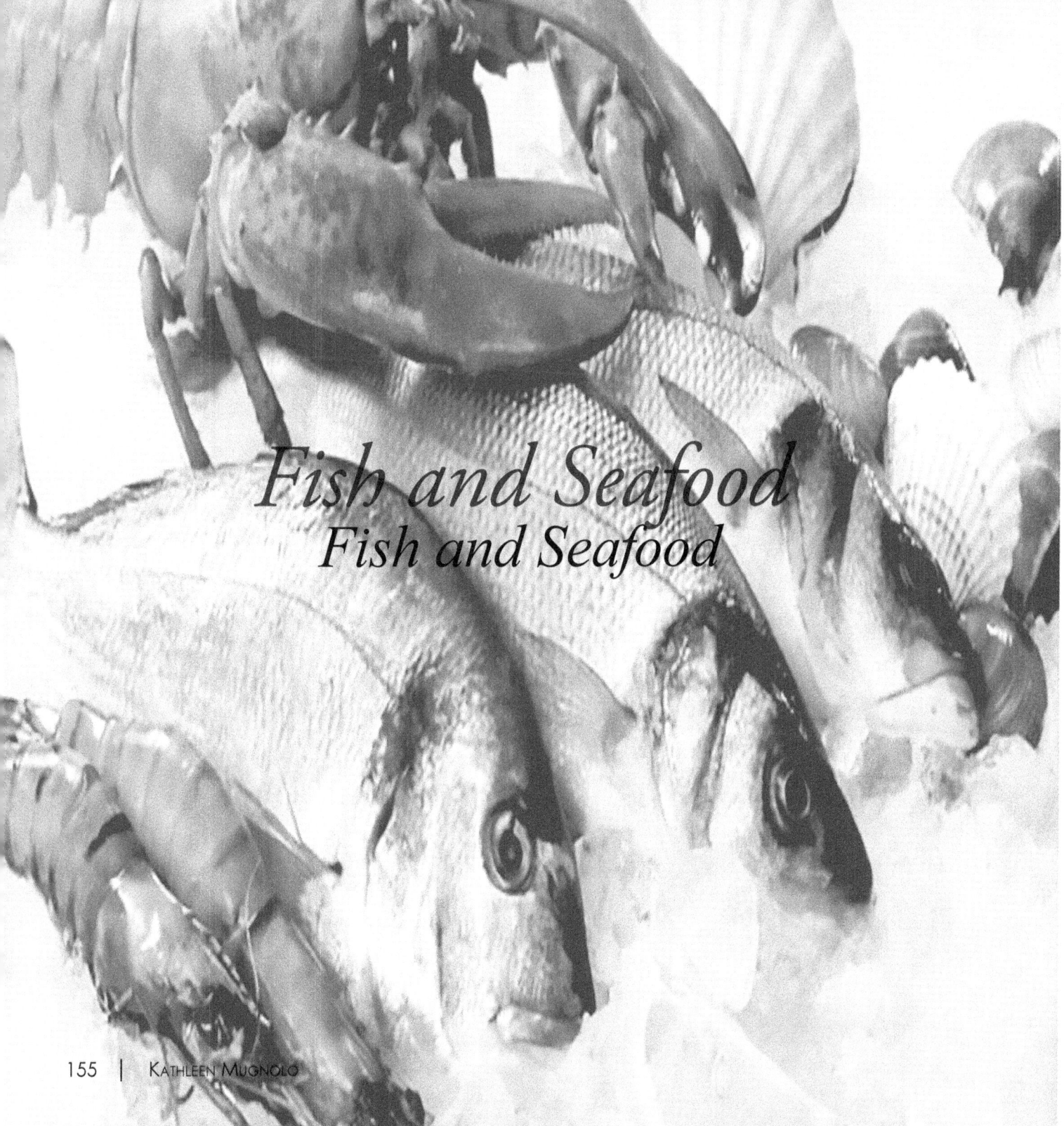

# Fish and Seafood

Fish and Seafood

# *Bacon-Wrapped Scallops on the Grill*

*Serves 6*

*A gourmet treat our son, Michael, and Milasy made for us on Christmas Eve.*

2 lb. scallops
8 slices bacon
2-3 tbsp. red wine vinegar
2-3 tbsp. olive oil
Black pepper to taste
8 wooden skewers

Soak the wooden skewers in water for an hour before needed.

Combine vinegar, olive oil and black pepper in a bowl.

Add scallops and toss to coat.

Cover and set aside for 5 – 10 minutes at room temperature.

Lightly sauté the bacon in a skillet until golden but still soft. Drain off grease on plate on paper towel. Cut each piece into thirds. Wrap a piece of bacon around each scallop and thread onto skewers. Should be 4 scallops to each skewer.

Preheat grill to medium-high. Lightly oil grill rack.
Place skewers on oiled grill and cook 3-4 minutes each side. Scallops are done when opaque in color.

Remove from grill and serve either as an appetizer or main dish with your choice of accompaniments, i.e., vegetable, salad, crusty bread, etc.

***Buon appetito!***!

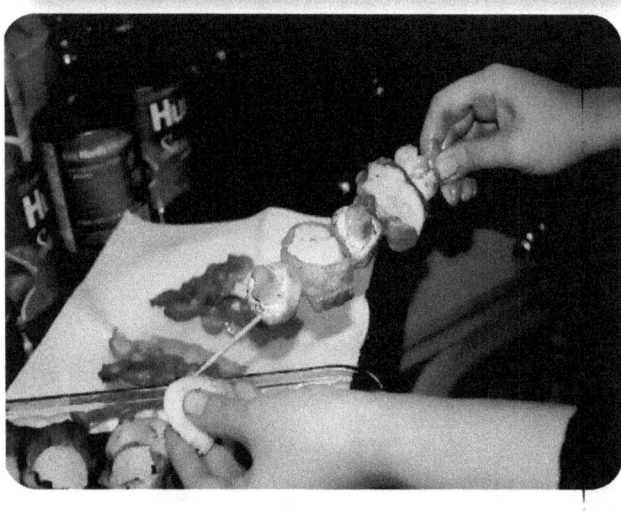

*(Milasy's hands)*

# Beer Battered Shrimp or Fish

*Serves 6*

*Easy method for batter fried shrimp or fish. Delicious!*

1 lb. large, cooked shrimp (cleaned and peeled, vein removed), or fish fillets
3 or 4 tbsp. baking mix*
1 cup baking mix*
½ tsp. salt
1 egg
½ cup beer

*I use Bisquick.

Lightly coat shrimp or fish with the 3 or 4 tbsp. of baking mix.

Mix the remaining 1 cup of baking mix with the salt, egg and beer till smooth.

Heat cooking oil in pan about 1 ½ inches deep. Use deep fryer heated to 350 degrees if you have one.

Dip shrimp or fish into batter (rub off excess batter on side of bowl because you want only a light coating once fried).

Fry in the oil till golden, about 2 minutes each side.
Drain on paper towels and serve with or without cocktail sauce for the shrimp or tartar sauce for the fish.
Enjoy!

# Baked Buttered Shrimp

*Serves 3 – 4 people*
*Nice as an entrée, especially for luncheons!*

1 lb. shrimp, peeled and deveined
1 stick butter, melted
½ tsp. crushed red pepper
¼ cup grated Romano
½ tsp. salt
2 to 3 tbsp. lemon juice
1 cup Italian breadcrumbs
2 tbsp. dry sherry or dry white wine

Devein shrimp. Grease an oblong casserole. Place shrimp in casserole.

Combine melted butter, breadcrumbs, cheese, salt, lemon, juice, and sherry or wine. Sprinkle crumb mixture evenly over shrimps. Bake uncovered in 325 degrees oven for approximately 20 – 30 minutes, until shrimp are cooked, and topping is golden.

Serve with a nice green salad, crusty bread and glass of wine or desired beverage.

# Fried Fish

*Just a little different, so easy and very good! Recipe given to us by friends who lived on a fresh water lake in North Carolina and who cooked the fresh fish they caught this way.*

**Clean fish fillets**
1 egg
1 tbsp. creole seasoning
8 – 10 dashes hot sauce.
Tabasco or Texas Pete)
Flour
Salt/pepper
Canola Oil for frying

Mix the egg, Creole seasoning, and hot sauce in a bowl and marinate fish in the marinade for at least an hour.

Dredge fillets in flour seasoned with the salt and pepper. Fry fillets in hot Canola oil a few minutes both sides until golden. Enjoy!

# *Calamari in Red Sauce with Wine*

*Serves 6*

*Christmas Eve in Jim's family was fish, the St. Joseph's Table. This recipe was a specialty of his mother's!*

2 lb. calamari, cleaned
1 tbsp. olive oil
2 or 3 cloves garlic, minced
4 cups tomato sauce
1 cup Italian red wine
1 – 2 tsp. crushed oregano
½ tsp. black pepper
½ tsp. crushed red pepper
1/3 cup grated Romano cheese
Pasta or your choice (spaghetti)

For other recipes for the St. Joseph's Table check index for:

Lentil soup
Fennel licorice tasting vegetable
Clams on the half shell
Baccala (fried cod fish)
Fried smelts
Crispy fried shrimp or fish
Stuffed artichokes
Fried bowties (Farfallette)
Pizzelles

Separate the tentacles from the long body of the calamari, if not done already.

Slice the body, or calamari tubes into rings about ½ inch thick. Set aside.

In saucepan, sauté minced garlic in the olive oil until just golden. Do not burn. Add the tomato sauce, wine, oregano, black pepper, red pepper, and half the grated Romano cheese.

Simmer on medium-low heat for about 30 minutes to blend flavors and allow the alcohol in the wine to evaporate

Add the calamari to the sauce. Continue to simmer slowly for an additional 20 – 30 minutes. Stir occasionally. Calamari is done when it is plump and opaque. Do not overcook or it will become rubbery.

Serve over your favorite pasta.

***Buon appetito!***

# Christmas Eve Crispy Crust Batter Fried Shrimp or Fish

*Jim's mother loved making shrimp and fish this way, and we all loved eating them!*
*It was a specialty of hers on Christmas Eve.*

Desired amount of fresh shrimp or fish
3 to 4 tbsp. flour
½ cup sifted all-purpose flour
¼ cup yellow cornmeal
½ tsp. baking powder
1 tsp. salt
½ tsp. garlic salt
¼ tsp. pepper
1 egg well beaten
1 to 2 tbsp. cooking oil
½ cup cool water
Cooking oil for frying
Cocktail sauce for the shrimp
Tartar sauce for the fish

Lightly coat shrimp or fish with the 3 or 4 tbsp. of flour.

Sift ½ cup flour, cornmeal, baking powder, salt and white pepper together. Combine with the beaten egg, cooking oil and water with a fork to make a smooth batter. Do not overmix.

Heat cooking oil in pan about 1 ½ inches deep. Use deep fryer heated to 375 degrees if you have one.

Dip shrimp* or fish into batter (rub off excess batter on side of bowl because you want only a light coating once fried). If coating is too thick after frying, add a little more water – if too thin, add a little more flour. Use batter ASAP once made. Fry about 2 minutes each side. Drain on paper towels and serve with or without cocktail sauce for the shrimp or tartar sauce for the fish.

Enjoy!

*Butterfly shrimp before dipping: Shell shrimp. Do not remove tail. Cut almost through each shrimp starting at the head down center of back to the tail. Open shrimp until they lie flat. Remove dark vein and discard. Rinse. Pat dry.

# Crab and Shrimp Quiche

*Yields 8 – 10 servings*
*A real gourmet treat!*

1 unbaked deep 9- inch pastry shell
8 oz. Swiss cheese, diced
2 tbsp. all-purpose flour
1 cup milk
3 eggs, beaten
½ tsp. salt
1/8 tsp. pepper
Dash ground nutmeg
1(6 oz.) pkg. frozen crabmeat and shrimp, thawed (or use either/or)

Prick bottom and sides of pastry shell with a fork.
Bake at 425˚ for 6 to 8 minutes. Set aside

Combine cheese and flour. Set aside.
Combine milk, eggs, salt, pepper, and nutmeg.
Mix well.

Stir in crabmeat and shrimp and cheese/flour mixture.
Pour into partially baked pastry shell.
Bake at 350 degrees for 50-60 minutes, Cool slightly before serving.

*Note: To freeze, bake only 40 minutes, wrap tightly in aluminum foil, and freeze.*
*To serve: thaw quiche and bake 15 to 20 minutes at 425 degrees.*

# Crab Casserole

*Easy!*

1 cup celery
8 slices bread
2 cups crabmeat
1 large onion
½ cup green pepper, chopped
½ cup mayonnaise
4 eggs, beaten
3 cups milk
1 can cream mushroom soup
Grated cheddar cheese
Paprika

Cook celery slowly 10 minutes in a little water. Drain.
Dice half the bread into a 4-quart baking dish. Mix crabmeat and onion, green pepper, celery and mayonnaise and spread over bread. Dice remaining bread and spread over crab mixture.

Mix eggs and milk together and pour over entire mixture. Refrigerate at least 4 hours or overnight.

Bake for 15 minutes at 325 degrees and then spoon soup over top. Sprinkle with cheese and paprika and bake till golden brown – about 45 minutes to 1 hour.

# Steamed Blue Crabs

*Serves 6*

*When our children were growing up they were on swim team and at the end of the swim season, the lifeguards held an all-you-can eat crab feast for us at the pool.*
*Jim used to run a race with our neighbor, Mary, and our daughter, Tara, as to who would be the last one still eating crabs! We also got together with our neighbors, the Bequettes, and cooked crabs in our back yards. This is the recipe for all time's sake!*

1 dozen live crabs
1 cup water
1 cup vinegar
1 bay leaf
2 ½ tbsp. salt
¼ tsp. cayenne pepper
Old Bay Seafood Seasoning or Phillips Crab House Seasoning or a combination of both (as directed on the package)

In the bottom of a large crab pot (steamer-type) place the water, vinegar and bay leaf. Put the live crabs in top part of the steamer. Steam approximately 40 minutes adding the seasonings when just about done cooking.

(Be sure water is at a rolling boil when placing crabs in top of the steamer so they will begin to cook immediately so they do not turn out mushy.)

A day out at the Crab Claw crab house at the harbor in St.Michael's, Maryland, one of our favorite places. Left: sister-in-law Suzanne Mugnolo; sister-in-law Carol Holley; brother-in-law Chuck Mugnolo; husband, Jim. Right: My sister, Mary Mugnolo; me; brother-in-law Richard Mugnolo; brother-inlaw Gary Holley.

# Crunchy Tilapia

*Serves 4*

*This is an oven-fried version of tilapia that is supposed to be better for you
than pan-frying. Good with fresh lemon drizzled over when served!*

1 lb. tilapia fillets
3 egg whites, beaten
¼ - ½ cup all-purpose flour
¼ tsp. salt
Dash of black pepper
¼ - ½ cup dried breadcrumbs
¼ cup cornmeal
1 tsp. parsley flakes or fresh, chopped

Stir together the flour, salt and pepper in shallow dish. Set aside.

Combine breadcrumbs and cornmeal. Dip tilapia filets first in flour mixture. Shake of excess. Drip into beaten egg whites. Then into bread crumb/cornmeal mixture. Shake off excess.

Spray a shallow baking dish with nonstick cooking spray. Lay tilapia fillets in the dish and bake in an oven preheated to 450 degrees for approximately 10 – 15 minutes, until fish is golden and flakes easily with a fork

# Fried Calamari

*Wonderful appetizer!*

2 lb. squid-cleaned and cut in rings
Oil for frying
1 cup flour
Salt
Lemon wedges

Heat 1 inch of oil in deep skillet. Dip calamari in flour. Shake off excess flour.

Fry until golden on both sides. Drain on paper towels and serve with lemon wedges and a nice red sauce for dipping and a good, crusty Italian bread.

*Note: For a good red sauce, see my spaghetti sauce recipe in this book.*

# Fried Cod (Baccala)

*Serves 4*

*Gourmet treat! Nice served with a side dish of pasta and/or nice salad.*
*Also served on the St. Joseph's table at Christmas.*

1 lb. of salted cod
flour
½ cup olive oil
Lemon juice of 1 lemon
Lemon wedges
Fresh parsley, chopped
Black pepper
3 eggs
flour

Make a marinade of some olive oil, lemon juice, and pepper. Cut the cod into 4 pieces and marinate overnight in refrigerator. Prepare batter by beating the eggs together with 3 tbsp. flour, salt, and pepper.

Heat olive oil in deep skillet. Dredge fish in the flour, dip into batter and fry until golden on both sides. Serve drizzled with lemon and garnished with a sprig of parsley and lemon wedge.

# Fried Smelts

*Serves 6*

*Jim's mother made these and they carried over to our families.*

1 lb. smelts, cleaned and headed*
½ cup flour
½ cup cornmeal
½ tsp. salt
¼ tsp. black pepper
¼ tsp. garlic powder
Cooking oil for frying

Soak smelts in cold water for 30 minutes. Drain well and pat dry. Mix together the flour, corn meal, salt, pepper, and garlic powder. Dredge smelts in this mixture.

Pour cooking oil into skillet to about ½ to ¾ inch. Heat to medium-high. Fry the smelts, in small batches, turning once or twice, 2 to 3 minutes each side until a nice golden brown. Drain on paper towels. Serve with lemon wedges and tartar sauce, if desired. *Smelts usually come cleaned and trimmed of their heads. You eat the entire fish. Try 'em. They're delicious.

# *Fried Scampi*

*Serves 6*

*A gourmet treat! Nice served with a side dish of pasta and a nice salad.*

3 lb. fresh shrimp or prawns, with shell
Cooking oil for frying
Sauce
½ cup olive oil
4 cloves garlic, minced
1 tsp. salt
¼ tsp. pepper
½ tsp. oregano
1 tsp. chopped parsley

Wash shrimp or prawns in cold water. Set out deep saucepan or automatic deep-fryer for deep-frying and heat oil to 360 degrees Fahrenheit. Peel shells from shrimp or prawns. Devein by cutting slit along back and remove vein. Rinse quickly in cold water. Drain on paper towels.

Fry only as many as will float uncrowded one layer deep in the oil for 3 to 5 minutes or until golden brown. Drain over the oil before removing to drain again on paper towels.

*Note: Shrimp and sauce can be put into a casserole and baked at 375 degrees for 15 minutes instead of frying process.*

*For sauce: Heat olive oil in skillet. Add minced garlic, salt, pepper, oregano. Pour sauce over shrimp on warm platter and sprinkle with chopped parsley.*

# Jim's Smoked Brined Salmon

*Serves 4*

*This is Jim's own method of brining and smoking salmon. It's a winner! Our sons
would love it if he would make it more often and give them some to take home!*

4 – 6 large salmon filets, skin on
Brining container (large crock)
1 Small, raw, clean, unpeeled fresh potato

**Brine\***

3 lb. coarse (kosher) salt
1 lb. brown sugar
2 tbsp. onion powder
1 tbsp. oregano
1 tbsp. Hot Shot (powder of black and red
   pepper blend)\*\*
2 tbsp. dillweed
2 tbsp. All Seasons spice
1 tbsp. dry mustard
1 tbsp. bay leaf, crushed

\*\*Double amount if you wish.

**For Smoking**
Throw away aluminum pan
Charcoal
Wood of your choice, i.e., flavored if you wish (apple,
cherry, cedar, etc.) Jim used a combination of bought
flavored wood chips.

Set out a large crock. * In the crock, put the amount of water needed to cover the salmon, Add the potato and let drop to bottom of container.

Slowly stir in the brine ingredients. As the brine works, the strength of the solution increases. The potato will become more buoyant. When it finally floats, you are ready to add your fish for brining. (This allows you to make the same strength brine the next time you brine.)

Now add the salmon, being careful it is completely covered. Weighing all down with a water filled jar works good.

Jim brined his salmon for 2 hours 15 minutes. Stir brine mixture occasionally with wooden spoon. If too salty first time you brine, simply decrease time your fish is in the brine next time and vice versa.

After brining, remove fish and rinse briefly to remove salt, then set aside to dry thoroughly. You may pat dry with paper towels.

# Jim's Smoked Brined Salmon continued

Smoking: Preheat smoker to 140 degrees to 150 degrees. Put the pan in the smoker with charcoal. Light charcoal. Have wood soaking in water constantly in bucket. Put some of the wet wood on top of charcoal.

Lightly greased or oil racks of smoker to avoid sticking. Arrange filets of salmon on racks, none of them touching each other. Skin side down. Put lid down on smoker. Check fish periodically. Brush with oil, butter or margarine during smoking if looking too dry.

Fish are done when pleasingly golden brown. A minimum of 4 hours smoking time is necessary to bring out the best in salmon. Feed more wood as needed during smoking. To test: press the flesh with a fork. When it flakes apart, it's done. You must be around to check the fish periodically. When done, cool and wrap in aluminum foil and store in refrigerator until needed. Keeps for a week or so.

*About curing and brining. Curing/brining reduces moisture content, retards formation of bacteria, and adds flavor. The salt dissolves into the fish while drawing out the moisture. Spices and seasonings help to tenderize and aid color of the finished product. Sugar is used to counter the hardening effects of the salt, which tends to dry the meat. While curing, seasonings are absorbed into the fish. Seasoning is a matter of taste. It is safer to refrigerate the entire brine container, if possible, to protect against spoilage. However, the length of time this recipe calls for (2 hrs. 15 mins.) is safer to do on the counter. Cure only in ceramic, glass, plastic, or enamel containers never metal, which reacts with salt and may taint your fish. Remember, smoking is an art, not a science, and you are continually watching and adjusting as you go. It's a matter of taste!

# Lobster Italiano

*Serves 4*

*Another gourmet treat! Nice served with a side dish of pasta and a nice salad.*

2 1 ½ lb. cooked lobsters
½ stick unsalted butter
6 garlic cloves, peeled and crushed
2 tsp. all-purpose flour
2 cups milk
2 ½ cups shredded Romano cheese
Salt, freshly ground pepper

*Note: Side dish of pasta optional.*

Halve the lobsters crack the claws. Remove the gills, the green sac behind the head, and the black vein running down the body.

Place the 4 lobster halves in a shallow ovenproof dish. Melt the butter in a small pan and sauté garlic until softened. Add flour and stir over medium heat for 1 minute. Remove from heat and gradually stir in the milk, stirring until the sauce thickens. Return to heat and cook, stirring constantly for 2 minutes until smooth and thickened. Stir in half of the Romano cheese. Pour sauce over lobsters. Sprinkle with remaining cheese.

Place dish in preheated 350 degrees oven and bake for 20 minutes until cheese is golden.

Serve with a nice mixed greens salad and a good white wine.

*Buon Appetito!*

# Maryland Crab Cakes

*Makes 6*

*A recipe my dear friend, Lori, gave me, and, in my opinion, the best!*

1 lb. fresh Maryland Crabmeat
1 cup crushed saltine crackers
1 large egg
¼ cup mayonnaise
1 tsp. Worcestershire sauce
1 tsp. dry mustard
½ tsp. salt
¼ tsp. white pepper
2 tbsp. fresh parsley, finely chopped
1 tbsp. onion, chopped fine

Mix all ingredients together. If mixture is too dry, add a little more mayonnaise.

Shape into crab cakes. Fry in cooking oil for about 5 minutes each side, or you may broil them. Serve with tartar sauce if you like.

Enjoy!

# Skillet Fried Tilapia

*Serves 4*

*This is my own method of cooking Tilapia and Jim and my family love it. So easy, so good!*

1 lb. tilapia fillets
¼ - ½ cup all-purpose flour
1 tsp. szechuan-style pepper blend
½ tsp. garlic powder
¼ tsp. salt
¼ tsp. black pepper
Olive oil for frying
Pat of butter

On a dinner plate, mix together with a fork the Flour, Szechuan style Pepper Blend, garlic powder, salt and black pepper. Lightly run each tilapia filet over this mixture on both sides.

Heat about 1/8 inch olive oil in bottom of skillet with a pat of butter. Sauté tilapia filets for approximately 4 minutes each side or until golden brown.

Remove from skillet and drain on paper towels on a plate and serve.

# My Mother's Tuna Fish and Macaroni

*Serves 2 – 4*

*From my sister, Mary's kitchen – the way our mother made it!*
*A "Friday dish" we grew up with and loved. Simple, wholesome and delicious.*

1 small or medium onion
½ stick butter
2 tbsp. flour
1 6 ½ oz. can water-packed tuna
1 cup milk
Macaroni (small shells or elbow are good)

Cook macaroni as directed. Drain and set aside. Sauté onion in butter until transparent (not brown).

Add flour and stir to blend. Add milk and tuna and blend until smooth and thickened. Add macaroni, stir and serve.

# Shrimp Pasta Supreme

*Serves 6*

*Good made with spinach fettuccini too!*

1 pkg. fettuccini, cooked and drained
1 pkg. (3 oz.) cream cheese, cubed and softened
1 ½ lb. medium shrimp, peeled and deveined
½ cup butter, softened
Salt/pepper to taste
1 can (10 ¾ oz.) cream of mushroom soup
1 cup sour cream
½ cup half-and-half
½ cup mayonnaise
1 tbsp. snipped chives
1 tbsp. chopped fresh parsley
½ tsp. Dijon mustard
¾ cup shredded Asiago cheese

Preheat oven to 325 degrees F. Combine pasta and cream cheese in medium bowl. Spread pasta mixture onto bottom of greased 13-by-9-inch glass casserole.

Cook shrimp in butter in skillet over medium-high heat until pink and tender, about 5 minutes. Season to taste with salt and pepper. Spread shrimp over noodles.

Combine soup, sour cream, half-and-half, mayonnaise, chives, parsley and mustard in another medium bowl. Spread over shrimp.

Sprinkle shredded cheese over top. Bake 25 minutes or until hot and cheese is melted. Serve garnished with fresh lemon slices.

# Seafood Coquille

*Serves 6 individual or 12 cocktail size*

*This is a favorite of mine I've served at various ladies' luncheons I have had in my home.*

1/3 cup minced onion
1 clove garlic, crushed
1/3 cup butter
¼ cup flour
½ tsp. salt
¼ tsp. black pepper
1 1/3 cups milk
2/3 cup white wine
1 (6 oz.) pkg. frozen cooked shrimp*
1 (6 oz.) pkg. frozen King Crab meat*
6 tbsp. shredded Swiss cheese, or try

grated Romano instead

*I always used Wakefield brand.

Cook and stir onion and garlic in butter till tender. Remove from heat. Blend in flour, salt and pepper.

Cook over low heat, stirring until mixture is bubbly. Remove from heat and stir in milk and wine. Heat to boiling, stirring constantly for 1 minute. Stir in crabmeat and shrimp.

Divide mixture among 6 large individual serving size (or 12 cocktail size) baking shells (real scallop shells) and top each with 1 tbsp. grated Romano for large size and 1 tsp. each for small size.

Do ahead of time, refrigerate and broil just before serving, 4 – 5 inches from heat for 3 to 4 minutes or until cheese is golden. Serve.

*Note: For my luncheons, I serve these filled shells (individual size) on a plate accompanied by Crunchy Broccoli Casserole (recipe in this cookbook), crusty roll and beverage such as iced tea or choice white wine. It has been a very popular luncheon dish! Serve the cocktail size as appetizers. You may also bake entire mixture in a buttered casserole and scoop the individual portions onto plates.*

# Seafood Mousse

*Yields 3 cups*

*Nice presentation unmolded on serving platter, garnished with snipped parsley.*

2 egg yolks
½ cup, plus 2 tbsp. heavy cream
½ (8 oz.) pkg. cream cheese, cut in pieces
2 tbsp. lemon juice
1 tbsp. lemon rind
1 tsp. Worcestershire sauce
¼ lb. crabmeat, shredded
1 envelope unflavored gelatin
3 tbsp. cold water
2 egg whites
Snipped parsley

In a 2-quart pan beat egg yolks and 2 tbsp. heavy cream. Stirring constantly, cook over medium to low heat until just heated through. Add cream cheese. Stir until cheese melts and mixture is smooth. Remove from heat.

Blend in lemon juice, rind, and Worcestershire sauce. Stir in crabmeat.

In small saucepan, soften gelatin in cold water 1 minute. Stir over hot water until dissolved. Cool. Blend in crabmeat mixture.

In small mixing bowl, whip egg whites at high speed until stiff. Set aside.

In medium bowl, whip remaining ½ cup heavy cream. Fold egg whites into whipped cream. Gently fold into crabmeat mixture.

Pour into a lightly chilled 3-cup mold. Cover and refrigerate at least 6 hours. Unmold, garnish, and serve with crackers or garlic-toasted baguette bread slices.

# Seafood St. Jacques

*Serves 6 – 8*

*A wonderful, easy seafood casserole!*

1 lb. sea scallops
1 cup white wine, dry
1 small onion, minced
1 tbsp. fresh parsley, minced
1 tsp. salt
1 can (3 oz.) sliced mushrooms
¼ cup butter
2 tbsp. lemon juice
4 tbsp. flour
1 cup light cream
1/3 cup gruyere cheese, grated
1/8 tsp. pepper
6 oz. cooked shrimp
7 oz. Alaskan King Crab meat
1 cup soft breadcrumbs, buttered

Combine wine, minced onion, parsley and salt in saucepan. Bring to boil. Add scallops. Simmer 5 minutes. Add mushrooms with the broth, 2 tbsp. butter and lemon juice. Simmer until butter is melted.

Drain liquid off the scallops and mushrooms but save the liquid.

Halve the scallops. Measure the liquid, adding water to make 2 cups.

Melt remaining butter. Blend in flour. Add saved liquid and the cream. Cook and stir over low heat till thick and smooth. Add cheese and pepper.

Stir until cheese melts. Stir in scallops, mushrooms, shrimp and crabmeat. Heat to serving temperature. Turn into a shallow 2-quart casserole. Sprinkle with buttered breadcrumbs. Brown under broiler. Serve with a nice salad and crusty roll, and don't forget a glass of white wine to go along with this tasty dish!

# Baked Stuffed Trout

*Serves 8*

*A real gourmet treat!*

2 cups breadcrumbs, plain white or Italian-style
2 ½ cups half-and-half cream
¼ tsp. salt
1/8 tsp. black pepper, fresh ground
2 tbsp. chopped fresh parsley
8 fresh trout, boned and butterflied
2 tbsp. butter
1 tbsp. shallots, chopped fine
¼ cup dry white wine
1/3 cup whipping cream
1 ½ cups Beurre Blanc
Fresh tarragon sprigs
Butter

Combine breadcrumbs, half-and-half, salt, pepper and parsley in a bowl. Mix well. Refrigerate for 1 hour. (This stuffing will be a smooth paste.)

Rinse trout. Pat dry. Open each trout. Lay skin side down on work surface. Season lightly with salt and pepper. Spread 3 tbsp. of stuffing on center of each trout and fold trout back together.

Preheat oven to 375 degrees. Butter a baking dish. Chop shallots and spread across bottom of baking dish.

Lay trout in baking dish.
Pour wine around trout.
Dot each trout with pats of butter.
Cover dish loosely. Bake in middle level of oven for approximately 20 minutes or until fish springs back at a light touch.

# *Baked Stuffed Trout continued*

Buerre Blanc (White Butter Sauce):
1 tsp. white peppercorns, crushed
¼ cup white wine vinegar
¼ cup dry white wine
2 tsps. Shallots, minced
1 cup butter, softened
Salt
½ cup whipping cream
Simmer vinegar, wine, shallots and pepper in saucepan until reduced to 1 ½ tbsps. Remove from heat. Whisk in butter 1 tbsp. at a time. Strain through a sieve. Add salt to taste. Keep warm over simmering water in double boiler. Do not beat as it will separape. Heat whipping cream till thickened. Whisk into the Buerre Blanc sauce.

When fish is done, remove from oven.
Set aside loosely covered and keep warm.
Prepare Beurre Blanc (see recipe to left) Add 1/3 cup whipping cream to saucepan and cook over medium heat until reduced to ¼ cup. Blend this into the beurre blanc with a whisk.

Transfer trout to waxed paper and one at a time, peel of the skin from both sides of each tour. Use waxed paper to gently roll trout over. Transfer trout to serving dish and spoon sauce over. Garnish with tarragon sprigs if desired and serve immediately.

# Breakfast/Brunch

Breakfast/Brunch

# Brunch Eggs

*Serves 4 – 6 people*
*Easy and tasty brunch/breakfast dish!*

½ cup seasoned breadcrumbs*
6 slices Swiss cheese
6 eggs, beaten
2 cups milk
¼ to ½ cup grated Romano cheese
Dash salt/pepper
½ tsp. dry mustard
1 tbsp. minced onion
4 to 6 slices bacon, crisp and crumbled

*I use Italian-seasoned breadcrumbs.

Spray bottom and sides of an 8-by-10-inch ovenproof dish with cooking spray. Sprinkle with breadcrumbs. Overlap with slices of Swiss cheese.

Beat eggs, milk and seasonings. Pour over Swiss cheese.

Sprinkle with grated Romano cheese. Bake in preheated 325 degrees oven for approximately 30 – 40 minutes, or until set and light brown. Serve.

# Mickey Mouse Pancakes

*The kids will just love making these with you!*

Pancake batter, homemade* or batter made from your favorite box mix such as Bisquick
Butter
Syrup
*See my Light and Fluffy Buttermilk Pancakes recipe in this book.

Make desired amount of pancake batter. Melt some butter into skillet or on griddle. Pour pancake batter into skillet or on griddle spacing several large pancakes.

Quickly pour small amounts to the right and left top sides of each pancake, thus forming the ears for what you now have, Mickey Mouse pancakes!

Serve immediately with butter and syrup.

# Buttermilk Biscuits

*Makes about 16 biscuits*
*Melt in your mouth good!*

2 cups all-purpose flour
2 tsp. baking powder
1 tsp. salt
¼ tsp. baking soda
1/3 cup cooking oil
2/3 cup buttermilk*
*I make my own buttermilk by adding a little lemon juice to regular milk and letting it sit until curdled.

*The biscuits will be lighter if you want to take the time to sift the flour.

Measure flour* and mix with baking powder, salt and baking soda in bowl.

Pour milk and oil at once into flour. Stir with fork until mixture comes away from sides of bowl and forms a ball.

Turn on waxed paper lightly floured. Fold waxed paper over pressing down firmly until roll is about ¼ to ½ inch thick.

Peel back waxed paper. Cut into biscuits with unfloured biscuit cutter or rim of a glass.

Place biscuits on ungreased baking sheet, touching or slightly apart.

Bake in preheated 325 degrees oven for approximately 10 – 12 minutes, or until golden brown.

Serve.

# Our family's Crispy Bacon

*Serves 4*
*Bacon done this way will not shrink and will be crispy and so delicious!*
*My mother-in-law taught me to make this when Jim and I were newlyweds.*

1 lb. bacon, or amount desired*
Flour
Pat or two of butter, if desired

*I recommend thin sliced bacon rather than thick

Note: I have never owned a bacon press but if you have one use it to press the bacon flat as it fries. Not necessary though.

Set out a heavy skillet or griddle.

Place some flour on a dinner plate.

Run each piece of bacon lightly over the flour to lightly coat each side.

Heat skillet or griddle to medium-high.

Melt butter on skillet or griddle.

Place slices of bacon on hot griddle. Fry, watching closely so as not to burn. Turn bacon over once or twice while cooking to brown evenly and "crisp" on each side. When golden and crisp, remove from griddle or skillet, drain off excess fat off (on paper towel on a plate).
Serve and enjoy!

# Italian Toast in the Oven

*Serves 4*

*Easy as can be and just a little extra special! I made toast this way so much
as the kids were growing up (and still do) that I have put away my toaster!*

1 loaf of fresh Italian bread
Butter

Cut the bread into fairly thick slices.
Place on baking sheet.

Spread each slice with butter on one side only.
Place under hot broiler in oven. Watch closely.
Toast top side only. Remove from oven and serve as is or with
your choice of butters, jellies or spreads.

Delicious as is. Enjoy!

# Rocky Mountain Toast

*Serves 4*

*Our kids loved this, and our grandchildren do too!*

1 or 2 slices bread per person
1 egg per slice of bread
Butter or margarine
Salt/pepper

Melt butter or margarine in skillet.
Cut a hole out of the middle of each slice of bread.
Place in skillet. Lightly "toast" one side. Turnover.

Crack an egg into each hole. Lightly salt and pepper each egg.
Fry lightly. Turnover. Cook other side until egg is cooked to
desired doneness. Serve alone with your choice of breakfast
meat. Enjoy!

# *Light & Fluffy Buttermilk Pancakes*

*Yields about 16 pancakes*

*The buttermilk makes all the difference! These are very
light, almost the consistency of crepes and oh so yummy! Kids love them*

1 cup all-purpose flour
1 tbsp. sugar
1 ½ tsp. baking powder
½ tsp. salt
½ tsp. baking soda
1 cup buttermilk*
1 egg, beaten
1 tbsp. salad oil
Butter for skillet or griddle

* I make my own buttermilk by adding 2 tbsp. lemon
juice or vinegar to 1 cup of regular milk

Combine dry ingredients. Combine remaining ingredients, except butter, and add to dry ingredients.
Stir just until flour is moistened. Batter will be lumpy.

Melt butter in skillet or griddle. Pour batter from a large spoon, cup or pitcher onto hot griddle into perfectly round pancakes.

Turn pancakes when puffed and full of "bubbles."
Turn and brown other side. Remove and keep warm between folds of paper towels or in a warm oven or warming drawer.

Do not stack them! Serve hot with butter and syrup and watch them ask for more!

Note: These are even lighter if you take time to sift the flour. Recipe doubles well and batter keeps well in refrigerator a couple of days.

# Kathy's Hash Browns

*Serves 4*

*My family claims no one else can make these like me!*

1 small-medium white potato per serving
Butter
Cooking oil
Salt/pepper to taste

Optional: Add chopped onion to grated potatoes – I do not

One of Jim's favorites for breakfast is:

2 eggs, fried over easy
Hash browns
Crispy Bacon
Italian Toast
Coffee or Tea (mostly hot tea)

He puts his eggs on top of the hash browns

Set out a non-stick skillet large enough for the grated potatoes to spread out kind of thin but thoroughly covering the bottom.

Wash, peel and grate the potatoes. I do this on paper towels. Once grated – dab – just "dab" the grated potatoes lightly with another paper towel to remove some of the moisture. DO NOT PRESS down on the potatoes or they will be mushy when cooked.

Put a light coating of cooking oil in bottom of skillet. Heat to medium-high. Add a pat or two of butter. As soon as the butter is melted and heat remains constant – add the potatoes. Spread lightly. When you see the potatoes are looking "crispy golden" around the edges – lift the potato "cake" formed all at once if possible and flip over in the skillet. Carefully spread any loose potatoes to the edge of the skillet. Sauté this side, watching closely. When the edges on this side are crispy golden, flip them over again quickly (You may have to use two spatulas!)

REMEMBER: DO NOT PRESS down with the spatula – just"flip" them. They will fry crispy golden. Then cut in wedges like a pie and serve.

# Mom's Scrambled Eggs

*Serves 4*

*Easy and delicious!*

1 or 2 eggs per person
Milk – 1 tbsp. for each egg
Grated cheese* - 1 or 2 tbsp. per egg
Onion, chopped – ½ tsp. per egg
Green pepper, chopped – desired amount
Mushrooms, optional – sliced – desired amount
Butter or margarine – ½ tbsp. per egg
Salt/pepper

* I use a variety of cheeses, but always some Romano if I have it on hand

Melt butter in skillet

Sauté the onion, green pepper and mushrooms until just soft and golden. Turn skillet off.

Crack the eggs into a deep bowl.

Add the milk and desired amount of grated cheeses.

Beat with whisk until blended.
Turn heat on under skillet.
Pour egg mixture over all in skillet and reduce heat to low. Lightly salt and pepper the eggs. When mixture starts to set at bottom and sides, spatula, turning skillet to cook all portions evenly. Flip and cook other side briefly. Remove to hot platter and serve at once.

# My Version of Sausage Gravy and Biscuits

*Serves 4*

*Easy does it! My grandchildren's favorite for breakfast.*

1 lb. breakfast sausage roll
¼ cup all-purpose flour
2 cups milk
Salt/pepper to taste
Prepared biscuits*

*I like to make buttermilk biscuits. See my recipe in this book, or plain biscuits are fine too.

Crumble and cook loose breakfast sausage in a large skillet over medium heat until browned.

Stir in flour. Gradually add milk and stir until flour and milk are blended in.

Cook sausage gravy until thickened and bubbly. Thin with a little more milk if too thick.

Lightly season with salt/pepper to taste. Serve over hot biscuits. Yum-yum!

# Mom's French Toast

*A regular in our house as the kids were growing up, and Jim and I still love it!*
*Simple to make and delicious!*

Thick slices of good bread (i.e., Italian style, etc.)
2-3 eggs
Some milk
Little vanilla extract (1/2 cap or so)
Butter
Confectioners' sugar, if desired.

Set out a heavy iron or nonstick skillet. Mix eggs and milk in a bowl with fork till blended. Stir in vanilla extract.

Soak each slice of bread quickly one side then the other in egg mixture till coated but not totally saturated.

Melt desired amount of butter in skillet on medium-high heat, quickly add as many coated bread slices as will fit comfortably in skillet. Brown first side, turn over and brown other side just till golden brown. Remove and serve while hot with your choice of syrup. Sprinkle with confectioners' sugar, if desired. Enjoy!

# Meat and Poultry

# 3 Soup Chicken

*Serves 4 – 6*

*I raised my children on this and Jim and I still love it.*

1 pkg. chicken thighs*
1 can cream of mushroom soup
1 can cream of chicken soup
1 can cream of celery soup
2 cloves garlic, minced
Olive oil
Rice

*Boneless, may use any boneless chicken parts.

Preheat oven to 400 degrees. Lightly coat the bottom of a rectangular baking pan with olive oil.

Lay chicken parts in pan. Sprinkle with the minced garlic. Roast open in pan approximately ½ hour turning chicken parts after 15 minutes to lightly brown meat.

Lower oven temperature to 350 degrees.

Pour all 3 soups over chicken parts, blending with spoon. Add another can of any of the soups if you want more gravy.

Roast an additional 45 minutes. Gravy will be bubbly and golden/brown around edges when done. Serve over rice.
This is "delicious!"

# 1943 Meat Puff (Kugali)

*Serves 4 – 6*

*My Mom called hers kugali, which I believe was derived from the Jewish kugel, or potato pie. My mom spoke four or five different languages and made meals from just as many, if not more ethnic areas she grew up around in Castle Shannon, Pennsylvania (outskirts of Pittsburgh) Also being war times, the ration card era, a homemaker had to make the most of leftovers and this dish would feed a family!*

1 ½ cups flour
2 tsp, baking powder
½ tsp, salt
2 well-beaten egg yolks
1 cup milk
1 to 1 ½ cups coarsely chopped leftover meat (My mom liked to use leftover pork)
2 tsp. minced onion
¼ to ½ cup grated potatoes
2 tbsp. melted shortening
2 stiffly beaten egg whites

Pour all your dry ingredients into a sifter together. Sift into a deep bowl.

Mix your beaten egg yolks and milk together and then add to the sifted ingredients. Stir well.

Add the minced onion, chopped meat, potatoes and shortening. Mix together well.

Fold in the beaten egg whites. Pour entire mixture into a well-greased 1-quart baking dish.

Bake at 425 degrees for 45 minutes. Serve as is or with a little brown gravy if you choose.

*Note: This dish looks wonderful when served, as it sits on your table with a nice, crusty golden brown top.*

# *Baked Stuffed Pork Chops*

*Serves 4*

*Worth the effort!*

4 rib pork chops, cut 1 ½ inches thick with pocket
Olive oil
2 cloves garlic, sliced
Salt
Black pepper
Toothpicks or String

Stuffing
1 slice bread for each chop, lightly toasted and cubed
1 small onion, diced
1 stalk celery, diced
Salt/pepper
3 tbsp. hot water

Make stuffing: Sauté onion and celery in a little olive oil in skillet. Add bread cubes, salt, pepper and water. Blend with fork.

Fill pockets of each chop with stuffing. Fasten with toothpicks or tie with string.

Sauté garlic slices in olive oil in skillet till golden. Remove. Sauté chops in skillet till browned well on both sides.

Place chops in a greased casserole with lid. Add water to drippings in skillet and stir to loosen brown sediment. Pour around chops.

Cover casserole and bake approximately 1 hr. in a preheated 375 degrees oven. Uncover for the last 15 minutes to brown chops.

I like to serve these with scalloped potatoes. See the recipe in this cookbook.

# Beef Stroganoff

*Serves 4 – 6 people*

*One of my children`s favorites from way back! First served to them by my friend, Lori, while eating over one day, and I`ve been making it ever since!*

1 pound ground beef, extra lean
½ pint sour cream
1 can cream of mushroom soup
(Campbell's is best)
Onion powder, to taste
Garlic powder, to taste
Salt
Black pepper
Dash Crushed red pepper,
optional 1 1b, spiral pasta (rotini)

Brown ground beef in large skillet in just a little cooking oil. Add the sour cream, cream of mushroom soup, onion powder, garlic powder, salt, and pepper(s). Stir to blend, Cook partially covered over medium-low heat for approximately ½ hour to blend flavors, Meanwhile cook ½ to 1 pound spiral pasta (Rotini) until al dente (just underdone) approximately 9 minutes. Drain pasta.

Serve stroganoff sauce over the pasta or mix sauce in with the pasta and then serve.

*Note: I usually double recipe for sauce and serve with 1 pound pasta cooked. Adjust to your liking.*

# Beef Teriyaki Barbecue

*Serves 6*

*Another recipe of a Japanese friend!*

6 steaks or fillets
3 tbsp. sugar
1 tbsp. sake
4 tbsp. soy sauce
1tsp. ginger
1 clove garlic, chopped fine

Make a marinade by mixing together all ingredients except the Steaks.

Marinate the steaks in the sauce for 30 minutes to one hour.

Barbecue until done as desired.

# Beef Tenderloin Steaks with Peppercorn Sauce

*Serves 4 – 8*

*Absolutely Scrumptious!*

**Sauce:**

2 tbsp. unsalted butter
¼ cup chopped shallots
1/3 cup brandy
1 cup beef stock or canned unsalted broth
1 cup whipping cream
1 tbsp. four-peppercorn blend peppercorns, crushed
8 (6 oz.) beef tenderloin steaks with peppercorn sauce salt/pepper
Szechwan seasoning
¼ cup vegetable oil

To Make Sauce:

Melt butter in heavy sauce pan over medium heat.
Add shallots and saute until golden, about 8 minutes.
Add brandy, bring to boil.
Add stock, boil until mixture is reduced to 1 cup, about 5 minutes. Add whipping cream and 1 Tbsp. peppercorn; cook over medium heat until reduced to sauce consistency, about 8 minutes. Season with salt. Chill and cover. (Can be made day before.)

Brush steaks with oil. Season with salt/pepper.*
Grill to doneness under broiler or on grill – medium high heat. (4 min. per side for medium-rare).

Bring sauce to simmer.

Transfer steaks to plates; spoon some sauce over.
Serve, passing remaining sauce separately.

*Note: Sprinkle with a little Szechwan seasoning too. Gives it a nice flavor even without the sauce. (Found in spice isle of grocery stores.)*

# Beef With Snow Peas

*Serves 4*

*Recipe from a Japanese friend. Authentic!*

½ lb. beef (lean cut like flank steak, top round or other)
½ lb. snow peas, strings removed*
1 tbsp. wine
3 tsp. soy sauce
½ tsp. salt
1 tsp. cornstarch
½ tsp. sugar
1 small clove garlic, crushed
2 thin slices of fresh ginger**
4 tbsps. cooking oil
4 tbsp. water
Cooked rice for 4

*Okay to use frozen snow peas
**Or use ginger powder sparingly

Cut beef into diagonal slices and marinate with wine, soy sauce, salt and cornstarch.

Heat 2 tbsps. oil in pan and stir-fry beef with ginger and garlic. When meat color changes, remove to a plate.
Heat rest of oil and quick cook snow peas.
Add ¼ cup water and cover 2 to 3 minutes.

Add sugar and beef to snow peas and thicken with 1 Tbsp. cornstarch mixed with the 4 Tbsps. water.

Mix well and serve with your choice of cooked rice.

# Italian Ground Beef Patties

*Serves 2 to 4*

*My sister, Mary's recipe. Very easy to prepare, and tasty!*

1 cup reduced fat ricotta cheese
½ tsp. garlic powder
½ tsp. onion powder
¼ tsp. pepper
½ tsp. salt
½ tsp. Italian seasoning
1 lb. lean ground beef
1 to 2 cans crushed tomatoes
4 slices part-skim mozzarella cheese

Simmer crushed tomatoes, adding Italian seasoning, for approx. 20 minutes.
Meanwhile: Season ground beef with garlic powder, onion powder, salt and pepper. Divide into 4 patties.

Brown on medium-high heat until dark brown but pink inside. Put in baking dish. Top with ¼ cup ricotta, ¼ cup crushed tomatoes, 1 slice mozzarella. Bake at 350 degrees for 20 min. or until hot and bubbly and cheese is melted.

# Bracciola di Manza (Beef Rolls)

*Makes 2 nice rolls (6 – 8 servings)*

*My own version of an old family recipe.*
*This is an absolute favorite of our children and Jim and me!*

Flank Steak (1 ½ to 2 pounds)
6 slices bacon – 3 per roll
3 Garlic cloves, minced
Italian Breadcrumbs
1 tbsp. Oregano
2 tsp. Parsley (fresh if available)
4 tbsp. Romano Cheese grated
Salt, to taste
Pepper, to taste
Crushed red pepper, optional
¼ cup olive oil
1 nice clove garlic cut in slivers
2 large cans Tomato Sauce
1 small can Tomato Paste

Select a flank steak thick enough to halve. Have the butcher halve it for you being sure to tell him you intend to stuff and roll each piece.

Lay each piece out on working surface. Pound with tenderizing mallet to flatten uniformly to rectangle shape.

Cover steak with next 9 ingredients, layering as you go and dividing ingredients in half for each piece of meat.

Roll steak up to enclose mixture. (help may be needed at this point). Turn sides of meat in as you roll which will aid in holding filling while cooking. Tie securely with string*

Heat oil in skillet. Sauté more slivers of garlic for flavor and discard. Add steak rolls and slowly brown on all sides. Add tomato sauce, paste and a little water. Cover skillet and simmer 1 ½ to 2 hours or until meat is tender. Remove string, slice and serve with your favorite pasta or other accompaniment.

*\*Jim makes a slip knot first, slides it over the beef roll, then proceeds to wind the twine around the roll width and finally lengthwise and then ties in knot, cutting the string.*

*"Bracciola"*

# *Braised Rack of Lamb*

*Serves 4 people*

*These are very tasty – a real gourmet treat!*

1 (8 point) rack of lamb
¼ cup olive oil
2 cloves garlic, chopped fine
¼ cup dry Sherry (drinking Sherry, not cooking
   Sherry)
1 jar Pommeray mustard
½ cup heavy cream
1/8 cup honey
Fresh sprigs of the herb Rosemary
Tomatoes, cold and diced

Cut rack of lamb into individual riblets. Heat oil in heavy skillet. Braise riblets approximately 2 minutes each side for medium rare. Add some chopped Rosemary and all of the chopped garlic. Shake pan to distribute oil and burst flavor of the herbs. Remove riblets and keep warm. Make sauce in pan by adding the Sherry, mustard, cream and honey. Stir until sauce is nice consistency.

Note: If the sauce breaks – separates – add a little more cold cream and stir to return.

Ladle enough sauce onto each serving plate to cover bottom. Place braised riblets (2 – 4 per person - to each side of plate on top of sauce.

Garnish with fresh diced tomatoes in center and a sprig of Rosemary on top. Serve immediately with a side dish of your favorite vegetable, roll and salad for a gourmet treat!

*Buon appetito!*

# Chicken Caccitore

*Serves 6*

*This is delicious! My very own way!*

1 whole chicken, cut up or chicken parts
(legs, thighs, breast)*
¼ cup olive oil
3 garlic cloves
Oregano, crushed dry leaves
Parsley, fresh if available
Salt/pepper
Crushed red pepper flakes, optional
Tomato sauce, 2 or 3 large cans
Pasta of your choice
Romano cheese, grated

*I use boneless chicken thighs most of the time.

Sauté chicken parts until golden in skillet in the olive oil, turn to brown each side. Chop the garlic cloves fine and sauté in pan with chicken again until just golden. (careful garlic doesn't burn.) Add desired amount of spices – oregano, parsley, salt and pepper, and crushed red pepper – if using.

Add tomato sauce, stir and cook over medium heat about 1 hour to allow chicken to cook and sauce to form an "irresistible" aroma.

Cook pasta of your choice in boiling water* until al dente. Drain. Top each serving of pasta with one piece of chicken and some sauce. Serve with grated Romano cheese and a crusty Italian bread.

*Buon appetito!*

*Note: I add a little cooking oil to the water when boiling the pasta. Reduces the starch so the pasta doesn't stick together while cooking and eliminates the need to rinse the paste when draining water off.*

# Chicken Croquettes

*Makes 8 croquettes*

*A delicious way my mother used leftover chicken.*

2 cups coarsely ground cooked chicken
1 cup (2 slices) soft breadcrumbs
2 eggs, well beaten
½ cup milk plus 2 tbsp.
1 tbsp. minced onion
1 tbsp. minced green pepper
½ tsp. salt
Dash of black pepper
¼ cup finely chopped, toasted almonds
(optional)
Melted shortening or cooking oil to make a 3-inch
    depth for frying

Veloute Sauce
½ stick butter or margarine
¼ cup sifted flour
1/8 tsp. pepper
1 can chicken consommé
¼ cup water
1 tsp. lemon juice

Melt butter or margarine in small saucepan. Remove from heat. Blend in flour and pepper. Gradually Stir in consommé and water. Cook over low heat, stir constantly until sauce thickens (1 minute). Stir in lemon juice. Serve hot.

Combine chicken, soft breadcrumbs, eggs, 2 tbsp. milk, onion, green pepper, salt, pepper and almonds in medium-size bowl. Chill about 2 hours.

Shape into 8 cylindrical croquettes, each 1 inch in diameter. Roll in fine dry breadcrumbs. Drip in ½ cup milk Roll again in crumbs. Brush off loose crumbs.

Heat fat or oil in deep heavy pot to 365-375 degrees (If you don't have a thermometer, a 1 inch cube of bread will brown in about 1 minute).

Fry croquettes 2 or 3 at a time for 2 minutes or until golden-brown.

Drain on absorbent paper. Serve warm with Veloute Sauce with your choice of vegetables.

Enjoy!

# Chicken Scaloppini With Lemon-Caper Sauce

*Serves 4*

*My sister, Mary's recipe. Delicious!*

1 lb. boneless chicken breasts
3 tbsp. all-purpose flour
¼ tsp. black pepper
¼ tsp. chili powder
1 cup fat-free, reduced sodium chicken broth
1 tbsp. lemon juice
1 to 2 tbsp. drained capers
Olive oil

Place chicken breasts between sheets of waxed paper. Pound each to ¼ inch thickness. Combine 2 tbsp. flour, pepper and chili powder. Dip chicken pieces in the flour mixture to lightly coat both sides.

Combine broth, lemon juice, remaining flour and capers in small bowl. Spray large skillet with nonstick cooking spray. Place chicken in hot pan in single layer. Cook for 1 ½ minute. Turn over. Cook 1 ½ to 2 minutes until chicken is no longer pink in center.

Repeat with remaining chicken (brush pan with ½ tsp. oil each time you add more pieces to prevent sticking. If cooking more than two batches, reduce heat to medium to prevent burning chicken.

Remove chicken to platter. Stir broth mixture and pour into skillet. Heat 1 to 2 minutes to deglaze pan and till thickened. Serve immediately over chicken.

Enjoy!

*Note: Serve both the chicken and the sauce over your choice of pasta, if desired.*

# Everyday Hamburgers

*Servings 4*

*Nice and easy and economical!*

1 ½ pounds ground round steak
1/3 cup dry oatmeal
1 ½ tsp. salt
¼ tsp. black pepper
3 tbsp. grated onion

Combine all ingredients in bowl.

Shape into 8 hamburger patties.

Heat frying pan; add patties and brown on both sides.

Serve as you wish, with mustard, ketchup, etc.

# Ground Beef Romano

*Makes 6 servings*

*So easy for busy nights!*

1 ½ lb. ground round steak or other good grade
   of beef
2 cloves garlic, crushed
1 egg
½ cup Italian-style breadcrumbs
1 tsp. oregano
1 tbsp. fresh parsley, chopped fine
1 tbsp. Romano cheese, grated fine
Pinch of salt
Pinch of black pepper
Pinch of crushed red pepper

Topping Mixture:
 ¾ cup (6 oz. can) tomato paste
1 tbsp. grated Romano cheese
6 slices mozzarella cheese (1 slice per portion)

Combine all ingredients in bowl. Shape mixture into a large square ¾ inch thick.

Cut into 6 portions. Arrange portions on broiler rack. Broil 2 inches away from heat sources approximately 10 minutes first side.

Turn, broil lightly and then spread with topping mixture. Broil until mozzarella cheese melts and is lightly browned.

Serve with a nice salad for an easy meal!

# Southern Fried Chicken, Italian-Style

*Serves 4*

*Marinating the chicken in the buttermilk overnight is what makes this fried chicken so good!*

Buttermilk
Olive oil
1 frying chicken, cut up or 2 to 3 lb.
chicken parts
½ cup all-purpose flour
1 ½ tsp. salt
¼ tsp. pepper
2 tsp. garlic powder
2 eggs, well beaten
¼ cup milk
1 tbsp. chopped parsley
½ cup grated Romano cheese
1 to 2 tbsp. water

Marinate chicken parts overnight in Buttermilk.

Pour ½ inch depth of olive oil into a heavy skillet having a tight-fitting cover.

Rinse and pat dry chicken with absorbent paper towels.

Coat chicken 2 or 3 pieces at a time in a plastic containing mixture of the flour, salt, pepper, garlic powder.

Combine well beaten eggs, milk and parsley. When oil is almost heated, dip each piece of chicken into egg mixture. Roll in grated Romano cheese.

Place pieces skin side down in skillet. To brown all sides. Turn pieces as necessary with tongs. When chicken is evenly browned, reduce heat and add 1 to 2 tbsp. water.

Cover tightly and cook slowly 25 – 40 minutes until tender when pierced with fork. Uncover last 10 minutes to crisp skin. Drain on paper towels and serve.

# Grandpa Joe's Favorite Swiss Steak

*Serves 2 – 4*

*From my sister, Mary's kitchen. Her version of the Swiss steak
she remembers my mother making for our father.*

1 lb. round steak
1 ½ cup ketchup
1 large onion, sliced
Water
1 tbsp. butter or margarine

Cut the round steak into serving-size pieces. Brown meat in the butter until dark.

Add the ketchup, water and onion. Simmer for 1 ½ to 2 hours or until fork tender.

*Note: Great served with mashed potatoes and a vegetable of your choice.
A man's meal!*

*You may choose to sauté the onion before or with the steak, then proceed with the recipe.
In my opinion, sautéing the onion first enhances the flavor of this dish.*

# Herb Crusted Flank Steak

*Serves 4*

*Recipe sent to me via an e-mail recipe exchange.*

1 lb. flank steak, visible fat removed
¼ tsp. salt
½ tsp. tarragon
½ tsp. garlic, minced
¼ tsp. fresh ground pepper
2 tbsp. Dijon mustard
¼ cup breadcrumbs, your choice
1 tbsp. fresh parsley chopped.

Preheat broiler and pan. Combine salt tarragon, garlic, pepper and mustard in a small bowl. Spread half of this mixture onto one side of the meat.

Broil mustard side up, about 4 inches from the heat for 4 minutes. Turn the meat and spread the remaining mixture, and broil for an additional 3 minutes. Combine breadcrumbs and parsley and pat evenly on meat. Broil 1 minute more. Let stand 5 minutes. Slice steak thin diagonally across the grain. Serve.

# Grilled Pepper Flank Steaks

*Serves 6*
*Non-fail delicious!*

3 flank steaks (1 ¼ lb. each)
¾ cup olive oil
1/3 cup red wine vinegar
4 ½ tbsp. Dijon mustard
4 large cloves garlic, minced
2 large shallots or green scallions, chopped
1 tbsp. coarsely ground black pepper
1 tbsp. fresh or 1 tsp. dried thyme
1 tbsp. fresh or 1 tsp. dried rosemary
1 tsp. salt
Garnish, fresh sprig of thyme or rosemary

Whisk olive oil, vinegar, mustard, garlic, shallots/scallions, pepper, thyme, rosemary and salt together.

Marinade meat in single layer in large, glass baking dish. Cover and refrigerate 4 hours or overnight. Remove from marinade and grill 4 minutes each side for medium-rare or longer to desired doneness.

Slices across the grain of the meat when serving. Garnish with a sprig of thyme or rosemary.

*Buon appetito!*

# Italian Pot Roast

*Serves 6-8 people*
*Nice "hearty" meal for a cold evening!*

3 lb. chuck or rump roast
¼ cup olive oil
4 to 5 carrots, cut into large chunks
1 stalk celery, cut in pieces
1 onion, chopped
2 cloves garlic, chopped
2 bay leaves
1 cup red wine
1 6 oz. can tomato paste
2 cups beef broth, warmed
Salt/pepper to tastes
Optional: 4 oz. can mushrooms, drained

Heat olive oil in dutch oven pot.
Sear beef roast in olive oil on all sides.
Add carrots, celery and onion and sauté till onion is golden.
Add garlic, bay leaves, mushrooms if using, salt and pepper.

Continue cooking over low heat approximately 5 minutes. Add the wine and tomato paste, diluted with the warmed beef broth. Cover. Cook minimum of 2 ½ hours over low heat until meat is fork tender. Serve with a nice, crusty Italian bread and red wine. Enjoy!

# *Italian Braised Beef*

*Serves 4*

*Nice served over cooked pasta! Very similar to Italian Pot Roast in this book.*

2 lb. beef rump roast
1 tbsp. olive oil
2 cloves garlic, minced
2 medium carrots, diced
2 stalks celery, diced
1 medium onion, diced
1 bay leaf
4 oz. fresh mushrooms, sliced
1 cup dry red wine
½ can tomato paste
2 cups beef broth

Heat a non-stick deep skillet. Add the olive oil.
Salt and pepper the roast, place in pan with olive oil and sear meat on all sides.

Add carrots, celery, onion and garlic. Sauté with meat until onion and garlic are golden brown but not burned.

Add the mushrooms. Mix beef broth and wine with tomato paste and pour over roast. Add bay leaf. Cook, covered, 350 degrees Fahrenheit oven for 1 to 1 ½ hours.

*To serve: Allow meat to rest on cutting board 3 to 5 minutes before cutting into thin slices.*
*Place meat on serving dish over cooked, warm pasta of your choice and ladle sauce overall.*

# *Italian Chicken-in-the-Oven*

*Serves 4*

*This is my husband's and children's favorite chicken recipe that I make.
Taught to me by my husband's grandmother. Nellie (DePasquale)
Rossi. It is the very first thing I learned to make in Jim's family.
The "aroma" of this dish cooking is absolutely irresistible!*

*(Grandma Rossi)*

1 chicken, cup up or equal parts (allow at least 2 parts
  per person)
3 or 4 cloves garlic, peeled and chopped fine
¼ to ½ cup olive oil
2 tbsp. dried oregano leaves
2 tbsp. parsley, fresh minced
5 potatoes, peeled and quartered
5 carrots, peeled and quartered
Pats of butter
Salt, black pepper to taste
Crushed red pepper to taste

Set out a 9 x 13 inch metal or glass roast pan.
Pour olive oil evenly in bottom of pan.
Place chicken parts, potatoes and carrots in pan,
intermingled.

Sprinkle with chopped garlic, oregano, parsley, salt, peppers.
Dot chicken with pats of butter.

Roast open in hot preheated 425 degrees oven for ½ hour.
Reduce oven to 375 degrees and bake approximately 1 hour
longer, turning pieces of chicken occasionally to brown on each
side and basting all with the juices as you turn the chicken.

Increase oven temperature again for an additional 15 minutes
at the end if needed to brown vegetables. Serve with your
favorite salad for a delicious meal-in one.

This dish tastes as good as it smells, and my family enjoys it
right down to the "crispins" they like to scrape up in the pan!

# *Italian Meat Balls in Sauce*

*Serves 6 – 8 people*

*I try to always have some of these meatballs made ahead and frozen to pop into
the sauce to cook on short notice for a nice meal.*

1 lb. ground beef
1 cup Italian breadcrumbs
2 tbsp. grated Romano cheese
2 tbsp. minced fresh parsley
2 tbsp. oregano leaves
2 to 3 cloves garlic, minced
1 egg
1 tsp. salt
¼ tsp. pepper
Pinch of crushed red pepper
2 (1 lb. 13 oz.) cans tomato sauce
1 (12 oz.) can tomato paste
1 large can water
Olive oil

Combine first 9 ingredients together in a bowl. Shape into meatballs.

Heat 2 tbsp. olive oil in skillet and brown meatballs on all sides. Pour off fat as it collects. (At this point, you can either drain the meatballs on paper towels, cool and freeze for later use, or continue below:)

Add tomato sauce, paste and water. Simmer on low heat long (minimum of 2 to 4 hours) covered loosely. Add water if needed. Stir occasionally.

Serve meat balls and sauce over your favorite spaghetti or other pasta. *Buon Appetito!*

# Italian Sausage and Peppers

*Serves 6 – 8*

*This is great served on sub rolls or eaten as is with a nice Italian bread served alongside for dipping. Another old family recipe, so easy and "so" delicious!*

2 lb. Italian sausage, hot and/or mild links
Olive oil
6 to 8 green bell peppers
2 large cans tomatoes
Italian bread or sub rolls

Coat the bottom of a skillet lightly with the olive oil.

Sauté the Italian sausage links until just golden.

Clean seeds out of the green peppers and slice each pepper into wedges. Add to skillet with sausage.

Do not drain the tomatoes but cut each tomato into quarters and add, with the juice, to the skillet with the sausage and peppers.

Cook all together over medium heat for about ½ hours or enough time for the sausage to be fully cooked, stirring occasionally.

Serve on rolls or as is with a nice Italian bread alongside for dipping.

*Note; If serving on rolls, you may want to vary this recipe by adding sautéed onions and mozzarella cheese on the roll placing under broiler for a delicious sausage sub. My family likes it as is. Enjoy!*

# *Italian-Style Hamburgers*

*Makes 8 patties*

*If you like hamburgers, you're in for a special treat with these.
They're absolutely mouthwatering! An old family recipe!*

1 ½ lb. ground round steak or other good grade
   of beef
2 cloves garlic, crushed
1 egg
½ cup Italian-style breadcrumbs
1 tsp. oregano
1 tbsp. fresh parsley, chopped fine
1 tbsp. Romano cheese, grated fine
Salt/black pepper
Pinch of crushed red pepper

Combine all ingredients in bowl. Shape into 8 patties. Heat fry pan; add patties.

Brown on both sides. Do not press hard with spatula when turning to retain juices! Serve and enjoy!

Note: You may also broil these or cook on your barbecue grill.

# *Marinated Flank Steak*

*Serves 6 – 8*

*Very tasty!*

½ cup cooking oil
¼ cup white wine vinegar
(I use Progresso.)
¼ cup soy sauce
2 tbsp. onion, chopped fine
2 cloves garlic, minced
1 tbsp. minced ginger root or 1 tsp. ground ginger
1 (1 ½ lb.) flank steak

In a shallow, oblong glass baking dish, combine all ingredients except the flank steak. Stir to blend. Add steak, turning once to coat both sides and pricking with the tines of a fork. Refrigerate, covered, turning occasionally, for several hours or overnight. Meat will turn dark and this is normal because of the marinade.

Remove the meat from the marinade. Discard marinade. Grill or broil 6 inches from heat sources 8 to 10 minutes for medium-rare, turning once. Broil longer for desired doneness. Serve, sliced thinly diagonally across the grain.

# Marinated Shish Kebab, I

*Serves 6*

*My own recipe, tasty and tender!*

1 ½ lb. beef cubes, good grade
2 cans beer
Fresh mushrooms
3 tomatoes, quartered
2 green peppers, cut in large cubes
1 large onion, cut in large pieces
Rice of your choice, white wild, or brown

Marinate beef cubes in beer in container in refrigerator 4 hours or longer, turning occasionally.

Alternate meat on skewers with the mushrooms, green peppers, tomatoes and onion. Broil about 4 minutes each side or until done to individual taste. Serve on bed of your favorite cooked rice.

# Marinate Shish Kebab, II

*Serves 6*

*Similar to No. 1, different marinade.*

1 ½ lb. beef cubes, good grade
1 ½ cups Italian dressing*
Fresh mushrooms
3 tomatoes, quartered
2 green peppers, cut in large cubes
1 large onion, cut in large pieces
Rice of your choice, white wild, or brown

See "Kathy's Italian Dressing," in this cookbook.

Marinate beef cubes in Italian dressing in container in refrigerator 4 hours or longer, turning occasionally.

Alternate meat on skewers with the mushrooms, green peppers, tomatoes and onion.

Broil about 4 minutes each side or until done to individual taste. Serve on bed of your favorite cooked rice.

# "Joe's Special"

*Serves 6 – 6*

*An easy, economical meal for busy nights. Another of my sister, Mary's recipes!*

1 lb. lean ground beef
2 cups sliced mushrooms
1 small onion, chopped
2 tsp. Worcestershire sauce
1 tsp. dried oregano leaves
1 tsp. ground nutmeg
½ tsp. garlic powder
½ tsp. salt
1 pkg. (10 oz.) frozen chopped spinach-thawed and
   drained but not squeezed dry
4 eggs, lightly beaten
1/3 cup grated parmesan cheese

Spray a large skillet with cooking spray. Add ground beef, onions and mushrooms.

Cook over medium-high heat 6 – 8 minutes until onion is tender, breaking beef apart with wooden spoon.

Add Worcestershire sauce, oregano, nutmeg, garlic powder and salt. Cook until meat is no longer pink.

Drain spinach but do not squeeze dry.
Stir into meat mixture.
Push mixture to one side. Reduce heat.
Pour eggs into other side of skillet. Cook without stirring 1 – 2 minutes or until eggs are set on the bottom.

Life edge to allow rest of egg to cook underneath.
Gently stir into meat mixture, heating through.
Serve.

# Marinated Rack of Lamb

*Yields 14 riblets*

*These are very tasty and a good dinner entrée served atop garlic mashed potatoes, or as an appetizer as is.*

2 (7 bone) racks of lamb
Coarse sea salt to taste
Garlic powder
Cracked black pepper
Olive oil
1 ½ cups Shiraz wine (or other red wine of
   your choice)
½ cup honey

Preheat oven to 400 degrees Season lamb with sea salt, garlic powder and cracked pepper.

In a medium cast-iron skillet over medium high heat, sear lamb on all sides in a little olive oil until evenly browned.

Place skillet with racks of lamb in preheated oven. Roast for 30 minutes

Remove lamb from skillet, reserving juices. Allow to rest 10 to 15 minutes before slicing rack into riblets.

Place skillet with juices over medium heat, and stir in the wine and honey. Cook until juices are reduced by about half. Drizzle over riblets and serve.

# Mike's Favorite Cube Steak and Gravy

*Serves 2 – 4*

*This was one of our son, Mike's absolute favorite meals when he was growing up.*

1 ½ lb. cube steak
1 medium onion, sliced
Flour
Olive oil
Salt/pepper
Gravy master or kitchen bouquet

Great served with mashed potatoes with the gravy overall.

Put about 1 cup or so of flour on a plate. Sprinkle with desired amount of salt/pepper.

Pour enough olive oil in a large non stick skillet to cover the bottom. Sauté the onion slices till golden.
Remove and set aside.

Run each piece of cube steak across the seasoned flour to coat lightly. Pour a little more olive oil in same skillet. Bring heat to medium-high. Place flour coated cube steak pieces in hot skillet and sauté all steak pieces until golden brown on both sides.

Once browned, mix an additional 2 tbsp. flour in 2 cups of water with 2 to 3 capfuls of gravy master or kitchen bouquet (browning agent). Add to skillet with the meat. Cook, covered, on low heat approximately 1 – 1 ½ hours until meat is tender, adding more water if liquid cooks down.

# Mock (or American) Wiener Schnitzel

*Serves 4*

*Try this for a nice change with chicken!*

½ shortening (I use Crisco)
½ butter mix
1 pkg. boned chicken breasts
1/3 cup flour
1 ½ tsp. salt
¼ tsp. black pepper
½ tsp. garlic powder
3 eggs, beat lightly with a little milk
1 ½ cup breadcrumbs
Lemon wedges
2 tbsp. melted butter
4 anchovy fillets, mashed
1 tbsp. lemon juice
Parsley, for garnish

Melt enough shortening and butter in a deep heavy pot or deep skillet to only 1/3 full.

Heat to 375 degrees (try and use a cooking thermometer). If not, watch oil closely.

Slice each chicken breast into 4 serving pieces. Pound each on flat working surface with meat hammer until ¼ inch thick.

Coat cutlets with mixture of flour, salt, pepper and garlic powder. Dip cutlets in egg mixture. Carefully drag cutlets through breadcrumbs to coat lightly. Let stand 5 minutes to seal coating.

Deep fry cutlets in the hot shortening/butter mixture as many as you can fit at one time not touching each other. Fry until golden brown – about 3 – 4 minutes each side. Use tongs to turn, not a fork.

Remove from oil. Drain on paper towels. Arrange on serving platter or individual Plates. Finish off with a sauced and heat the remaining 2 tbsp. butter with the mashed anchovy fillets; add the tbsp. of lemon juice. Pour over cutlets and garnish with a sprig of parsley.

*Buon appetito, Americano!*

# My Chop Suey

*One of my kid's favorites to this day!*

1 – 1 ½ lb. lean beef cubes
1 medium onion, chopped
1 green pepper, chopped
2-3 stalk celery, cut into bite-sized pieces
1 can Chinese-style vegetables
1 small can water chestnuts
1 can bean sprouts
Soy sauce*
Cooking oil
2 cups water
1 to 2 tbsp. cornstarch
Gravy master or kitchen bouquet
(browning sauce)

Heat cooking oil in skillet just to lightly cover bottom.

Sauté onion till golden. Remove to plate and set aside.

Sauté the beef cubes on high heat tossing occasionally until browned.

Return onion to pan with the beef cubes and add the chopped green pepper and celery, Chinese-style vegetables, water chestnuts, bean sprouts and 3 or 4 tbsp. soy sauce.*

Mix cornstarch in the water and add to skillet. Darken sauce with a little Gravy master or kitchen bouquet as desired.

Cook covered for about 1 – 1 ½ hours until meat is fork tender. Serve over rice and pass more soy sauce.

*Remember, soy sauce is salty, so add sparingly. You can always add more.*

# My Meat Loaf

*Serves 6 – 8 people*

*I raised my children on this and, it's as good leftover!*

1 1/2 - 2 lb. ground beef
½ lb. ground pork
½ lb. ground veal
2 eggs, beaten
2 cups soft breadcrumbs
½ cup minced onion
¼ cup minced green bell pepper
1 tbsp. horseradish (bottled)
1 tsp. salt
¼ cup milk
¼ cup ketchup
1 tsp. dry mustard

Note: Some stores have meat loaf mixture already made up, a combination of beef, pork, and veal.

Add eggs to meat; blend lightly with fork. Add remaining ingredients; mix thoroughly but lightly as too much tends to toughen loaf.

Shape into oval loaf or loaves.
Place in shallow pan that has been greased.

Before baking, make a crease down length of the top of the meatloaf; pour ketchup along indentation for a nice finishing touch.

Bake 1 hour in hot 400 degrees oven.

*Note: Nice served with fluffy mashed potatoes and a nice green vegetable or salad on the side.*

Tip: For a healthy touch, my mother used to add a handful of dried oatmeal to the meatloaf mixture, which I often do as well. I think it was a method started during the Depression days to stretch the meal! It's good!

# *Marinated Beef Tenderloin*

*Serves 8 – 12 people*

*Recipe given to me by my friend Juanita. It is so tender and non-fail delicious! Better make extra!*

1 (4 to 6 lb.) beef tenderloin
1 cup ketchup
2 tsp. prepared mustard
½ tsp. Worcestershire sauce
1 ½ cups water
2 (7 oz.) envelopes Italian salad dressing mix (Good Seasons is what we use.)

Combine all ingredients except the tenderloin.
Mix well.
Spear the meat in several places on board or pan.
Place meat in a heavy-duty plastic bag you can either tie or close tightly otherwise.

Pour the marinade over meat. Seal bag tightly. Place in refrigerator for 8 hours or overnight. Turning occasionally.

Drain marinade off after the 8 hours.
Do not save. Roast in a pre-heated 425 degrees oven 30 – 45 minutes for rare. *Thermometer (if using) registers 150 degrees for medium-rare; 160 degrees for medium.

Let rest on counter on cutting board a few minutes.
Carve and serve, and listen for the oohs and aahs!**

*My husband, Jim, likes to cook this on the grill outside. Only danger there is you might have to invite the neighbors in!
**Option: Serve a pat of either Herb Butter (recipe on pg. 236) or Maître D'hôtel Butter (recipe on pg.248) of this book atop each slice or any of the sauces like Bearnaise you can make from store bought packs.

# Pan Seared Veal Chops

*Serves 4*

*Delicious!*

Olive oil
2 garlic cloves sliced
4 loin or rib veal chops, cut ¾ thick inches
Salt
Cracked black pepper

Pour enough olive oil in bottom of heavy skillet to coat Bottom. Heat to medium-high heat.
Quickly sauté the garlic slices and remove from skillet when golden, flavoring the olive oil.

Place the veal chops in the skillet and sear on both sides on medium-high until nicely browned. Add a little salt and cracked black pepper.

Cover and simmer till done, approximately 20 minutes. Remove lid and sear uncovered a couple minutes just before serving to give a nice glaze to the chops.

Serve immediately with a rice side of pasta of your choice and salad or vegetable. Oh … and don't forget the wine! *Buon Appetito!*

# Roasted Leg of Lamb, Italian-Style

*Serves 6*

*Cut 5 or 6 slits in the skin of the lamb roast. Cut garlic cloves into slices. Into each slit, place a slice of garlic (and a sprig of Rosemary if using)*

5 lb. spring leg of lamb
3 nice cloves garlic
Rosemary (optional)
Sea salt/black pepper
Olive oil
Wine Vinegar

Rub a little olive oil over the roast
Drizzle a little wine vinegar over the roast. It acts as a tenderizers and takes the strong lamb taste away.
Lightly salt and pepper it.
Place it in an open roast pan. Roast at 350 degrees till done to your liking, about 1 ½ to 2 hours for medium.

Serve with accompaniments of your choice. We roast potatoes and carrots in with the roast, basting as it all roasts several times with the juices. Enjoy!

My sister-in-law, Carol, marinates her roast overnight in a large baggie with a cup of wine vinegar. Then coats the roast with a paste of a little olive oil, minced garlic, a little salt and a little oregano before it goes in the oven.
Bake at 425 degrees 30 minutes, then lower to degrees above in recipe.

# Roasted Lamb's Heads

*Serves 4*

*Jim's mother served these as a meal with roasted potatoes and considered them a delicacy.
They are actually served in some Italian restaurants in Chicago as a specialty item and you must
call well ahead to order*

2 spring lamb's heads, cleaned and cracked in half
   by the butcher
¾ cup olive oil
½ cup red wine
1 tbsp. crushed oregano
3 to 4 cloves garlic, finely minced
1 tsp. salt
1 tsp. fresh ground pepper
Crushed red pepper
6 to 8 white potatoes

Remove the eyes and tongue and discard.

Soak heads in salt water to clean few hours.
Drain. Place in fresh water to cover in deep pot and parboil for
10 minutes. Drain.

Make a marinade by combining ½ cup of the olive oil, the
red wine, 1 tsp. oregano and ½ the minced garlic. Pour over
heads while warm and marinade for 1 hour, turning occasionally.
Remove heads from marinade. Discard marinade.

Pour remaining olive oil in roast pan and place lamb's heads in
pan. Peel potatoes, quarter and place in roast pan around lamb's
heads. Sprinkle remaining minced garlic, oregano, salt and a little
crushed red pepper over lamb's heads.

Roast at 325 degrees for 1 ½ hours, basting all from time
to time.
Serve with salad and crusty Italian bread.
***Buon Appetito!***

# *Roasted Pork Loin*

*Serves 4 – 6*

*Another family favorite and so easy to prepare.*
*Great for company as you can vary it so many ways.*

4 lb. pork loin
Garlic
Olive oil
Oregano, dry leaves
Salt/pepper
Crushed red pepper (optional)
Potatoes
Carrots

Pour enough olive oil on bottom of open roast pan to coat.

Place pork loin in pan.
Cut slits in top of roast. Insert slivers of garlic into slits.

Sprinkle over meat desired amount of oregano leaves, salt/pepper, and crushed red pepper.

Peel, rinse, and quarter potatoes and carrots and lay around roast in pan. (one potato and carrot per person, more as desired).

Roast open in pan in preheated 400 degrees oven for 1 – 1 ½ hours till done (185 degrees on meat thermometer). Baste everything every 20 minutes to keep from drying and aid browning.

Nice served with an Italian salad (see my dressing in this book) or as is. Enjoy!

# Sam's Fried Chicken

*Serves 4*

*Sam is our dear friend who worked for and with us at our place on Lake Anna.
It was always a special treat to see Sam show up toting a tray of his freshly fried, crispy,
delicious chicken! In our minds, nothing can compare!*

Chicken parts (whole chicken cut up or buy
   desired parts)
Flour, white all-purpose
1 tsp. Mrs. Dash's original blend seasoning
Garlic salt
Salt/black pepper
Paprika – about 1 tsp.
2 eggs
Milk, whole
Cooking oil for frying

*Only fry as many pieces of chicken that will fit well in
the oil – do not crowd

Bear with me Sam doesn't measure!

In a bowl, mix together 2 eggs and a little milk (I'd say 1/8 cup).

Soak chicken parts in this mixture in a large sealable plastic bag for at least a couple hours.

Remove chicken. Combine the flour, garlic salt, salt/black pepper and paprika in a brown paper bag or in a bowl. Put a couple pieces of the chicken in bag or bowl and dredge with flour mixture until coated.

Heat cooking oil (Sam uses Crisco) in a deep pan (or heavy iron skillet is best if deep enough) enough to cover chicken while frying. (No more than half the pot in oil as oil expands with frying.)

Cover pan lightly. Cook chicken in the hot oil* for 20 minutes, turning chicken to brown evenly. Remove from oil. Drain on paper towels and immediately sprinkle Mrs. Dash's seasoning. Enjoy!

# Southern Fried Chicken

*Serves 4*

*Marinating the chicken in the buttermilk overnight is what makes this fried chicken so good!*

1 chicken, cut into parts, or about 4 lb.
chicken parts
2 cups buttermilk
1 – 2 tbsp. Tabasco sauce
1 ½ cups flour
Paprika
Cooking oil for frying
Salt/pepper

Rinse the chicken in cold water; pat dry with paper towels.

Combine buttermilk and Tabasco. Pour over chicken parts in bowl. Cover with plastic wrap. Refrigerate 4 hours or overnight. Remove chicken from refrigerator. Place chicken in colander to drain excess buttermilk mixture off.

Heat cooking oil in a deep cast iron frying pan over medium-high heat. Preheat oven to 200 degrees F. Line a baking sheet with paper towels.

In a deep bowl, combine the flour, 2 tsp. salt, 1 tsp. pepper and paprika. Dredge the chicken parts in the flour mixture. Shake off excess.

Place half of the chicken in the hot oil and fry, turning often until the chicken is golden and cooked through – about 20 minutes.

Transfer to prepared baking sheet and keep warm in the oven until all the chicken is fried. Serve.

# *Steak on a Skewer*

*Serves 6*

*Great for casual summer get-togethers. Serve with your favorite rice or
baked potato, salad and nice, crusty bread!*

1 ½ lb. flank steak, partially frozen (for ease in slicing)
1 green pepper, cut into 12 pieces
12 cherry tomatoes
6 large mushrooms, sliced in half through stems

Marinade
1/3 cup burgundy wine
¼ cup salad/cooking oil
¼ cup finely chopped onion
1 clove garlic, crushed
½ tsp. salt
1/8 tsp. coarsely ground pepper

Combine ingredients for marinade in shallow baking dish; mix together well.

Slice partially frozen flank steak across the grain into 1/3-inch-thick pieces (12 slices). Add to marinade and refrigerate covered for 2 hours.

Meanwhile, Simmer green pepper in boiling water 5 minutes, till just tender.

Thread steak slices onto six long skewers with cherry tomatoes, green pepper and mushroom slices in a ribbon-like fashion. Brush with olive/cooking oil.

Grill 6 inches from prepared coals or broiler for Approximately 2 – 4 minutes each side, depending on doneness desired.

Serve.

# Swiss Steak, Mom's Style

*Serves 4*

*My Mom didn't have a recipe! She made this just about every
Sunday after church for my father and it smelled as good as it tasted!
Hopefully comes close.*

1 ½ pounds round steak, 1 ½ inches thick
2 tbsp. flour
1 tsp. salt
1/8 tsp. black pepper
2 tbsp. melted fat, or shortening (Crisco)
1 cup hot water
3 large onions, peeled, sliced
¼ to ½ cup ketchup, optional or 1 medium
 can Hunt's tomato sauce
½ tsp. prepared mustard, optional

Trim excess fat from meat; cut into serving pieces.
Combine flour, salt and pepper. Place meat on breadboard; sprinkle with half of the flour mixture. Pound it into meat using rim of a saucer.

Turn meat. Pound remaining flour into other side. Melt fat or Crisco in heavy frying pan or Dutch Oven.

Brown meat on both sides over medium heat. Remove meat from pan and set aside. Sauté onions in pan juices until golden, adding a little more fat or Crisco if needed.

Add water and ketchup if using or tomato sauce (Mom used ketchup) Cover. Cook over low heat 1 ½ to 2 hours or until meat is tender. More water may be added while cooking if needed. Great served with mashed potatoes!
Enjoy!

# *Veal Marsala*

*Serves 4*

*A "standard" in our house as the children were growing up.*
*Also served on buffets at our dinner parties.*

2 cloves garlic, peeled and sliced thin
¼ cup olive oil
5 tbsp. butter, room temperature
8 pieces of veal scaloppini, pounded thin
¼ cup flour
½ tsp. salt
1/8 tsp. black pepper
¼ cup sweet marsala wine
¼ cup dry marsala wine (or ½ cup of either and ¼ cup white wine)
¼ cup water
¼ tsp. chopped parsley (fresh is best)
2 cups sliced mushrooms (optional)
1 tbsp. lemon juice (optional)

Heat olive oil and 2 tbsp. butter in large skillet and sauté garlic till golden. Discard garlic. Coat veal with flour/salt/pepper combination.

Add veal to garlic flavored olive oil in skillet and sauté slowly on both sides. Remove veal from pan and pour off remaining butter. Keep veal warm.

Return pan to medium heat. Add the marsala wine, water, and chopped parsley. Simmer 30 seconds. Add lemon juice if using, then add 5 tbsp. butter chunks. When butter is melted, add mushrooms, if using.
Simmer until the mushrooms are cooked (about 1 minutes). If mixture is too thick add small amount of water.

Pour sauce over veal and serve with your choice of accompaniments. Goes very nicely with fettucini alfredo. (See Easy Alfredo Sauce recipe in this cookbook.)

# Veal Piccata

*Serves 4*

*"Impressive, easy to prepare, and so delicious!"*

1/3 cup flour
8 pieces scaloppini veal, pounded thin
6 tbsp. butter, room temperature
3 cloves garlic, peel and slice thin
2 tbsp. olive oil
2 cups white wine
½ cup lemon juice
5 to 6 tbsp. cold butter, cut in chunks
¼ cup capers
¼ cup chopped parsley, fresh is best

Lightly flour the veal.

Heat 3 tbsp. butter and 1 tbsp. olive oil in a skillet over medium heat. Sauté garlic till golden. Add 4 pieces of veal. Sauté veal for 2 minutes on each side until done. Remove from pan. Pour off remaining butter.

Return pan to heat and add the remaining 3 tbsp.
butter and 1 tbsp. olive oil; sauté the remaining 4 pieces of veal as above. Remove veal from pan.
Pour off remaining butter again.

Return pan to stove over medium heat.

Deglaze pan by adding the wine and reduce 1 minute. Add lemon juice. Cook 2 – 3 minutes to reduce liquid by half. Add 5 – 6 tbsp. cold butter chunks to pan. Swirl the butter into reduced liquid; the sauce will emulsify. Add the capers.

Place two pieces of veal on each plate; pour sauce over. Sprinkle with chopped parsley. Serve with your choice of pasta, i.e., fettucini alfredo, or roasted potatoes, salad and a good crusty bread. Ahh, that's Italian!

# Veal Rolls with Asparagus

*Serves 6 – 8*

*Impressive, easy to prepare, and delicious!*
*You may make these ahead of your guests coming and keep warm until serving.*

16 asparagus spears
8 veal scaloppini
8 thin slices mild Italian cheese
(Provolone works well)
8 thin slices of mortadella with pistachio nuts
6 tbsp. butter
4 tbsp. extra-virgin olive oil
6 tbsp. dry marsala wine or blush ok for substitute
All- purpose flour
Salt/pepper
Garlic powder, optional

Wash asparagus, break off woody ends at bottom by snapping off gently. Blanch asparagus in boiling, salted water for 3 minutes. Drain but reserve 6 tbsp. of the liquid.

Season each scaloppini with salt and pepper. Trim or fold the mortadella and cheese slices until just a bit smaller than the veal. Place on each veal slice along with two asparagus spears at one end and roll each veal slice up tightly, tie in place at each end with string.

Roll in flour seasoned with salt and pepper. Add a little garlic powder to the flour if desired. Heat the butter/olive oil in frying pan. Sauté the rolls over low heat approximately 10 minutes, until golden and tender. Turn frequently. Remove rolls to a hot serving platter and keep warm.

Add marsala to the skillet with reserved asparagus liquid and a pat or two of butter. Simmer on low approximately 4 – 5 minutes scraping the bits from pan. Spoon over veal rolls and serve with your favorite side – i.e., pasta, roasted potatoes, salad, crusty bread for a meal your guests won't forget.

**Buon appetito!**

# Veal With Mushrooms

*Serves 8*

*An "easy" way to serve veal. Similar to stroganoff.*

2 cans (4 ½ oz.) mushroom caps*
¼ cooking oil
3 lbs. veal, cut in 1 inch cubes
2 cans condensed cream of mushroom soup
1 cup white wine
½ cup chopped onion
1 tsp. oregano
1 cup sour cream
8 cups cooked rice

*Use fresh baby mushrooms if you like.

Drain mushroom caps, if using canned. SAVE LIQUID and add water to make 1 cup.

Heat oil in saucepan.
Add veal and sauté until golden brown.

Stir in mushroom liquid (or 1 cup water if using fresh mushrooms), mushroom soup, one-half cup of the wine, onion and oregano. Bring to boil.

Cover and reduce heat. Simmer until veal is tender (1 ¼ hours approx.), stirring occasionally.
Just before serving: Add remaining ½ cup wine, mushrooms and sour cream.

Serve over your choice of cooked rice.

# *Veal, Potatoes and Peas*

*Serves 8*

*A sort of veal "stew" in the oven.*
*A favorite recipe taught to me by my mother-in-law and*
*my husband. Now a favorite of my family.*

1 lb. veal cutlets, cut into bite-sized pieces
2 – 3 cloves garlic, minced
Olive oil
1 to 2 large cans (1 lb. 13 oz.) of Italian plum tomatoes,
   undrained, cut into bite-sized pieces
Salt
Pepper
1 to 2 tsp. dry Oregano leaves
3 potatoes, pared, rinsed and cubed*
1 bag (8 oz.) frozen peas

*par cook the potatoes if you wish to speed overall cooking time in the oven

Coat the bottom of a deep skillet with olive oil. Sauté the veal cutlet pieces on both sides till golden.

Add the minced garlic and sauté till golden.

Place veal/garlic mixture into a lightly greased 9 x 13-inch glass oven dish. Immediately add the canned plum tomatoes, salt, pepper and oregano. Add frozen peas and potatoes overall and stir.

Cover with foil and bake for approximately 1 to 1 ½ hours until veal and potatoes are tender.

Serve with a nice crusty Italian bread.
***Buon appetito!***

# Fiesta Chicken

*Serves 4 - 6*

*My daughter, Tara's recipe – delicious!*

1 pkg. chicken thighs (6 – 8 thighs)
Bell peppers, green and red (2 each)
1 medium onion, sliced thin*
¼ cup Olive oil
Butter (1 pat on each chicken piece)
Garlic powder, to taste
Parsley, to taste
Black pepper, as desired
Tomato salsa, 2 cups

* Use sweet (Vidalia) onion if desired

Put olive oil in rectangular glass baking dish.

Place chicken parts in dish. Core peppers, remove seeds and cut in quarters. Add to chicken. Top with all remaining ingredients except salsa, as desired.

(Salsa goes on last 30 minutes.)

Bake at 350 degrees for 1 ½ hours uncovered, adding the salsa in the last 30 minutes of baking.

Great served with Mexican Rice (see recipe in this cookbook.)

# Chicken Bog

*Serves 6*

*Our son, Carl's recipe – he's our South Carolina boy now that he and his family
live in Myrtle Beach! And this is a South Carolina dish, a hardy meal that tastes as
good as it smells while cooking!*

2 – 3 lbs. of chicken pieces (boneless chicken thighs
   work well)
6 cups water
1 tbsp. salt
1 medium onion, chopped fine
1 – 1 ½ lb. smoked sausage, sliced
2 cups long-grain rice
2 tbsp. herb seasoning and/or
1 packet chicken and herb seasoning
1 tsp. black pepper

Use a heavy pot with lid.

Put water, salt, onion and chicken in pot.
Boil until chicken is tender – approximately 1 hour.
Cut chicken into bite-size pieces.

Slice smoked sausage into ½ inch pieces.
Add sausage, pepper, rice and seasonings to chicken.

Simmer until broth is absorbed and rice is cooked.

# Beer Can Chicken

*Serves 4*

*More than just a conversation piece – delicious!*

1 roasting chicken or fryer – 3 ½ lbs.
1 can beer
4 tbsp. of your favorite spice rub
2 tsp. cooking oil

Prepare the beer can. Cut the top off with a can opener or punch 3 big holes into top of beer can with opener. This will allow more flow of moisture of the beer to the chicken.

Next: Dispose of half the beer in can. (I'll leave that up to you!)

Add ½ of the spice rub to the beer and stir.

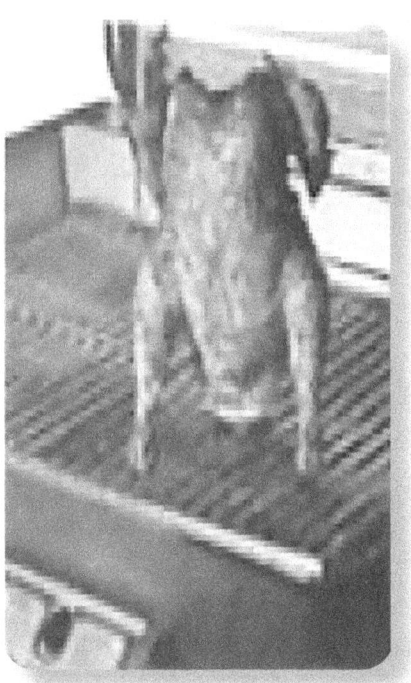

Rub the chicken with the cooking oil. Rub other half of the spice rub all over the chicken, under the skin, to allow the flavor to reach the meat – and – inside the chicken for best flavor.

Lift the chicken up onto the beer can carefully and pull the legs of the chicken forward, creating a "tripod." The beer can act as the back of the tripod. Set the beer can on the grill (be sure the cover has room to close). Close lid. Cook chicken on can on the grill at 300 degrees - 325 degrees for about 1 – 1 ½ hours. (Check the chicken as it cooks. If skin is getting too brown, cover with a tent of aluminum foil and remove last 15 minutes to finish browning. Remove chicken with beer can to platter. Let it rest for about 5 minutes. Be careful not to spill any beer still in can to avoid getting burned. Remove chicken from can. Carve and serve with sides of your choice and watch 'em dig. Delicious!!"

# *Fall-Off-the-Bone Baby Back Ribs Steamed Baked in Oven*

*Serves 4*

*A fail-proof, easy and delicious way to make tender, fall-off-the-bone, delicious ribs every time!*

1 full rack baby back ribs
Dry rub
3 tbsp. Brown sugar
2 tbsp. Paprika
1 tsp. dry mustard
1 tsp. garlic powder
1 tsp. onion powder
2 tsp. chili powder
2 tsp. sea salt
1 tbsp. fresh ground pepper
1 tsp. cumin (optional)
Olive oil
Barbecue sauce (your choice)
Aluminum foil

Preheat oven to 275 degrees. Lay ribs on a large sheet of heavy aluminum foil. Mix dry rub mixture together. Rub both sides of ribs with olive oil lightly. Coat both sides of ribs generously with the rub. Pull up sides of aluminum foil to create a loose tent over the ribs. (This allows the ribs to steam cook.) Bake in the oven for 1 ½ to 3 hours.

Remove from oven. Open tent slightly to let steam out and to check ribs. Careful, the steam is hot! Ribs should be cooked and falling off the bone.

Remove from oven. Coat with barbecue sauce. Return to oven, turn oven to broil. Broil ribs till you have a nice glossy finish. Remove. Cut in portions. Serve. Finger-lickin' good!

Note: You may wish to serve the ribs dry and pass the barbecue sauce, your preference. Also: In the early stage, once you coat both sides of ribs with the rub, you may wish to place in a large baggie and refrigerate overnight in the rub. Enjoy!

*Ribs on the Green Egg*

# Thanksgiving Turkey with Italian Sausage and Bread Stuffing

*A nice touch to that traditional Thanksgiving dinner.*

Turkey- size you want
1 round Italian loaf of bread
1 lb. Italian sausage
2 tbsp. olive oil
½ cup (1 stick) butter
2 medium sweet onions, chopped
4 sticks celery, then cut across into
    small pieces
4-5 garlic cloves, chopped or minced
4 eggs
½ cup heavy cream
½ turkey broth or chicken broth
1 cup grated Romano cheese
¼ cup fresh parsley, chopped coarsely
(We use either Italian or curly parsley)

Cut bread into thick slices. Butter slices. Toast slices under broiler until golden. Cut into cubes. Set aside.

Remove sausage from casings. Sauté in skillet in a little olive oil breaking sausage into little pieces until browned.

Pour off fat and transfer browned sausage to large bowl. Set aside. Melt butter in skillet. Cook the onions, celery and garlic until golden.

Add vegetables and bread cubes to sausage. Whisk together the eggs, ½ cup cream, chicken or turkey broth, cheese and parsley.

Stir egg mixture into the stuffing. Cool. Stuff turkey then roast as desired until golden and done.
*Serve with all the trimmings and enjoy!

*I rub my turkey with softened butter before roasting and sprinkle with some cracked pepper. Also, I place a tent of aluminum foil loosely over my turkey while roasting to retain moisture, and then remove it during the last ½ hour to bring the turkey to a nice golden color. Follow instructions on turkey for roasting time according to weight.

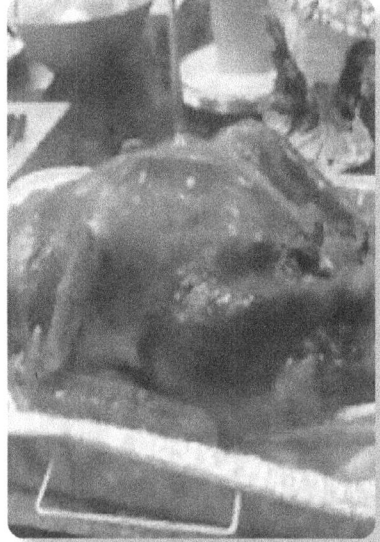

*Thanksgiving Turkey*

# Miscellaneous

Miscellaneous

# Apple Sauce

*This is my easy, sugar-free recipe.*
*So good you don't miss the sugar! Yummy!*

5 lbs. apples*
Cinnamon

* I like to wait until the apples are in at the apple orchards in our area. Golden Delicious is my favorite but a combination of apples is good too.

*Food Mill*

Set out a large dutch oven pot.
Pour just enough water in to lightly cover the bottom of the pot.

Wash the apples. Cut them into eighths.
It's perfectly fine to leave skins on, seeds in.
Cook apples in the dutch oven pot over mediumhigh heat until the apples begin to cook down.

Lower heat. Continue cooking, stirring the apples to allow all sections to cook down.

When all are cooked down and soft, place a hand-turn food mill over a large bowl.

Put 2 to 3 cups of the cooked apples in the food mill and turn the handle running the apples through into the bowl, thus forming the apple sauce and leaving the peels and seeds behind.

When all is through the mill, sprinkle with desired amount of cinnamon, stir and store in jars or freezer bags in freezer until needed.

*Note: If you don't have a food mill, you have to remove the seeds and skins from the apples before cooking them down. Then, once cooked, you just stir to mash and add cinnamon, as desired – no sugar needed.*

# Broccoli-Chicken Quiche

*Serves 6 to 8*

*For a more hearty quiche, try this!*

Pie crust mix*

2 cups shredded Swiss cheese

1 ½ cups chopped cooked chicken

1 (10 oz. pkg. frozen, chopped broccoli

½ cup chopped onion (Vidalia sweet onion or regular onion okay)

1 1/3 cups milk

3 eggs

½ tsp. salt

¼ tsp. pepper

* For homemade crust, see my recipe in this cookbook. Or follow directions on boxed mix. Also, the stores now have wonderful pie dough rounds already formed and frozen in boxes, 2 to a box.
Very convenient.

Heat oven to 400 degrees F. Grease 10-inch glass pie plate or quiche dish.

Prepare pie crust and place in pie plate or quiche dish.

Combine the cheese, chicken, broccoli and onion. Place in pie/ quiche dish.

Combine remaining ingredients in bowl and blend with electric mixer at high speed until smooth. Pour over ingredients in pie/ quiche dish.

Bake 25 to 30 minutes until knife inserted in center comes out clean. Cool 5 minutes before slicing. Serve garnished with tomato wedges, if desired.

*Note: Omit the chicken for a meatless quiche and increase the broccoli to two 10 oz. pkg.*

# Chinese Egg Rolls

*Yields 36 – 40 rolls*

*Jim's mother made these for the family. Every once in a while
she ventured out of the Italian way. Very good.*

¾ lb. cooked pork, chopped fine
¼ cup soy sauce
1 tbsp. dry sherry
1 clove garlic, minced
1 tbsp. cornstarch
1 tbsp. brown sugar
1 tsp. grated ginger
½ tsp. salt
2 tbsp. cooking oil
4 green onions, chopped fine
1 ½ cups shredded celery cabbage
½ lb. fresh bean sprouts
1 can water chestnuts, drain & chop
1 pkg. (16 oz.) egg roll wrappers

Combine soy sauce, sherry, garlic, cornstarch brown sugar, ginger and salt. Set aside.

Stir fry onions and celery cabbage in large pan or wok for 2 to 3 minutes in the cooking oil.

Add pork, sprouts, water chestnuts and soy sauce mixture. Cook 3 minutes. Stir constantly. Chill mixture.

To assemble:
Cover wrappers with damp towel. Place 2 tbsp. filling in center of each wrapper. Begin folding, fold in sides, and continue rolling. Moisten ends with water and press to seal.

Fry in hot deep fat (cooking oil) at 365 degrees for 3 to 4 minutes until golden. Serve with your choice of dipping sauces or soy sauce

*Note: To make appetizer egg rolls, cut the wrappers in half before filling and
use only 1 tbsp. filling for each.*

# Cold Horseradish Cream

*Makes 2 cups*

*Great served with cold, rare roast beef or broiled steak.*

½ cup thinly sliced, peeled fresh horseradish*
3 – 4 tbs. Distilled white vinegar
3 tbsp. finely minced white onion
1 ½ cups sour cream
½ cup heavy cream
1 tsp. salt
½ tsp. freshly ground pepper
3 tbsp. chopped fresh dill or chives, optional

* May use 5 tbsp. prepared horseradish but fresh root is better

Place the horseradish and 3 tbsp. vinegar in a food processor fitted with metal blade or do in blender.

Puree until smooth.

Transfer to a bowl. Stir in remaining ingredients until well mixed, adding another tbsp. of vinegar, if needed, for tartness and flavor balance.

*Note: This sauce can be warmed gently over low heat and spooned over hot rib eye or filet steaks.*
*Great on cooked salmon too.*

# Crab Quiche

*Serves 4*

*For the seafood lovers in your life – "dee-licious!"*

½ cup mayonnaise
2 eggs, beaten
2 tbsp. all-purpose flour
½ cup milk
1 lb. crabmeat, preferably fresh
8 oz. Swiss cheese, cubed
Small jar pimentos, drained
9-inch unbaked pie shell

Mix the mayonnaise, eggs, flour and milk until well blended. Add the rest of the ingredients.

Pour into a 9-inch pie crust.

Bake at 350 degrees for 45 minutes. Let stand 10 minutes before cutting into pie-shaped wedges for serving.

Enjoy!

# Spinach Quiche

*Serves 6 to 8*

*Another delicious quiche!*

One 9-inch unbaked pie shell
1 small onion, chopped fine
2 tbsps. melted butter or margarine
1 10 oz. pkg. frozen creamed
spinach, thawed
2 tbsps. flour
1 tsp. salt
¼ tsp. pepper
¼ tsp. nutmeg
2 eggs, beaten
1 cup Half & Half
2 tbsps. grated Romano cheese

Preheat oven to 400 degrees. Bake pie shell for 5 mins. Set aside. Sauté onion in butter lightly. Add spinach, stir well.

Cook 2 minutes. Add flour, salt, pepper and Nutmeg. Mix well.

Combine eggs, Half & Half and Romano cheese. Beat well. Stir in spinach mixture.

Pour into pie shell. Bake for 35 minutes at 400 degrees.

# "Hash"

Serves 4 - 6

*Our "poor man's meal" for those nights you want a quick but good meal. My family loves it!*
*Very economical too!*

6 large, white potatoes
1 large onion, Vidalia or yellow
1 lb. ground beef
salt/pepper
Butter
Milk

Melt some butter in a skillet. Slice the onion and sauté it in the butter. Remove from skillet and set aside. Sauté the ground beef in same skillet until browned.

Meanwhile:
Peel potatoes, rinse clean and quarter them. Cook in boiling, salted water on top of stove approximately 20 to 25 minutes or until fork tender. Drain. Mash with desired amount of butter and milk.

Combine the sautéed onions and ground beef with the mashed potatoes. Add a little salt and black pepper. Serve on plates with a dollop of real butter in center of potatoes and there you have it — we call it "Hash!"

# Herb Butter

*Great on steaks, veal chops, broiled chicken or salmon.*

½ cup chopped green onions
½ cup chopped fresh parsley
2 cloves garlic, minced
1 tsp. basil (2 tbsp. fresh)
1 tsp. marjoram (1 tbsp. fresh)
1 tsp. tarragon (1 tbsp. fresh)
1 tsp. dill weed (1 tsp. fresh)
1 tsp. black pepper
Dash of Tabasco
1 lb. unsalted butter

Mix all ingredients together into a nice herb butter.

Wrap in logs and store either in refrigerator until ready to use or you can freeze it for up to 2 months.

When ready to use, slice off a portion and place on top of just cooked meat/salmon to melt over and add flavor.

*Grandchildren in my herb garden*
*Front to back: Anna, Mason, Jennifer, Aaron*

# *Quiche Au Fromage*

*Serves 6 to 8*

*A delicious quiche that also makes up nicely in
small muffin tins as "mini quiches" to serve as hors d' oeuvres.*

Pie crust mix
1 tsp. butter
6 slices lean bacon, cut in ¼ inch pieces
2 eggs, plus 2 extra yolks
1 ½ cups heavy table cream
½ tsp. salt
Pinch of white pepper
¾ cup grated imported Swiss cheese
2 tbsp. butter, cut in tiny pieces

<u>Note</u>: For mini quiches, take walnutsize pieces of dough and spread out in each mini muffin pan section (grease pan first). Proceed as for full-size quiche, baking for just about as long as for the full-size.

Make pie crust to fit 9-inch pie plate or quiche dish (grease dish before placing pie crust in dish). Preheat oven to 375 degrees. In heavy skillet, melt the butter over moderate heat. When foam subsides, cook bacon until brown and crisp. Remove bacon from skillet with slotted spoon and drain on paper towel. Cool bacon, then crumble into small bits.

Using wire whisk or electric beater, beat eggs, extra yolks and cream together with seasonings in large mixing bowl. Stir in grated Swiss cheese. Scatter the bacon bits over the bottom of pie crust and gently ladle the egg-cheese mixture over it. Sprinkle the top with dots of butter and bake in the upper third of the oven.

Bake for 25-35 minutes or until the quiche has puffed and browned and a knife blade inserted in center comes out clean (dry).

# Candied Violets

*Yields Quite a few*

*Very pretty on petit fours, or as a garnish – completely edible too!*

Violets (pesticide free)
2 egg whites
Confectioner's sugar

Pick violets (flowers) only – no stems, in the sun.
Beat egg whites lightly, just so they are broken up.
Sift Confectioner's sugar into a saucer. Dip each violet in egg whites, then the sugar. Shake off excess sugar.
Dry in a warm place on a baking sheet or in the oven at lowest temperature.

# Carmel Apples

*An "autumn treat" I used to make for my kids and Jim, a favorite of Jim's to this day!*

1 bag (14 oz.) caramels
2 tbsp. water
5 apples
Wooden skewers
Chopped nuts, optional

Combine the caramels and water in top of a double boiler. Heat over 2 inches of boiling water in bottom of the double boiler until caramels are melted, stirring frequently.

Dip apples, held by wooden skewers, into the hot caramel sauce, turning apples until coated. Scrape sauce from bottoms of apples and place them on waxed paper. Chill until firm!

*Note: You may wish to roll the coated apples in chopped nuts once dipped before chilling. Enjoy!*

# Italian (Lemon) Ice

*Makes about 4 to 6*

*My husband, Jim's absolute favorite!*

4 to 6 whole lemons*
1 quart water
2 cups sugar
1 ½ cups lemon juice**
Zest of 2 lemons, finely grated

*Save the lemon shells once you squeeze juice from lemons.
**Okay to use some reconstituted lemon juice to make it to the 1 ½ cups if not enough juice

Mix water and sugar and let stand until clear. Make a syrup by boiling the water and sugar for five minutes.
Cool completely.

Add the strained lemon juice and zest. Pour into cups or hollowed out lemons (pulp removed). Cut tip off bottom of lemons slightly to sit flat.

Freeze until serving time. Serve right in the lemon

*Note: You may freeze mixture in a freezer tray first and "shave" it before serving in dessert dishes or lemon shells, but we like to freeze and serve it right in the lemon shell on a paper doily on a small dessert plate with a sprig of mint to garnish. Nice presentation and quite a hit!*

# Grappa Cranberry Jelly

*Makes about ¾ cup*

*Delicious addition to that already festive, Thanksgiving table!*

lb. frozen cranberries (4 cups)
1 ½ cups sugar
1 ½ cups cold water
¾ cup grappa
2 envelopes unflavored gelatin
    (about 4 teaspoons) glass mold

Bring cranberries with the sugar, 1 cup water, and ½ cup grappa in heavy pot to boiling. Simmer, partially covered, stirring occasionally, until most of the cranberries have burst open and mixture has thickened. Strain through a fine mesh sieve or jelly bag into a bowl, pressing hard then discarding solids.

Stir together gelatin and remaining ¼ cup water. Bring 1 cup cranberry liquid to a simmer. Add gelatin mixture. Stir. Add rest of grappa. Pour mixture into lightly oiled mold and chill till set (about 12 hours..covered with plastic wrap).

To unmold: dip mold in large bowl of warm water. Halfway up mold 5 seconds. Run thin knife around edge of mold. Turn out onto plate and serve.

# Mom's Pizza

*One of our kids' favorites – and they can make it better than me now!*

Dough
1 cup lukewarm water
1 – 2 pkgs. rapid-rise dry yeast
½ tsp. salt
2 cups all-purpose flour

Topping
Small can of tomato sauce
Oregano flakes
Slices of pepperoni
Slices of cooked Italian sausage
Salt/pepper, to taste

Any Other Topping Desired
Chopped green pepper
Sliced mushrooms
Mozzarella cheese, shredded

Note: This recipe doubles well as we never make just one pizza!

*Son, Michael*

Grease a round pizza pan well with shortening. Dissolve yeast in lukewarm water. Add salt and flour. Stir to blend to a nice dough. Pour out on floured board. Add more flour if necessary and knead to a nice, pliable dough – not sticky. Place dough into a greased bowl, turn once to bring greased side of dough face up, cover with a kitchen towel, and set aside to rise until double, approximately 25 minutes.

Place round of dough on greased pan. Using your fingers, gently spread dough to outer edges of pan.

Add topping(s): tomato sauce, oregano, salt, pepper, pepperoni, sausage, and/or whatever toppings your prefer. End with topping of shredded mozzarella cheese.

Bake in preheated 420 degrees oven for approx. 20 – 25 minutes until crust is golden and crisp. Slice and serve.

# Mom's Pizza Too

*Serves 6 to 8*

*Another version of Mom's umm-m-m!*

## Dough:
2 pkgs. rapid rise dry yeast
1 ¼ cups warm water or milk*
1/8 cup melted shortening or cooking oil
1 tsp. sugar
1 tsp. salt
2+ cups all-purpose flour

*Use lukewarm milk – makes a better crust (or half water/half milk)

## Toppings:
1 ½ cups sieved tomatoes or 1 can tomato sauce
Pepperoni or cooked Italian
sausage in desired amount
Sliced mushrooms
1 green pepper, diced
¼ cup grated Romano cheese
1 cup Mozzarella cheese
1 tsp. salt
½ tsp. black pepper
2 tsps. oregano flakes
Crushed red pepper flakes,
Optional

Note: Add any other toppings of your choice

Lightly grease two pizza pans, round or rectangular. Dissolve yeast in ¼ cup warm water. Combine remaining lukewarm warm water or milk, melted shortening or cooking oil, sugar and salt. Blend well and add the dissolved yeast.

Then add the flour one cup at a time beating after each addition with a long wooden spoon until mixed well. Turn dough out onto a floured board or surface. Knead for several minutes, adding more flour if dough is sticky. Knead only until the dough is nice and pliable, not too soft and not too stiff

Cut dough into two portions and place in greased bowls to rise, turning the dough once to bring oiled dough surface to top. Cover with towels and let stand to rise at room temperature approx. 25 minutes or until doubled but not overly light.

Press each ball of dough out on a greased pizza pan, taking the dough to the edge of the pan and up sides. Let stand approximately 15 minutes in pan, meanwhile preheating the oven to 400 degrees.

Next: Puncture pizza dough with fork and bake in center of preheated oven approximately 10 to 12 minutes. Remove. Cool slightly. Puncture any areas of dough that puffed up with a fork. Top with any or all toppings and finish baking for an additional20 to 25 minutes on center rack of oven until bottom crust is browned and crisp but not burned. Cut in wedges and serve.

# Mom's Mini Pizzas

*Serves 4*

*I made these lots of times for my kids' school lunches and for quick "after school" treats.
And our grandchildren took them to school as well.*

1 container of refrigerated biscuit dough

Toppings:
Small can of tomato sauce
Oregano
Mozzarella cheese, grated
Salt/pepper to taste

Any other topping desired such as:
Chopped green pepper
Sliced mushrooms
Sliced Pepperoni
Sliced Italian Sausage

Crack open the container of frozen biscuits.

Spread each biscuit into a "mini" pizza about 3- or 4-inches round on a non-stick pan.

Top each mini pizza with your choice of toppings.

Bake in preheated 400 degrees oven until done per biscuit package directions (10-12 minutes).

Remove from baking sheet and either serve or cool and send off and running with your children wrapped for later eating. Reheat well. Great cold.

*Note: This is something to involve the kids in with you – they love them – and they enjoy making them with you!*

# Mustard Cream Sauce

*Makes 2 cups*

*Great complement for roast beef, sautéed filet of beef or broiled veal chops.*
*Also nice with sautéed or roasted chicken, roast pork loin, or salmon.*

2 tbsp. unsalted butter
2 tbsp. all-purpose flour
1 cup chicken stock, heated
5 – 6 tbsp. Dijon mustard
1 cup heavy cream
2 tbsp. chopped fresh tarragon, optional (use other herb to your liking)
2 tbsp. chopped fresh chives, optional
Salt/pepper to taste

Melt the butter in a saucepan over medium heat.
Add the flour and cook, stirring a few minutes.
Gradually add the stock, whisking constantly.

Whisk in the mustard and cream.
Simmer until slightly thickened, about 5 minutes.
Stir in herbs, if using, and season to taste with salt/pepper.

Note: Also, very good on a host of vegetables including beets, carrots, green beans, or simple boiled potatoes.

# Mustard-Chive Butter

*Makes about 2/3 cup*

*Great on steaks, veal chops, broiled chicken or salmon.*

1 tbsp. dry mustard
1/ 2 tsp. sugar
2 tbsp. distilled white vinegar or water
¼ cup Dijon mustard
½ cup plus 2 tbsp. unsalted butter, room temperature
¼ cup minced fresh chives
salt/pepper to taste

Note: Stores well wrapped in waxed paper and refrigerated or freezer (form into log) in freezer wrap.

Dissolve the dry mustard and sugar in the vinegar or water in a small bowl.

Stir in the Dijon mustard.

Transfer to food processor fitted with metal blade (or you may use a blender).

Add the butter and chives. Process to blend thoroughly Season to taste with salt/pepper.

# Roasted Pumpkin Seeds

*When our kids were growing up, carving the pumpkin at Halloween time always*
*meant collecting the pumpkin seeds which I would then wash and roast in the*
*oven – the wonderful aroma filled the house and they didn't last long!*

Pumpkin seeds from 1 or 2 pumpkins
(about 1 – 2 cups)
1 to 2 tbsp. butter
Salt
Large baking sheet

Wash the pumpkin seeds to remove all the pulp and place in a bowl. Melt butter in a pan and then pour into the seeds, tossing them as you go. Just enough butter to lightly coat the seeds.

Add salt. Spread the seeds out over a baking pan and bake in an oven preheated to 250 degrees, turning occasionally, until crisp and a light golden brown color. Do not overcook as this will cause the seeds to be tough and lose flavor. Remove from oven, cool and enjoy. Oh, and Happy Halloween!

# Nuts & Bolts

*Serves 6 to 8*

*A "snack" I make that the kids and Jim still love!*
*Great Super Bowl snack or anytime. Enjoy!*

1 box croutons, plain flavor
3 cups Wheat Chex cereal
1 ½ cups Rice Chex cereal
Pretzels
1 jar dry roasted nuts
¾ cup cooking oil
¾ tsp. garlic salt
½ tsp. Accent
A little savory salt
2 – 4 tbsps. Worcestershire sauce
Butter
1 to 2 pkgs. corn nuts

Mix all dry ingredients together.
Mix Worcestershire sauce, oil, butter and salts together.

Pour over dry mixture on a 13 x 9-inch pan with sides. Bake in 275 degrees oven for 45 minutes. Stir occasionally to help dry.

Remove from oven, cool on pan and store in air-tight containers.

# Pierogi

*Yields 5 – 6 dozen*

*As close as I can get to the way my mother made them!*

Dough
2 tbsp. melted butter
2 tsp. salt
4 egg yolks, well beaten
1 ½ cups lukewarm water
6 cups flour

Filling
5 large potatoes
1 medium-size onion
¼ lb. American cheese
1 tsp. salt

Other
Butter
Another onion

Add flour to make a stiff dough. Knead on floured surface only until mixture is smooth. Brush top with melted butter, cover and let stand about 30 minutes.

Roll fairly thin and cut into 3 – 4 inch circles with rim of drinking glass. Fill with following:

Filling: Peel, wash, quarter potatoes. Cook in rapidly boiling water approx. 25 min. or just until tender. Drain and hold. Slice onion and sauté in butter. Add sautéed onion, cheese, salt and a little butter to potatoes. Beat as for mashed potatoes until all ingredients are blended nicely.

Place a tsp. of filling in center of each circle of dough. Wet edge of one-half of each circle and fold over to seal, thus forming the "pierogis." Press edges with tines of fork to be sure they are sealed. Boil in salted water 10 – 15 minutes till done. Drain, rinse and serve with butter – or – sauté the cooked pierogis in butter and onions and serve.

"Delicious!"

# Old Fashioned Hard Candy

*Jim's mother loved making this candy during the holidays. It isn't that hard to make for those who want something extra special to have or give during the holidays.*

1 cup sugar
½ cup butter
¼ cup light molasses
2 tbsps. water
½ tsp. vanilla
½ tsp. peppermint extract or flavor(s) of your choice
Candy thermometer
Confectioner's sugar for dusting finished candy

Note: Jim's mother made several batches and added a different flavor to each batch.

Combine first 4 ingredi ents in a heavy 2-quart pan. Stir over low heat until sugar is dissolved. Cook over medium heat to 300 degrees (hard-crack stage), stirring gently and continually. Remove from heat. Stir in vanilla and peppermint or other extract.

Pour into buttered 8 x 8 x 2-inch pan. Do not scrape saucepan.

Before candy cools, mark quicky into squares or odd shapes with sharp knife. Set aside to cool. When hard, break into pieces. Dust with confectioner's sugar and store in tightly covered container in a cool, dry place.

# Roquefort Butter

*Makes about ¾ cup*

*Delicious on steaks, veal chops or tucked into hamburgers!*

3 oz. Roquefort cheese
6 tbsp. unsalted butter, room temperature.
2 tbsp. cognac
1 tsp. freshly ground pepper
¼ cup chopped walnuts, optional

Place cheese, butter, Cognac and pepper in a food processor fitted with the metal blade.

Process thoroughly.
Transfer to a bowl and fold in the walnuts, if using.

# 'Taffy Apples

*Yes, I really did make these for my kids when they were growing up.*
*They are every bit as good as I remember you could buy at fairs when I was growing up!*

6 apples
1 cup sugar
1 cup light corn syrup
½ cup cold water
Few drops red food coloring
Few drops cinnamon flavoring
Candy thermometer

Wash and dry apples, remove stems and insert wooden skewers in stem end. Combine sugar, corn syrup, cold water and red food coloring in saucepan.

Cook over medium heat, stirring to 280 degrees on candy thermometer — or until a little mixture separates into hard but not brittle threads when let to drip from spoon into cold water. Remove from heat. Add cinnamon flavoring. Dip Apples in syrup, twirling to cover entire surface of Apple. Cool on greased pan or waxed paper. Yummy!

# Maître D'Hôtel Butter

*Yields 2/3 cup*

*A wonderful accent to meats and vegetables!*

1 stick butter, softened
2 tbsps. fresh parsley, minced fine
2 tbsps. chives, minced
2 tbsps. lemon juice

* Italians usually prefer to use flat-leaved Italian parsley which is far more flavorful than the curly variety.

Blend softened butter, parsley & chives in small bowl.
Add lemon juice, add a little at a time.
Turn out onto waxed paper. Shape into a 1 ½ inch wide roll.

Wrap tightly and refrigerate until firm. *Cut into slices and serve 1 slice on each serving meat

# Anna's Devilled Eggs

*Granddaughter Anna gave me this recipe for how she makes deviled eggs when she was around 12 years old, and I have made mine like this ever since!*

6 hard-boiled eggs, cut in half
¼ cup mayonnaise
2 tbsp. pickle juice (your choice, sweet or sour)
(I also add 1 tsp. yellow mustard.)

Cook 6 eggs to hard-boiled stage.
Peel the eggs; cut each in half.
Scoop out the yolk carefully.
Mash and stir the yolk till nice and finely blended.

Add mayonnaise, mustard, pickle juice. Mix well.

Evenly heap teaspoons of yolk mixture into each egg white half. Serve or refrigerate for later.

Enjoy!

*Anna's Devilled Eggs*

# Pasta and Sauces

Pasta and Sauces

# *Andy's Saucepan Pasta*

*Serves 4 to 6*

*An easy, versatile pasta recipe! Ready in minutes! Very good with cooked Italian sausage!*
*Andy Spence is an attorney friend of mine who loves to cook and experiment with food!*

1 medium onion, chopped, ½ cup
2 cloves garlic, minced
2 tbsp. cooking oil
2 large (16 oz.) cans tomatoes, cut up
2 cups packaged dried pasta
(rigatoni, mostaciolli, etc.)
1 ¼ cups water
1 2 ½ oz. jar sliced mushrooms, drained
1 tsp. dried Italian seasoning, crushed
(i.e., oregano)
1/8 tsp. crushed red pepper, or red pepper
   flakes (optional)
1 ½ cups chopped cooked chicken or turkey
Grated Romano cheese

Sauté onion and garlic in the hot oil in large saucepan until tender but not brown.

Stir in undrained tomatoes, pasta, water, mushrooms, Italian seasoning, and crushed/flaked red pepper.

Bring to boiling; reduce heat. Cover and simmer about 20 minutes or until pasta is tender but slightly firm (al dente), stirring occasionally.

Stir in cooked meat; heat through.

If desired, garnish with fresh basil leaves. Serve with fresh grated Romano cheese, tossed or musculin salad, and don't forget the wine!

*Buon Appetito!*

*Note: If using Italian sausage, either remove sausage from casings before sautéing or use bulk Italian sausage, either way – breaking into bite-sized pieces as cooking.*

# Cheese and Pasta in a Pot

*Serves 8*

*A recipe given to me years ago by a friend. It's not something I would have normally made my family. But – I tried it on them one day and, to my surprise, they liked it! So goes the old saying, "Try it, you just might like it!"*

2 lbs. ground beef
Olive oil
2 medium onions, chopped
1 or 2 cloves garlic, minced
2 cups Spaghetti sauce, preferably homemade
1 can (1 lb.) tomatoes
1 small can broiled in butter
sliced mushrooms
8 oz. shell or spiral pasta
1 ½ pints sour cream
½ lb. sliced provolone cheese
½ lb. mozzarella cheese, slice thin

Brown ground beef in a little olive oil in a large, deep fry pan. Drain. Add onions and garlic and sauté them.

Add Spaghetti sauce, tomatoes, and undrained mushrooms. Mix well.

Simmer 20 minutes.

Meanwhile: Cook pasta in boiling water to al dente stage (just underdone) about 6 to 8 minutes. Drain and rinse with cold water. Pour ½ of the cooked pasta into a large, greased casserole suitable for baking. Cover with ½ of the sauce. Top with ½ of the sour cream. Top with provolone cheese. Repeat the process, ending with mozzarella cheese.

Cover and bake in preheated 350 degrees oven for approximately 40 minutes. Remove cover and continue baking until mozzarella melts and turns golden brown.

*Buon appetito!*

# *Easy Alfredo Sauce*

*Serves 2-4*

*My grandchildren, especially Aaron, love Fettuccini Alfredo!*
*This is an easy Alfredo Sauce to whip up in a hurry!*

*Grandson, Aaron, 13 yrs. old's "favorite" dish!*

¼ cup butter
1 cup heavy cream
1 clove garlic, crushed or minced
1 ½ cups fresh grated Romano cheese*
¼ cup chopped fresh parsley
*You may use other cheeses if desired, such as Parmesan or Asiago, grated

Melt butter in a medium saucepan over medium-low heat.

Add crushed/minced garlic. Sauté only until garlic is a golden color. (Do not brown.)

Add cream and simmer for 5 minutes.
Add cheese.

Whisk quickly, heating through. Stir in parsley and serve over fettuccini or your choice of pasta.
Delicious!

# Gorgonzola Cheese Sauce

*Servings 8*

*Great served over beef tenderloin or your choice of pasta!*

3 tbsp. butter
3 tbsp. all-purpose flour
3 cups milk
1/3 cup Gorgonzola cheese, crumbled
¼ tsp. salt
¼ tsp. pepper

Parsley (chopped and sprinkled over optional)

Melt butter in a medium saucepan over medium-low heat. Stir in flour, then the milk.

As mixture thickens, stir in the cheese.

Cook until cheese is melted, and the sauce is of desired consistency.

Season with salt and pepper and serve.

*(left to right: Granddaughter Anna (8), Grandson Aaron 13, Husband Jim, Daughter Tara)*

# Lasagna, My Way

*Serves 6 – 9 people*

*Another family favorite! Nice to make ahead and freeze
to have on hand for that unexpected company.*

1 1b. Lasagna noodles
Spaghetti Sauce (Gravy)*

Filling:
1 1b. ground beef
1 lb. Italian sausage, loose (or links removed from casings)
1 – 2 tsps. garlic powder
1 – 2 tsps. dried oregano
¾ lb. Mozzarella cheese, grated
2 eggs
2 tbsp. Fresh chopped parsley
¼ cup grated Romano cheese**
Salt/Black pepper to taste
2 lbs. ricotta cheese

*.Jim's family calls spaghetti sauce "gravy"
** Locatelli

For sauce: See "Spaghetti Sauce ("Gravy") in this cookbook.
For Lasagna, boil lasagna noodles approx. 8 to 10 min. to al dente stage (just underdone). Drain and rinse with cold water. Set aside.

Filling:
Sauté the ground beef and Italian sausage till browned.
Drain off most of the grease and set meat aside to cool.

In a bowl, combine the sautéed meat with the ricotta cheese, 2 eggs beaten, ½ the grated mozzarella and Romano cheeses, parsley, oregano, salt & pepper.

To assemble Lasagna: (about 3 layers) pour ½ cup sauce in bottom of a 9 x 13-inch lasagna dish to coat bottom. Alternate layers of noodles, meat/cheese mixture and sauce, ending with a layer of noodles on top. Top with sauce and the remainder of the Mozzarella and grated cheese(s) sprinkled over (add more cheese if desired).

Bake in preheated 350 degrees oven approx. 30-45 min. till bubbly. Let stand 5 – 10 minutes out of oven to set layers. Cut into squares and serve. Pass a tureen with extra sauce and a bowl of grated Romano cheese. Serve with your favorite salad, Italian bread and wine.

*Buon Appetito!*

# Mushroom Sauce

*Serves approximately 8*

*My "original" recipe! Good sauce recipe
for those vegetarians in your life. Very tasty!
I devised this recipe for an old friend of ours who used to
run marathons here in D. C. and was a vegetarian but wanted
pasta to build up his carbs before the marathon.*

8 oz. fresh mushrooms, chopped or sliced
4 tbsp. butter
2 – 3 cloves garlic, minced
1 – 2 tsp. dried oregano
1 tsp. parsley flakes
Salt, to taste
Crushed black pepper, to taste
Tomato Sauce, 2 large cans
Pasta or your choice

Melt butter in skillet or deep sauce pot. Sauté minced garlic, just till golden. Add chopped/sliced mushrooms.

Sauté till mushrooms are golden, turning occasionally, over medium-high heat. Add tomato sauce. Add ½ cup water.

Add the oregano, parsley, salt and pepper to taste.

Cook partially covered for a minimum of 1 hour. Add water as needed to maintain desired consistency of your sauce.

Serve over your choice of pasta. Enjoy!

# *Pierogi*

*Yields 5 – 6 dozen*

*As close as I can get to the way my mother made them!*
*Easy to make and so delicious. Another economical, wholesome meal.*

Dough:
2 tbsp. melted butter
2 tsp. salt
4 egg yolks, well beaten
1 ½ cups lukewarm water
6 cups flour

Filling:
5 large potatoes
1 medium-size onion
¼ lb. American cheese*
1 tsp. salt
Butter

*Or cheese of your choice

## Dough

Blend butter, salt, beaten egg yolks and water.
Add flour to make a stiff dough. Knead on floured surface only until mixture is smooth. Brush top with melted butter, cover and let stand about 30 minutes.

Roll fairly thin and cut into 3 – 4-inch circles with rim of drinking glass. Fill with following:

## Filling

Peel, wash, quarter potatoes. Cook in rapidly boiling water approx. 25 min. or just until tender. Drain and hold. Slice onion and sauté in butter. Add sautéed onion, cheese, salt and a little butter to potatoes. Beat as for mashed potatoes until all ingredients are blended nicely.

Place a tsp. of filling in center of each circle of dough. Wet edge of one-half of each circle and fold over to seal, thus forming the "pierogis." Press edges with tines of fork to be sure they are sealed. Boil in salted water 10 – 15 minutes till done. Drain, rinse and serve with butter – or – sauté the cooked pierogis in butter and onions and serve. Delicious!

Note: The amount of filling you put into each dough circle depends on the size of the circle. Larger circle, use 1 tbsp. filling instead of 1 tsp.

*"Making Pierogi"*

# Spaghetti Sauce (or Gravy)

*Serves approximately 8*

*My "original" recipe! A good basic sauce - Jim's parents called it "Gravy!"*
*Make ahead and freeze to have on hand for that unexpected company.*

Meatball mixture:
1-1 ½ lb. ground beef
1 cup Italian breadcrumbs
2 tbsp. grated Romano cheese
2 tbsp. minced fresh parsley
2 tbsp. oregano leaves
2 – 3 cloves garlic, minced
1 egg
1 tsp. salt
¼ tsp. black pepper
Pinch of crushed red pepper
3 (1 lb. 13 oz.) cans tomato sauce
1 (12 oz.) can tomato paste
1 large can water
Olive oil

1 lb. Italian sausage links,
hot or mild or combination

Combine first 10 ingredients together in a bowl.
Shape into meatballs. Heat 2 tbsp. olive oil in a deep skillet or sauce pot and brown meatballs on all sides. Remove meatballs from skillet/sauce pot and drain on plate on paper towels.

Place sausage links in same skillet/sauce pot and sauté till browned on both sides. Drain off most of the fat.

Add tomato sauce, tomato paste and water. Stir to blend. Simmer on low heat a minimum of 2 to 4 hours, low and long, stirring occasionally, loosely covered. Add water if needed for thinning the sauce. I add the the browned meatballs to only the last 1 – 1 ½ hours of cooking so they remain on the firm side but go ahead and add them to the skillet/sauce pot with the cooked sausage then adding the sauce, etc. if you like.

Serve sauce over your favorite spaghetti or other pasta.

*Buon Appetito!*

# *Quick and Easy Spaghetti Sauce*

*Serves approximately 6 - 8*

*Amazingly good sauce and so easy! Our dear friend, Jim Graham,
now deceased, always "loved" Italian sausage so this was an easy recipe
for him to make – that is, when I didn't make it for him!*

1 or 2 lbs. Italian sausage, hot or mild – your preference
3 or 4 cloves of garlic, minced
Oregano, to taste
Tomato sauce – 3 1lb. 13 oz. cans
Grated Romano cheese

Sauté the sausage in a deep dutch oven pot.
Drain off half the fat.

Add the minced garlic to the pot. Sauté until golden.
Watch closely so it doesn't burn.

Add the oregano and tomato sauce. Bring to bubbling.
Turn heat down and simmer on low for 2 – 3 hours.

Serve with your favorite pasta, crusty bread and salad.
Sprinkle with a little grated Romano.

Enjoy immediately or freeze in small portions for a quick & easy
meal later.

*Note: My husband prefers serving this sauce over Rigatoni pasta!*

# Spinach Gnocchi

*Serves 2 - 4 people*

*Nice served along with a garlic/butter sauce or cream sauce or, nice accompaniment to beef, lamb, pork or veal.*

1 cup thawed frozen chopped spinach
8 oz. ricotta cheese
2 small eggs, lightly beaten
½ cup freshly grated Romano cheese
Salt/fresh ground pepper
½ - 1 cup all-purpose flour

Sauces
I prefer to serve these with either the Gorgonzola Cheese Sauce or Easy Alfredo Sauce (recipes in this book under Pasta & Sauces)

Squeeze excess moisture from thawed spinach. Place in food processor with ricotta cheese, eggs, Romano cheese, salt/pepper and blend until smooth. Pour into a bowl and add enough flour to form a soft, dough slightly sticky. Pour out onto floured board and mix in a little more flour by hand until still pliable but no longer sticky.

Break off small pieces, roll by hand to pencil shape. Cut into pieces about ¾ inch long. Curl each piece by pressing lightly and rolling off the tines of a fork toward you forming the shell shape or gnocchi.

We freeze gnocchi on floured baking sheets removing them to be stored in freezer bags once frozen. Freeze up to 2 months until ready to cook.

To cook, gradually add the frozen gnocchi to rapidly boiling water to which you have added a little olive or cooking oil (keeps pasta from sticking once drained. Boil approx. 5 minutes till gnocchi rise to surface.

Remove with slotted spoon or small colander to serving dish. Taste for doneness. Serve with your favorite sauce, finely grated Romano cheese, a nice salad and nice Italian wine if desired.
**Buon Appetito!**

# *Our Family's Homemade Ravioli*

*Yields about 3 dozen*

*An "original" family recipe! We make about 500 of these at Christmas and they are what we traditionally serve as this family's Christmas dinner, along with "Gavadios" (Gnocchi)*

Basic Noodle Dough:
4 cups all-purpose flour
½ tsp. salt
4 eggs
6 tbsp. cold water
4 tbsp. cooking oil

Filling:
One lb. ground beef
One 2 lb. container Ricotta cheese
2 cloves garlic, minced
2 cups grated Mozzarella cheese
¼ cup grated Romano cheese
2 tbsp. chopped parsley
1 tsp. oregano
Salt/pepper to taste
½ tsp. crushed red pepper, optional
1 or 2 eggs

*This recipe is especially long and "detailed" to benefit future family members who may want to continue on this "family tradition."*

Put flour in large mixing bowl.
Make well in center.
Add, one at a time, mixing slightly after each addition the eggs, water, salt and cooking oil.

Mix well to make a stiff dough. Turn dough onto a lightly floured surface and knead. Cover with lightly dampened towel and let rest while you make the filling.

*(Kathy making the dough)*

Filling: Sauté minced garlic in a little oil in skillet until golden. Remove to plate. Brown ground beef in same skillet. Set aside to cool. Once cool: Add sautéed garlic back into skillet with meat. Add the Ricotta cheese, grated Mozzarella, Romano, parsley, oregano, salt/peppers, and egg(s).

To form and fill Ravioli:

We have a metal ravioli plate set (see picture) that comes in two parts. We also have a Dough Machine (see picture). If you have these, fine. If you don't – that's ok – you can roll the dough by hand. We advise having both however as they are both worth their weight in gold.

Assuming you have the plates and dough machine.

1.  Cut a portion of dough off ball. Clamp dough machine on side of counter. Adjust numbers on machine as you work the dough through to find desired # for consistency of dough you want. Not too thin, not too thick.

*Son, Carl, and granddaughter*

*My husband, Jim*

2.  Turn handle and pull dough through machine. Jim works his numbers down as he goes and runs each piece of dough through at least twice, maybe three times.

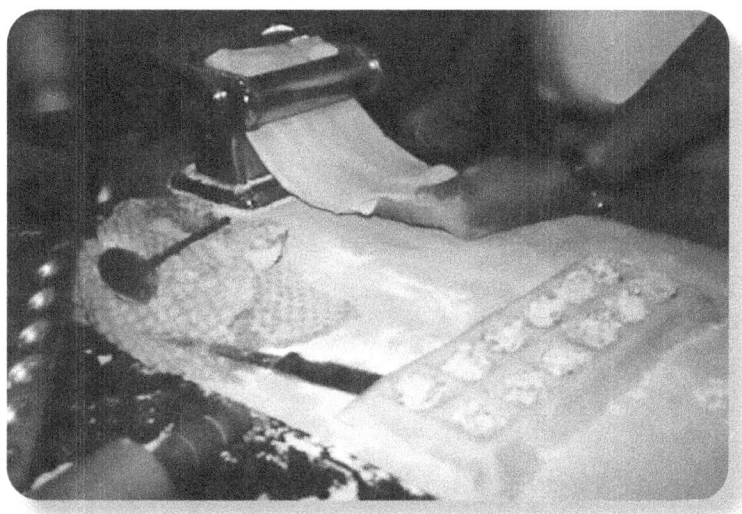

3.  Place strip of dough on bottom metal plate (with the holes in) on a floured surface (and flour the plate so dough doesn't stick).

*(Daughter, Tara & Grandson, Mason)*

4.  Place top plate on top of dough and press lightly to make impressions in the dough (pockets).

5.  Put a scant teaspoonful of filling into each pocket.

6.  Wet the bristles of a pastry brush lightly and wet all edges of dough around filling.

7.  Place top strip dough on.

8.  Roll over the plate now with a rolling pin to seal and cut between each individual ravioli.

*(My father, Joseph Ambrose, putting ravioli on trays to freeze.)*

9.  Flip plate over onto floured surface, separate ravioli, and place them on a floured pan if freezing, not touching.

10. Place pan in freezer. Once frozen, remove from pans and place in freezer bags and return to freezer for later use.*

*Jim's parents used to make the ravioli and lay a clean, white sheet out on their bed and dried their ravioli there, since they intended to cook them later that day.

To prepare: Heat a large, deep pot of water on stove to boiling, add a little olive oil or cooking oil to keep the ravioli from sticking, add the ravioli; cook for approximately 8 to 10 min. Ravioli rise to the surface as they cook. Test one for desired doneness. We like ours al dente. See recipes in this book for sauce to serve with.

Give them a try. They're worth all the effort and it makes for a fun afternoon of family and friends gathering to make them. If you come to my house, I've probably got some in the freezer! *Buon Appetito!*

*(The spread on the island in our kitchen, grandson, Aaron in background)*

# Stuffed Pasta Shells

*Makes about 2 - 3 dozen*

*Jim's mother made these often and she and I made a couple hundred of these for our neighbor at Lake Anna who was retiring from the FBI and having quite a crowd down to their lake home and were wondering what to serve – Mom solved that problem when she offered to make these. They were a big hit to say the least!*

1 box of large pasta shells
Spaghetti sauce (see recipe in this book)

Filling:
One lb. ground beef
One 2 lb. container Ricotta cheese
2 – 3 cloves garlic, minced
2 cups grated Mozzarella cheese
¼ cup grated Romano cheese*
2 tbsp. fresh parsley, chopped
1 tsp. oregano
Salt/pepper to taste
½ tsp. crushed red pepper, optional
1 or 2 eggs

*Or locatelli

Cook pasta shells in boiling, salted water to which a little cooking oil has been added to keep the pasta from sticking to al dente stage (just underdone). Drain pasta. Set aside.

Filling
Sauté minced garlic in a little oil in skillet until golden. Remove to plate. Brown ground beef in same skillet. Set aside to cool.

Once cool: Add sautéed garlic back into skillet with meat. Add the Ricotta cheese, 1 cup of the grated Mozzarella, Romano, parsley, oregano, salt/peppers, and egg(s). Stir just enough to mix ingredients together. Spoon filling into each shell. Arrange shells in a rectangular baking dish. Ladle sauce generously overall. Sprinkle remaining cup of mozzarella over top. Bake in preheated 350 degrees oven approximately 30 – 45 minutes. Serve with more sauce, nice green salad, fresh grated Romano or Locatelli cheese to sprinkle over and a nice, crusty Italian bread. *Buon appetito!*

# *Italian Macaroni & Cheese*

*Serves 4 - 6*

*Great comfort food dish!*

1 stick butter
¼ cup flour
salt/pepper to taste
2 cups whole milk
1 cup half & half cream
3 tbsp. olive oil
1 lb. macaroni (cooked al dente) *
1 cup Ricotta cheese
1 lb. mozzarella, shredded
1 large tomato or 2 small, diced
½ cup Romano cheese, fresh grated
½ cup Italian breadcrumbs

* I use penne pasta.

Melt the butter in a large sauce pot on low heat.

Stir in the flour, salt, pepper.
Gradually stir in the milk and half & half. Stir until well blended. Continue to cook over medium to mediumlow heat until mixture begins to thicken, stirring constantly.

Mix together the cooked pasta, above sauce, olive oil, diced tomatoes, ½ the breadcrumbs, shredded mozzarella, Romano cheese and ricotta cheese.

Spoon mixture into a large, greased casserole.
Sprinkle with remainder of breadcrumbs.

Bake at 350 degrees for 30 minutes. Serve.

*Note: You can also add cooked Italian sausage for a heartier meal. Serve with garlic bread and a nice salad. Easy dish to prepare ahead to pop in the oven when you get home from work for an easy dinner!*

# *Spinach Tortellini*

*Makes 6 – 8 servings*

*Also called Little Hats by some. Delicious!*

Fresh Pasta for Tortellini
3 cups flour
1 tsp. olive oil
2 eggs
Water
Salt

Put flour in bowl. Make a well in center. Pour into well the eggs, water, olive oil and salt. Mix together with fingers or fork to a nice dough. Knead on floured board or counter for approx. 8 min. Form a ball and cover with plastic wrap.

Filling
1 cup Ricotta cheese
3 tbsp. chopped spinach
1 egg
¼ cup Romano cheese, fresh grated
¼ tsp. black pepper
1 egg mixed with 1 tsp. water

Roll out the dough on floured surface. Cut dough into 3- or 4-inch circles with round cookie cutter or drinking glass.

Place ¼ tsp. filling in the center of each circle. Brush the bottom half of each circle with the egg wash. Fold dough over filling to seal.

Form tortellini by folding each filled dough round back around your finger and pinching the edges together.

Bring some water to a rapid boil in a deep pot. Add a capful of olive oil to the water as it boils. (This keeps the pasta from sticking once cooked and drained.)

Cook tortellini in batches 3 – 6 minutes or until they float to the surface.

Remove from water and drain in colander. Serve with your favorite white or red sauce.

Note: See recipes in this book for Alfredo (white) sauce, or a Spaghetti Sauce (red) recipe. Also, very good served just tossed while hot in butter and sprinkled with fresh chopped parsley and fresh grated Romano at the table!

*Buon Appetito!*

# Penne Gorgonzola with Prosciutto

*Servings 4 - 6*

*Another very easy, tasty pasta dish!*

½ lb. pkg. Penne pasta, cooked al dente
1 pint half & half
1 cup gorgonzola cheese, crumble fine
¼ lb. prosciutto ham, sliced thin
¼ cup fresh Italian parsley, chopped*
Fresh grated Romano cheese

Note: Curly leaf parsley fine too.

In a deep pot, over medium heat, bring half & half to a boil, stirring constantly so it doesn't burn. Boil 3 – 4 minutes.

Whisk in the Gorgonzola cheese. Cook, stirring constantly, until you have a smooth and creamy sauce.

Add the cooked Penne pasta, the Prosciutto and parsley. Stir. Heat through.

Serve immediately with your favorite salad, crusty bread and nice wine if desired. Pass some fresh grated Romano cheese to sprinkle over!

*Buon Appetito!*

# Capellini (Angel Hair) Fritters

*Makes about 1 dozen fritters*

*Just a little something different. Serve as an appetizer or
light lunch or light dinner with the sauce and a nice salad on the side.*

½ lb. pkg. Capellini (Angel Hair)
pasta
3 eggs
¼ cup Romano or Locatelli cheese, freshly grated
Black pepper, to taste
2 – 3 tbsp. olive oil

Pasta sauce – red – see recipe in this book or buy already prepared sauce of your choice.

Break pasta into fourths. Cook to al dente stage. Drain.

Beat eggs in a bowl with the Romano or locatelli cheese and black pepper. Stir in cooked Capellini.

Heat olive oil in a non-stick skillet.

Drop Capellini mixture into skillet using 1/8 to ¼ measuring cup depending on size fritters desired.
Press down very lightly and cook on both sides just until lightly golden/brown.

Drain on paper towels. Continue cooking until all fritters are made, adding more olive oil to the skillet as needed.

Serve with warm sauce. Enjoy!

# Capellini With Lobster

*Serves 4*

*Lobsters are scant along the coasts of mainland Italy and
therefore, considered quite a gourmet treat!*

1 lb. pkg. Capellini pasta
1 ¼ cups dry white Italian wine
½ cup onion, chopped fine
2 tbsp. heavy table cream or half & half
¾ cup butter
2 tbsp. lemon juice
1 tsp. lemon rind
1 tbsp. fresh chives

1 lb. fresh pea pods*
2 or 3 carrots*
2 (1 – 1 ½ lb.) lobsters
4 tbsp. olive oil
¼ cup sliced ripe olives

* blanch the pea pods & carrots
2 minutes & cut in strips

Cook lobsters and split length-wise.

In a pot combine the wine, and onion. Bring to boil.
Boil approx. 2 – 3 minutes. Stir in heavy table cream, butter,
lemon juice and lemon rind.

Cook, stirring, until butter melts and mixture thickens and is
creamy.

Remove from heat. Stir in the chives.

Cook the pasta to al dente stage and drain. In large bowl,
combine the cooked pasta, pea pods, carrots strips and ½ cup
of the butter lemon sauce. Cover.
Keep warm.

Put 2 -3 tbsp. olive oil in large skillet. Heat on medium-high. Add
each lobster half, meat side down (still in the shell) and cook for
2 minutes to lightly brown.

Serve each lobster half atop some Capellini mixture on individual
plates. Garnish with sliced olives (or capers) and pass remaining
lemon butter Sauce at the table. Enjoy!

# Gnocchi My Way

*Serves approximately 6 people*

*Just a little different than the potato version. I was introduced
to making Gnocchi this way by Patti Bray, one of the original owners
of the "Italian Gourmet" store in Vienna, Virginia years ago.
They have become a "way of life" in our family!*

3 -4 cups all-purpose flour
Salt
1 container (15 oz.) ricotta Cheese
Grated Romano, finely grated
Your choice of Sauce (see recipes in this book)
1 egg
Small handful grated Roman Cheese

In bowl, add the egg and Romano cheese to the ricotta cheese stirring in before adding the flour, combine 2 cups flour, pinch of salt and ricotta cheese. Mix thoroughly, adding more flour as need to make nice dough. Turn our and knead on lightly floured board until dough is smooth. Set aside. Cover with damp towel.

Break off small pieces, roll by hand to a pencil shape. Cut into pieces about ¾ inch long. Curl each piece by pressing lightly and rolling off the tines of a fork toward you, forming the shell shape of Gnocchi.

Once Gnocchi are made, we freeze them on floured baking sheets. Then, take them off the baking sheets and store them in freezer bags. Freeze up to 2 months until ready to cook. To cook, gradually add the frozen Gnocchi to rapidly boiling water*. Boil 5 – 10 minutes till Gnocchi rise to surface. Test tenderness by pressing a Gnocchi against side of pan with fork or spoon. Drain in colander. Rinse with cold water. Serve with your favorite sauce, finely grated Romano cheese, a nice salad and – don't forget the wine! *Buon Appetito!*

*To which a little cooking oil has been added to keep pasta from sticking together.

*Note is: You can find a Gnocchi board on-line to use in place of a fork. Very easy to use.*

"Making Gnocchiie"

# Linguine With Clams & Sun-dried Tomatoes

*Serves 4*

*The sun-dried tomatoes give a robust flavor to this dish!*

8 oz. pkg. linguine, fettuccine, or spaghetti

2 6 ½ oz. cans chopped or minced clams

1 medium onion, chopped

2 cloves garlic, minced

2 tbsp. olive oil

¼ tsp. crushed red pepper

½ cup dry white wine

1/3 cup oil-packed sun-dried tomatoes, drained and cut in strips

2 tbsp. snipped fresh parsley

(or 1 tbsp. dried)

Cook pasta to al dente stage. Drain and set aside.

For sauce: Drain clams. Reserve liquid. In medium saucepan cook the onion, garlic, and crushed red pepper in hot oil.

Stir in clam juice and wine. Bring to boiling. Gently boil for about 10 min. or until sauce is reduced to about 1 cup.

Stir in clams, tomatoes and parsley.

Arrange cooked pasta on individual plates or one large platter. Garnish with sprigs of fresh parsley if desired. Enjoy!

# *"Gavadios"*

*Serves approximately 6 people*

*According to Jim's mother this is the authentic version, although today you'll find many, many variations. Also, she called these "Gavadios" and most people know them as Gnocchi. Very delicious!*

3 medium-sized potatoes
1 to 2 cups all-purpose flour
Dash of salt
Grated Romano, finely grated
Your choice of Sauce

Wash, pare, quarter and cook the potatoes in boiling, salted water to cover until potatoes are fork tender as for mashed potatoes. Drain, leaving very little water to mash nicely until free of lumps. Cool slightly.

Measure flour into bowl. Make a well in center.
Add the warm mashed potatoes and a dash of salt.
Mix well to make a soft dough. Turn on floured board or surface and knead a few minutes.

Break off small pieces of dough, roll by hand to pencil shape. Cut into pieces about ¾ inch long.

I form the Gnocchi as follows: *

Place a fork right side up with the tines facing you on floured surface. Holding fork with left hand (if right-handed), place a piece of dough between your right thumb (supporting the piece of dough underneath) and your index and middle finger (supporting the piece of dough on top.

Roll the piece of dough off the fork toward you, pressing with the top two fingers and removing your thumb from underneath as you roll, keeping top fingers vertical as you press on the dough as you roll toward you off the fork, thus forming the "shell" we call "Gavadios" or "Gnocchi!"

Place formed Gnocchi on floured cookie sheets and place in freezer. Once frozen, remove Gnocchi and put in freezer bags. Freeze up to 2 – 3 months until ready to cook.

To Cook, bring a pot of water 2/3 full to a rapid boil to which you have added a cap or two of cooking or olive oil (which keeps the pasta from sticking).

Boil 5 – 10 minutes until Gnocchi float to the surface and are cooked to the al dente stage (just underdone).

Remove one and taste for desired doneness. Drain water off Gnocchi in colander. Rinse with cold water (or – if you added the cooking oil during cooking no need to rinse).

Serve Gnocchi with your favorite red or white sauce (see recipes in this book) and a nice mixed green salad. Pass finely grated Romano or Locatelli cheese at the table to sprinkle over.

*Buon Appetito!*

# Salads and Dressings

# *Overnight Layered Salad*

*Yields 6 to 8 people*

*A salad, our entire family loves. Also called 7-Layer Salad.*
*Interestingly different and delicious!*

5 cups shredded lettuce
Salt, pepper to taste
6 hard boiled eggs, sliced
1 (16 oz.) bag of frozen peas (do not thaw)
1 lb. bacon, cooked crisp and crumbled
1 bunch scallions, chopped (optional)
2 cups Swiss cheese*, shredded
2 cups of mayonnaise blended with
2 tsp. sugar)

* use a couple different kinds of cheeses, if desired –
i.e., Swiss, cheddar, Italian Romano

Place half the shredded lettuce in a 9 x 13-inch glass dish.
Sprinkle with salt and pepper.

Arrange the egg slices over lettuce.
Layer the peas over egg slices.
Layer rest of lettuce over peas.
Layer bacon over this layer of lettuce.
Layer chopped scallions over bacon (optional).

Spread mayonnaise/sugar mixture overall.
Top with layer of shredded cheese(s).

Cover tightly with plastic wrap.
Chill for 24 hours.

At serving time, sprinkle salad with a little Paprika.

Enjoy!

# Loretta's Coleslaw

*Yields 1 1/3 cups dressing*

*"Simply delicious!"*
*Recipe of my youngest sister-in-law.*

1 medium head of cabbage
2 tbsp. plus 1 tsp. vinegar
3 tbsp. sugar
¼ Kraft Miracle Whip
½ cup plus 1 tbsp. mayonnaise
¼ cup evaporated milk
½ grated carrot, optional

Mix vinegar and sugar till sugar dissolves. Add Miracle Whip and mayonnaise and the evaporated milk.

Mix well with a whisk or wire spoon to be sure sugar is dissolved. Refrigerate 2 hours to blend.

Shred cabbage and toss with 8 or 9 ice cubes in a bowl and refrigerate about an hour to crispen.

Drain cabbage just before serving and remove any chunks of ice. Toss with dressing* and serve (adding the optional grated carrot while tossing, if desired).

* Use as much dressing as desired.

# Pappy's Cucumber Salad

*Serves 2 - 4*

*Our grandchildren call my husband, Jim, "Pappy." And this is a very simple salad
I make for him as he loves cucumbers. This has become one of his absolute favorites!
Great served alongside steak, chicken or most any meat.*

2 large cucumbers
1 very small onion, or ½ medium*
Mayonnaise
Salt/black pepper, to taste

*Sweet onion, or Vidalia, may be used if you can't eat regular onions.

Peel cucumbers or, if desired, score length-wise with a peeler leaving skin partially on for a decorative touch. Gives cucumber a "striped" look.

Cut cucumbers in half length-wise. Remove seeds if you want (I do not). Then cut halves into slices, as thick as you want them. Peel the onion. Cut in half and slice each half as thin as you want the slices.

Put the sliced cucumbers and sliced onions in a deep bowl with enough mayonnaise to coat the cucumbers. Stir to blend cucumbers and onions.
Sprinkle with salt/pepper to taste. Serve.

# Creamy Dressing

*Makes ½ pint*

*This dressing is so good!*

3 tbsp. olive oil
1 tbsp. mayonnaise
1 tbsp. sour cream
2 tbsp. lemon juice
1 tsp. brown sugar
Salt
Cracked pepper
1 clove garlic, crushed
1 tbsp. fresh chives, chopped
(optional)

Combine all ingredients. Marinate minimum of 1 hour, or better, overnight on counter.

Shake well before pouring over Romaine lettuce.

# Easy Caesar Dressing/Salad

*This makes an elegant Caesar Salad and
is quick and easy! I always make this during the holidays
to serve with our Ravioli/Gnocchi Pasta Christmas dinner.*

2 egg yolks
½ tin anchovies
½ cup olive or vegetable oil
¼ cup red or white wine vinegar
2 cloves garlic, minced
½ tsp. dry mustard
½ tsp. salt
¼ tsp. fresh ground black pepper
Large garlic clove, peeled & halved
Fresh lemon cut half
Salad greens (Romaine lettuce)
Garlic/cheese croutons
Romano cheese

Blend all ingredients except salad greens, croutons and Romano cheese.

Stores well in refrigerator for up to 2 weeks.

When ready to make your Caesar Salad:

(Preferably use a wooden salad bowl if you have one*)

Rub bowl with a fresh, peeled garlic clove you have cut in half. Rub bowl next with lemon halves, squeezing slightly as you rub.

Break Romaine lettuce into bite-sized pieces. Toss in bowl with desired amount of dressing. Top with garlic/cheese croutons and grated Romano cheese.

Use pepper mill to grate fresh cracked pepper over salad servings as desired. *Buon Appetito!*!

# Romano Lettuce Salad

*Makes 6 servings*

*Quick, easy and good!*

1 head crisp iceberg lettuce
6 green scallions
1 (10 oz.) package frozen peas, thawed
Garlic powder
Fresh ground black pepper
¼ cup olive or vegetable oil
1 tbsp. red or white wine vinegar
Grated Romano cheese
Italian croutons

Tear lettuce into bite-size pieces. (Do not cut with knife as that will cause the lettuce to "rust."

Slice the scallions (tops as well). Combine with lettuce and peas. Toss.

Add oil and vinegar and toss again. Sprinkle with finely grated Romano cheese. Top with croutons.
Serve immediately.

# Artichokes and Avocado Salad

*Serves 4*

*A nice change from the usual green salad.*

1 medium avocado, cut into chunks
1 (14 oz.) can artichoke bottoms*, drained and cut
  into fourths
½ tsp. crushed fresh garlic
½ tsp. salt
¼ cup lemon juice
¼ tsp. dried dill weed
¼ cup vegetable or olive oil
Black pepper, to taste
Crushed red pepper (optional)
*Note: Ok to use artichoke hearts

Place avocado and artichoke pieces in small bowl.

Combine garlic, salt, lemon juice, dill weed, and pepper.
Slowly stir in oil.
Pour over avocado and artichoke mixture.
Marinate a while.

Serve on 4 individual leaves of curly leaf lettuce.

(May also be served as an appetizer with toothpicks on a bed of lettuce leaves.)

# Asian Salad

*Makes 8 to 10 servings*

*The salad my sister, Mary, took to our boating "Cruiser Club" get togethers
and everyone raved about it (men too!) and wanted the recipe!*

2 3 oz. pkgs. beef-flavored Ramen Noodle
Soup Mix
2 8.5 oz. pkgs. slaw mix
1 Cup sliced almonds, toasted
1 Cup sunflower seeds, shelled
1 Bunch green scallions
½ Cup sugar
¾ Cup vegetable oil
½ Cup wine vinegar

Remove flavor packages from soup mix and set aside.

Crush noodles and place in bottom of large bowl.

Top with slaw mix.
Sprinkle with toasted almonds*, sunflower seeds, and scallions.

Whisk the flavor packets with sugar, oil and vinegar.
Pour overall. Cover, seal with lid or saran wrap, and refrigerate
24 hours. Toss just before serving.

* Toast almonds by either placing almonds in skillet with a little
butter and heating until just golden – or do the same on low heat
on a pan in the oven.

*(My sister, Mary, and me)*

# My Chicken Salad

*Yields 6 to 8 servings*

*So easy and everyone seems to like it!*
*A great ladies luncheon dish!*

3 cups cooked chicken, cubed
1 cup chopped celery
1 – 2 tbsp. chopped onion
¼ cup toasted slivered almonds
Salt/pepper to taste
Mayonnaise, 3 or 4 tbsp. or amount desired
Lettuce leaves (I use red leaf lettuce)

Combine first six ingredients in a bowl.
Chill until ready to serve.

To serve: Line a pretty salad bowl with the lettuce leaves.

Fill with the chicken salad and serve.

*Note: What makes this chicken salad so good is the chicken. I use - our "Italian Chicken-in-the-Oven" leftovers (see recipe in this book) or if I don't have leftovers and no time to cook, I buy a "honey-baked" chicken from the grocery store. Either one gives the chicken salad such a good flavor! You may vary this recipe so many ways, i.e., one by adding red seedless grapes halved. Enjoy!*

# Italian-style Chicken Salad

*Makes 6 to 8 servings*

*A new "twist" to an old-time favorite!*

3 cups cooked chicken, cubed

1 (6 oz.) jar marinated artichoke hearts, drained

1 (3 ½ ox.) can pitted ripe olives, drained and sliced

1 cup chopped celery

8 oz. bottled Italian dressing (or freshly made – see recipe for Italian dressing in this book)

Lettuce leaves

Tomato wedges

Combine first five ingredients. Chill until ready to serve.

To serve: Line a salad bowl with the lettuce leaves. Fill with the chicken salad.

Garnish with the tomato wedges and serve.

# Dijon Spinach Salad

*Makes 6 servings*

*So good, and so good for you!*

1-pound fresh spinach, torn

6 slices bacon, cooked & crumbled

2 hard cooked eggs, chopped

1 cup sliced fresh mushrooms

¼ cup vegetable oil

¼ cup olive oil

1 clove garlic, minced

2 tbsp. lemon juice

1 tbsp. white wine vinegar

½ tsp. Dijon mustard

¼ tsp. salt

¼ tsp. crushed black pepper

Garlic/Cheese Croutons

Combine first 4 ingredients in a large salad bowl. Toss gently.

Combine remaining ingredients in a jar; cover tightly. Shake vigorously.

Chill.

To serve: pour chilled dressing over spinach mixture; toss gently.

Serve with croutons.

# Greek Salad

*Yields 2 to 4 servings*

*My version of a Greek salad I enjoy at a family restaurant in Fairfax, Virginia.*
*Often served with garlic toast alongside.*

1 head crisp lettuce
1 cucumber, peeled, seeded and sliced
1 tomato, sliced
Onion (optional)*
Greek or Calamata olives
Feta cheese, amount desired, crumbled
A few Pepperonci peppers
Parsley
Oregano
Taziki sauce

* I prefer to omit the onion.

Taziki Sauce
1 (8 oz.) carton plain yogurt
1 small cucumber, peeled and shredded
1 clove garlic, minced fine
1 pinch of dried dillweed
1 tbsp. lemon juice
¼ tsp. seasoned salt

Tear lettuce into bite-sized pieces.

Add the cucumber, onion (if using), tomato, olives, feta cheese and pepperonci.

Sprinkle with just a bit of parsley and dried oregano.

Toss with desired amount of Taziki sauce and serve heaping on platter.

Enjoy!

# Italian Pasta Salad

*Yields 6 to 8 servings*

*This salad has always been especially popular
in our family during the summer months.*

1 lb. pasta (penne, rotini, etc.)
8 oz. of Italian dressing*
1 medium onion, finely chopped
1 medium green pepper, finely chopped
1/3 cup grated Romano cheese
½ cup sliced green olives
½ cup sliced black olives
1 ½ tsp. oregano leaves
1 tsp. garlic power
¼ cup parsley (fresh chopped or dried flakes)
¼ cup Genoa salami, diced*
1 can artichoke hearts, drained & quartered
Salt/Cracked pepper
Little crushed red pepper flakes, optional or *pepperoni

Cook pasta al dente and drain well. In a large bowl, combine hot pasta and salad dressing.
Chill for a couple hours, stirring occasionally.

When cold, add remaining ingredients and mix well. Chill 4 hours or overnight, stirring occasionally.

# Tomatoes in Garlic and Oil

*Serves 4*

*This is a salad traditionally served in Jim's family that goes way back. Jim likes to dip Italian bread in the oil that remains once the tomatoes are gone. Buon Appetito!*

6 to 8 fresh tomatoes
¼ cup olive oil
2 cloves garlic, chopped fine
¼ tsp. salt
½ tsp. Oregano
1/8 tsp. black pepper

Wash tomatoes, remove stem ends and cut into quarters or eighths. Place in nice serving bowl. Set aside.

Combine olive oil with remaining ingredients.
Pour olive oil mixture over tomatoes, stir to blend seasonings and serve immediately or refrigerate until serving time.

# Kathy's Italian Dressing

*Makes ½ pint*

*Marinating the cloves of garlic in the oil is what makes this dressing so good!*

1 cup Extra-Virgin Olive Oil
½ cup Red Wine Vinegar (Progresso)
3 Cloves of garlic, peeled and cut in half
Oregano, to taste, optional
Black pepper, to taste
Dash salt
1 tbsp. Romano cheese, grated fine*

*Can omit while marinating and either add later or omit and just sprinkle some grated Romano right on the salad greens when serving.

1 tbsp. Balsamic Vinegar, optional

Pour the olive oil in dressing jar. Add the peeled and cut garlic cloves. Marinate minimum 1 hour, or better, overnight on counter.

Next: Add remaining ingredients. Shake well and use as desired on salad, antipasto, etc. Store unused portion in refrigerator away from coldest part of refrigerator to keep oil from setting*.

Note: I often keep an attractive salad dressing jar with a cork in top on my counter with just the olive oil, vinegar and garlic cloves marinating. Then I shake the jar to blend the oil & vinegar at time of serving, pour desired amount over my salad and sprinkle remaining seasonings over salad as desired, then toss again. I always sprinkle grated Romano over all just before serving.

* If you plan to use dressing within a few days, no need to refrigerate.

# Olive Salad

*Makes 4 cups*
*Something a little different!*

1 head garlic (about 6 cloves)
1 green bell pepper, quartered
1 red bell pepper, quartered
5 celery stalks, cut in half
1 ½ lbs. mushrooms
4 (10 oz.) jars large pimiento stuffed olives (10 cups), drained
2 cups vegetable oil
2 cups white vinegar
2 tbsp. ground black pepper
2 tbsp. lemon pepper
2 tbsp. garlic powder
2 tbsp. onion powder
2 tbsp. sugar
1 medium onion, chopped

Chop vegetables. In bowl of food processor fitted with metal blade, place garlic, red and green bell peppers, celery, mushrooms and olives.

Process with short pulses until coarsely chopped. (This can be done in batches.) Cook the seasonings: In 2-quart saucepan, combine oil, vinegar, pepper, lemon pepper, garlic powder, onion powder and sugar over med-high heat.

Bring mixture to a boil and add onion. Remove from heat and cool. Combine all ingredients in a large bowl, stirring together vegetable and seasoning mixtures till well blended. Cover, refrigerate overnight.

Can be stored, refrigerated, for up to 1 month.

# Shrimp & Pasta Salad with Caper Dressing

*Yields 4 servings*

*Good summertime salad. Cool and refreshing!*

1 cup dried medium shell pasta
12 ozs. Shrimp, deveined – raw or frozen
2 green onions, sliced
l red or green bell pepper, diced
2 tbsp. olive oil
3 tbsp. wine vinegar (red or white)
1 tbsp. capers
1 clove garlic, minced
Salt/pepper to taste
1 tsp. snipped fresh dill or
½ tsp. dried
1 cup fresh pea pods or 6 oz. pkg.
frozen, thawed
Spinach or lettuce leaves (optional)

Cook the pasta to al dente stage. Drain and rinse with cold water.

If raw, cook shrimp, uncovered, in boiling water 1 to 3 minutes till shrimp turn pink. Drain. Rinse with cold water.

Combine pasta, shrimp, red or green bell pepper and green onions. Toss.

Prepare dressing: Combine in a jar the vinegar, oil, capers, dill, garlic, salt and pepper. Cover. Shake well. Pour dressing over pasta mixture. Toss gently.
Cover and chill for 3 hours to overnight.

Add the pea pods just before serving, cutting the pods in half crosswise. If desired, serve on a bed of spinach or lettuce.

Tip: Make this one easy, purchase shrimp, steamed, at your local grocery store.

# Blueberry Congealed Salad

*Yields 4 servings*

*Good summertime salad. Cool and refreshing!*

2 large pkgs. grape Jello-O
1 cup boiling water
1 can blueberry pie filling
1 large can crushed pineapple

Topping
8 oz. cream cheese
8 oz. sour cream
½ cup sugar

Chopped nuts, if desired (walnuts, almonds, pecans, etc.)

Mix Jell-O, boiling water, pie filling and crushed pineapple together.

Let mixture congeal.

Blend cream cheese, sour cream, sugar together.
Spread across top of salad once congealed.
Sprinkle with chopped nuts, if desired.

# Strawberry Congealed Salad

*Yields 4 servings*

*Mix Jell-O, boiling water, strawberry pie filling, and crushed pineapple together.*

2 boxes Strawberry Jell-O
1 cup boiling water
1 can strawberry pie filling
1 small can crushed pineapple
1 cup chopped pecans

Topping
1 (8 oz.) cream cheese
½ cup sour cream
1 cup sugar

Mix Jell-O, boiling water, strawberry pie filling, and crushed pineapple together.

Set aside to congeal.

Mix together cream cheese, sour cream and sugar.
Once salad is congealed, spread topping overall.

Sprinkle with the chopped pecans, if desired.

# Mediterranean Orzo Salad

*Yields 8-10 serving*

*Wonderfully delicious! This is a big hit at dinner parties for something different!*

1-1 ½ cups dry orzo
½ cup pitted Kalamata olives
¾ cup cherry tomatoes, halved
1 red pepper, chopped
12. oz. artichoke hearts, drained
½ cup feta cheese, crumbled
¼ cup chopped parsley
2 tbsp. capers
1 tsp. honey

Dressing
¼ cup lemon juice
1 clove garlic minced,
½ cup extra-virgin oil
Salt/pepper, lots

Cook the orzo according to package directions. Drain. Set aside to cool.

**Dressing**
Combine lemon juice, garlic, honey, salt/pepper in food processor. Process slowly drizzling in the olive oil. Combine the cooked orzo with remaining ingredients drizzling enough dressing over to coat. Toss and serve or refrigerate until ready to serve.

# Sandwiches

# *The History of Sandwiches*

The first recorded "sandwich" was made by the famous rabbi, Hillel the Elder, who lived in the first Century BC poor but a scholar. He began the process of "sandwiching" during Passover—sandwiching a mixture of fruit, nuts, spices and wine between two matzohs. This was the start of the Seder and is named after him.

And down through history, the sandwich was introduced to America by Elizabeth Leslie (1778-1858) through her Directions for Cookery. She gave us a recipe for ham sandwiches she felt worthy as a main dish.

With the Industrial Revolution underway, bakeries then began to sell bread, presliced. Americans were overjoyed at the ease of making a sandwich.

So, we can thank Elizabeth Leslie for introducing us to the ease and convenience we so enjoy today with the endless combinations we know as sandwiches!

# Ratatouille on the Roll

*Different, quick, great tasting, healthy, economic!*

Olive oil

Garlic cloves, crushed with press

1 large onion, yellow or sweet

2 Bell Peppers (red, green, etc.)

1 Hot banana peppers, optional

2 zucchini squash

1 large eggplant

Plum tomatoes (or any kind)

Fresh basil leaves (optional as accent on sandwich
 or chopped over pasta)

Salt/pepper

Italian sub rolls

Grated Locatelli/Romano

Cheese (to sprinkle over optional)

Note: Make a large batch and have some on hand for a quick, easy dinner or lunch. Keeps well for a week refrigerated.

Set out a large, deep skillet. Saute desired amount of minced garlic cloves and the onion (sliced to desired thickness) in ¼ cup olive oil until golden. (I also add a large pat of butter for flavor but that can be omitted.)

Cut peppers into quarters length-wise. Cut zucchini and eggplant into approx. ½ inch thick slices. Cut tomatoes in half length-wise.Add to garlic/onion mixture.

Continue to simmer on top of stove in skillet until vegetables are tender (or place in oven in oven-proof skillet) and roast at 400 degrees until tender. (10 – 15 minutes). Stir occasionally.

To serve: Layer into rolls and serve. Delicious! Options: Chop leftover ratatouille and toss with cooked pasta for an easy, delicious lunch or supper! Great served alongside any meat as an accompaniment! Enjoy!

# Sausage, Peppers & Tomatoes

*Serves 6 to 8*

*Such a favorite Italian "Sub" you're likely to find at craft fairs and food and wine festivals everywhere...this is my own version...and we often eat this as a meal, serving it on a plate and dipping Italian bread in the sauce!*

2 lbs. Italian Sausage, hot or mild
4 to 5 green bell peppers
2 large cans tomatoes, Italian plum is best, or use equal amount of fresh tomatoes
Submarine rolls or rolls/bread of your choice
Olive oil

Set out a large skillet. Sauté the sausage in a little olive oil, turning sausage until all sides are a golden brown.

Drain off some of the fat.
Core and remove seeds from bell peppers.
Cut in long slices. Add peppers to skillet with sausage.
Cut tomatoes in large chunks and add to skillet.

Cook together, lid on, over medium heat until done (approximately 1 hr.) Watch while cooking and stir occasionally to keep from burning.

Serve hot on Sub rolls as a sandwich or "as is" as a meal with Italian bread for dipping.

# *Italian Meatball Sub*

*Makes 8 Patties*

*Quick and easy sandwich with made ahead meatballs and sauce.* *

Meatballs
1 ½ lbs. ground round steak or other good grade
   of beef
2 cloves garlic, crushed
1 egg
½ cup Italian-style breadcrumbs
1 tsp. oregano
1 tbsp. fresh parsley, chopped fine
1 tbsp. Romano cheese, grated fine
Pinch of salt
Pinch of black pepper
Pinch of crushed red pepper
Tomato Sauce
Slices of Mozzarella Cheese

Combine all ingredients in bowl.
Shape into walnut-size or little larger meatballs.
Brown well in skillet.
Add tomato sauce to cover.
Cook no less than 2 hours in sauce. Cool.

When ready to serve subs, slice the rolls almost through. Place desired amount of meatballs on roll, ladle with just enough sauce, top with slice of Mozzarella.

Place under broiler just until cheese is melted.
Serve immediately.

* Makes good use of leftover meatballs and sauce

# Italian-Style Hamburgers

*Makes 8 Patties*

*If you like hamburgers, you're in for a special treat with these.*
*They're absolutely mouthwatering! An old family recipe!*

1 ½ lbs. ground round steak or other good grade
  of beef
2 cloves garlic, crushed
1 egg
½ cup Italian-style breadcrumbs
1 tsp. oregano
1 tbsp. fresh parsley, chopped fine
1 tbsp. Romano cheese, grated fine
Pinch of salt
Pinch of black pepper
Pinch of crushed red pepper

Combine all ingredients in bowl.
Shape into 8 patties. Heat fry pan; add patties.
Brown on both sides. Serve.

Note: You may also broil these patties or grill on your barbecue
grill. Adjust herbs to your own taste. **Buon Appetito!**

# Fried Bologna & Onion Sandwiches

*Yields 2 Sandwiches*

*A favorite of Jim's to this day!*

Bologna, beef or part beef/ part pork
1 medium onion, sliced
4 slices bread*
Butter

* toast the bread lightly, if desired

Set out a large skillet.
Melt a couple pats of butter.
Sauté the onion slices until translucent and a light golden/brown but not burned.
Remove onion slices and set aside.
Place bologna slices (I usually use 3 slices per sandwich) in skillet. Brown on both sides, cutting a "slit" in each slice as cooking to lie flat.
Place some of the fried bologna and fried onion slices on top one bread slice, top with the other bread slice. Serve.
One of the tastiest sandwiches you'll ever eat! Enjoy!

# Fried Egg & Tomato Sandwiches

*Yields 4 Sandwiches*

*One of "my" favorites! So easy, so good!*

8 slices bread of your choice*
4 eggs
butter
salt/pepper
Tomato slices
Mayonnaise
Lettuce leaves

*Lightly toast bread if you wish

Melt a couple pats of butter in a skillet.
Fry the eggs to desired doneness. Spread each slice of bread with desired amount of mayonnaise.

Place one fried egg on each of 4 slices of bread.
Top each with a slice of tomato, a little salt and pepper and some lettuce. Place another slice of bread on top of each.
Serve and enjoy!

# *Greek Pita Sandwiches*

*Makes 3-6 servings*

*If you like Souvlaki, you'll love these!*

1 ¼ lb. lean boneless pork
Olive oil
3 pita bread rounds, halved
Thinly sliced onion, optional
Thinly sliced tomato, optional
Lettuce, shredded or sliced in shreds
Feta cheese, crumbled
Marinade:
¼ cup olive oil or cooking oil
¼ cup lemon juice
2 tbsp. prepared mustard
2 cloves garlic, minced
1 ½ tsp. dried oregano, crushed
Taziki Sauce:
1 8 oz. carton plain yogurt
1 small cucumber, peeled and shredded
1 clove garlic, minced fine
1 pinch of dried dillweed
1 tbsp. lemon juice
¼ tsp. seasoned salt

Partially freeze pork. Thinly slice into bite-size strips. Place pork in plastic bag set in deep bowl. Prepare marinade: Combine oil, lemon juice, mustard, garlic, and oregano. Mix well. Pour over pork strips in bag. Seal bag. Marinate in refrigerator 6 hours or overnight, turning bag occasionally.

Prepare sauce: In small bowl, combine yogurt, cucumber, garlic, dillweed, lemon juice and seasoned salt. Cover and chill 6 hours or overnight.

At serving time: Drain pork. Discard marinade. (DO NOT KEEP.) In large skillet, stir-fry pork in a little oil half at a time, over medium-high heat about 3 min. or till pork is no longer pink. Using slotted spoon, remove pork from skillet. Spoon into pita halves.

Stir cucumber sauce and spoon atop meat. Garnish with the thinly sliced onion (optional), tomato, lettuce and crumbled Feta cheese. Serve.

NOTE: Another way to serve this sandwich is to serve it with the pork open faced atop whole pita round mixed in with Greek Salad* and some of the cucumber sauce and topped with desired amount of crumbled Feta Cheese. Then you have open-faced "Souvlaki!" Enjoy!

* See Greek Salad recipe in this cookbook.

# Healthy Veggie Pita

*Yields 1 pita sandwich*

*A quick & healthy meal full of vitamins & proteins. A Forsythe family recipe.*
*(My niece & nephew)*

1 whole wheat pita
½ cup fat-free cottage cheese
1 large handful baby spinach
¼ cup chopped yellow pepper
½ avocado
2 tsp. olive oil
¼ cup chopped red pepper
Pinch of salt/pepper
Fresh slice of pineapple or cantaloupe

Smash avocado with spoon in a bowl with cottage cheese. Meantime, heat olive oil in a pan and lightly sauté spinach and peppers until warm. Do not overcook spinach. Veggies should be slightly al dente.

Mix veggies and avocado mixture together And add a pinch of salt and pepper.

Cut pita in half. Fill each side. Serve with fresh pineapple or cantaloupe slice alongside.

# Onion Sandwiches for Daddy

*One of my father's favorite treats my mother made for him!*

White onions*
Bread of your choice
Butter
Salt
Pepper

*Vidalia or sweet onions may be the choice of the ladies.

Pour salted ice water over thin slices of onion.
Let stand for a while to extract the strong flavor.
(Skip this step if using sweet onions.)
Drain the onion.

Place between buttered slices of bread. Season with salt and pepper. Enjoy!

Note: When growing up, I could never imagine wanting to eat an onion sandwich! Then, at a women's club function, there they were – tiny rounds of onion sandwiches served as appetizers. And, would you believe, they were delicious! Try one!

# Hot Roast Beef & Gravy

*Yields enough for 6 to 8*

*An old stand-by I made when the kids were growing up. Serve open or closed-faced with a side of mash potatoes & the brown gravy! Yummy! And I'm still making them just for the two of us!*

1 3–4 lb. chuck roast of beef
1 medium-sized onion (yellow or sweet Vidalia)
Water
Flour
Gravy Master or Kitchen
Bouquet
Salt
Black pepper

Lightly coat the bottom of a heavy, deep skillet with olive oil. Heat to medium-high.

Place chuck roast in skillet and sear/braise it on all sides to seal in juices.

Dissolve 2 Tbsp. flour in a large glass of water with a few drops of Gravy Master or Kitchen Bouquet (browning agent found in spice section of grocery store).

Add to skillet around meat with a little salt and black pepper. Cover with lid, reduce heat to simmer on low until meat is cooked and tender (falling apart) – approximately 2 – 3 hours, adding more water/flour mixture if necessary as it cooks to form a nice amount of brown gravy.

I serve this meat "open-faced" on top of a slice of bread and ladle the gravy over the meat. I also serve mashed potatoes on the side also "smothered" with gravy. Enjoy!

# Italian Beef

*Makes 6 servings*

*Authentic "Italian Beef" consists of thin slices of roast beef, dripping with meat juices, served inside crusty rolls most often with the roasted green pepper. The sandwich is often dipped in the "gravy" when eaten (pan juices from roasting).*

1 4 lb. rump roast
salt/pepper
3 to 5 garlic cloves
2 cups beef stock
1 tsp. dried oregano leaves
1 tsp. dried thyme leaves
1 Bay leaf
1 medium onion, diced
2 tbsp. Worcestershire sauce
2 – 3 green peppers, seeded and sliced
Crusty Italian rolls or bread

*This is "made-from-scratch" Italian Beef, my way! I'm told it's pretty darn close to the real thing!*

Preheat oven to 325 degrees. Season roast with salt and pepper. Place on a rack in roasting pan. Poke holes in roast and insert half of the garlic cloves in slices. Mince remaining garlic cloves and spread over roast with the onion.

Roast in oven until medium-rare to medium (140 degrees on meat thermometer if using one) or about 1 – ½ hrs. Remove roast to cutting board, cover loosely and let rest for about ½ hour.

Meanwhile, leave juices in pan and add remaining ingredients except bread. Simmer all in pan on top of stove 15 – 20 min.

Slice the beef thinly on board. Strain juices and pour over beef in pan. Refrigerate with the green pepper and juices 8 hours or overnight. Next day: heat the beef and juices. Serve on crusty Italian rolls, spooning some of the juices and green pepper over for a delicious sandwich we know as "Italian Beef" and enjoy!

# History of Italian Beef

Early immigrants to Chicago from Italy first made a dish they called "Italian Beef", slow roasting the tough beef they brought home to make it more appealing. They added spices while roasting. When done, they sliced it thinly and served it with the juices on fresh Italian bread. It became very popular as it was inexpensive but "delicious!"

# Italian Sub

*Serves 4*

*My very own recipe which my children and my husband love.*

Crusty Italian Sub Rolls
Desired amount of sliced
Genoa salami
Prosciutto
Capacola (Italian ham)
Provolone cheese
Onion, sliced very thin
Tomato, slice thin
Hot cherry peppers, cut into rings*
Oregano (dried crushed leaves)

*Optional (use mild if desired or pepperonci)

Slice rolls not quite to the end and fold open. Drizzle with a little of the juice from the jar of peppers. Layer all ingredients as desired across each roll. Be sure the onion is the top layer, sprinkled with a little oregano.

Place on pan in oven under broiler. Watch carefully until the onion is cooked but not burnt and the cheese is melted. Remove from oven, close and serve immediately.

Note: My family prefers this sandwich served hot right from the broiler, but you can prepare and serve it cold if preferred and not broil. "Enjoy!"

# Open-faced Melted Cheese Sandwiches

*One of my children's favorites when growing up and so easy and quick on those nights when we just didn't want a heavy dinner or on sports nights!*

1 block Velveeta cheese
Milk
Black pepper (optional)
Bread of your choice

In a pot on top of stove, over low heat, melt the block of Velveeta cheese adding milk a little at a time, until just a nice pouring consistency but not too thin and heated through.

Place a slice of your choice of bread on a plate. Pour melted cheese over. Season with black pepper. Eat with fork while warm and enjoy. Comfort food!

# Pizza Burgers

*Serves 4 - 6*

*My memory of these goes way back to my high school days when they were served to us there
by some of the mothers who manned the school cafeteria – An "original" old hometown recipe!*

1 lb. ground beef
2 small onions, chopped
2 cans tomato paste
½ can tomato soup
¼ cup grated Romano cheese
1 tsp. garlic powder
1 tsp. oregano
American cheese slices

Brown ground beef in skillet with a little oil and the chopped onion.

Mix together the tomato paste, tomato soup, Romano cheese, garlic powder and oregano. Add to meat mixture and simmer briefly. Scoop onto open buns, top each with American cheese slice. Bake 8 to 10 minutes in 400 degrees oven.
Serve hot

# Sloppy Joes

*Serves 4*

*Another great standby I raised my family on! Quick and easy!*

½ cup onions, sliced
½ cup green pepper, diced
2 tbsp. fat or shortening
1 (1 lb. 13 oz.) can peeled tomatoes, diced
½ cup mushrooms, diced optional
1 lb. ground beef
1 cup tomato juice
1 tsp. salt
½ tsp. black pepper

Rolls of your choice

In skillet, saute the onion and green pepper in the fat/shortening till lightly browned.

Add ground beef and saute till browned.
Add the tomatoes, mushrooms if using, tomato juice, salt and pepper.

Cover and cook over low heat for approximately to 20 minutes. Thicken juices if desired with a little flour or cornstarch dissolved in a little water and added. If too thick, thin with a little water. Serve on rolls and enjoy!

# Club Sandwiches

*A sandwich no one made like my mother! A "triple decker!" She never wasted
anything, and this is one "delicious" way she used up her leftovers!*

Leftover roast chicken or turkey*
Bread slices of your choice**
Cooked bacon slices
Fresh tomato slices
Fresh lettuce leaves
Mayonnaise
Salt/pepper

*Or any leftover cooked meat
** Lightly toasted if you wish

Take 3 slices of bread of your choice (white, whole wheat, etc.)

Spread first slice with light coating of mayonnaise.
Lay slices of leftover chicken or turkey, etc. on slice.
Top with thin slice of fresh tomato. Salt lightly. Add fresh lettuce
leaves.

Add second slice of bread, spread lightly again with mayonnaise.
Add slices of cooked bacon.
Add another thin slice of fresh tomato. Salt lightly.
Add fresh lettuce leaves.

Top with last slice of bread. Cut in half and serve.
Enjoy!

# Tea Sandwiches

*Great for luncheons/picnics.*

Good quality bread (white, wheat, pumpernickel, rye)
Unsalted butter, room temperature
Mayonnaise, if desired
Choice of fillings, i.e., chicken, egg or tuna salad; thin slices of luncheon meat (ham, etc.); smoked salmon, cream cheese, cucumbers

Cut the crusts off the bread (never serve end slices).

Lightly butter slices (keeps sandwiches from becoming soggy before serving). Butter should be room temperature. You can also add a light spread of mayonnaise over the butter if desired.

Spread first slice of bread with choice of filling or thin meat slices. Top with second slice. Cut sandwiches into 4 triangles or other fancier shapes with cookie cutters. (Tea sandwiches are meant to be delicate.)

Decorate tops of each, if desired, with a dollop of mayonnaise and thin slice of pimento-suffed green olive (which I do). If serving later, cover sandwiches loosely with a sheet of waxed paper and then a damp kitchen towel to keep them from drying out. (Never place a damp towel directly on bread.) Refrigerate until time to serve. Allow a serving of 4 triangles per person.

# Prosciutto & Brie

*Makes 4 sandwiches*
*A little something special!*

4 ciabatta rolls*
¼ lb. prosciutto, sliced thin
¼ lb. Brie cheese, thin slices
½ cup fig confit**

*Ciabatta is a chewy, classic Italian bread – wide, flat, flourdusted; comes in loaves or rolls

** For Fig confit
1 cup dried figs (Calimyrna),
½ cup dry white wine
½ cup water
3 tbsp. honey
1 tsp. rosemary leaves, chopped fine (optional)

First make fig comfit. In a heavy saucepan, stir together the dried figs, wine, water, honey, and rosemary leaves if using. Simmer, covered, approx. 15 – 20 min.

Remove lid and simmer until most of the liquid evaporates and is thickened, stirring occasionally to avoid burning.

Puree fig mixture in food processor to coarse texture. Bring to room temperature before using.

**Sandwich**
Halve rolls or cut loaf diagonally into 4 pieces, and cut each piece in half. Spread each with the fig confit, prosciutto slices and Brie.

*Buon Appetito!*

# Egg Salad Sandwiches

*Yields 1 Sandwich*

*A sure favorite!*

For each sandwich:
Two slices of bread
1 hard-cooked egg
2 tbsp. diced celery
1 tsp. onion, chopped fine
1/8 tsp. salt
Dash of pepper
2 tbsp. mayonnaise
Lettuce

For each sandwich
Mash the egg. Stir in the mayonnaise.
Add in the celery, onion, salt and pepper.
Spread filling on one slice of bread.
Top with torn lettuce pieces.
Enjoy!

*Note: Double the recipe as many times as desired to make enough filling. Makes delicious "finger" sandwiches too – cut bread in small desired shapes, fill and serve on trays.*

# Grilled Cheese Sandwiches

*Yields 1 Sandwich*

*A sure favorite in our house as the kids were growing up!*

For each sandwich
Two slices of bread
Slice(s) of American cheese*
Butter
*Or your choice of cheese

For each sandwich:
Butter the bread slices. Place slice(s) of cheese between the bread. Place in oven and broil each side until bread is toasted and cheese melts. Serve hot.

*Note: Aside from broiling these in the oven, often times I would fry them in a skillet in melted butter, turning to brown each side. Either way, they were a favorite!*

# Soups and Stews

Soups and Stews

# *Beef Chop Suey*

*Serves 6*

*My version of chop suey. Another dish I raised my family on and to this day, they love it.*

1 – 1 ½ lb. beef chuck or rump roast
2 tbsp. fat (or cooking oil)
1 ½ cup diced celery
1 cup diced green pepper
1 cup diced onion
1 tsp. salt
½ tsp. pepper
2 tbsp. soy sauce*
2 cups water
Gravy Master or Kitchen Bouquet (optional)
4 to 5 cups cooked white, long-grain
rice (cook according to box)

*Add more according to taste

Cut the beef into bite-size cubes, trimming away excess fat. Sauté in fat in skillet till browned.

Remove meat and set aside.

Sauté onion, celery and green pepper in same skillet till lightly browned. Add meat back in. Add salt, pepper, soy sauce, and water. I also add a cap or two of gravy master or kitchen bouquet to darken sauce, but this is optional. Add the Chinese vegetables, bean sprouts, water chestnuts.

Cover and cook over low heat approximately 45 minutes to 1 hour, thickening juices if desired with a couple tablespoons of cornstarch dissolved in a little more water and added, if desired.

Serve over cooked rice.

# Cream of Broccoli Soup

*Serves 8*

*My sister, Mary's recipe. Delicious!*

2 cups water
¾ cup chopped onion
¼ cup butter or margarine
6 cups 1% milk
1 tsp. white pepper
1 (16 oz.) pkg. frozen broccoli cuts
½ cup all-purpose flour
4 chicken bouillon cubes
1 cup shredded cheddar cheese

Cook broccoli in boiling water for about 7 minutes. Remove from heat and let sit.

Sauté onion in butter until tender. Stir in flour until smooth. Add milk gradually and bouillon cubes.

Cook over medium-high heat until mixture thickens, stirring almost constantly. Put ½ the broccoli in blender and puree.

Finely chop the rest of the broccoli.

Combine both mixtures and salt and pepper. Simmer about 30 minutes. Stir occasionally. Stir in ½ cup cheese until it melts. Serve soup garnished with the rest of the cheese.

# *Creamy Cauliflower-Romano Cheese Soup*

*Serves 6*

*An elegant dinner party soup served with delicious "Romano cheese toast!"*

1 large head cauliflower, or 1 bag frozen
5 cups chicken broth
2/3 cup light cream or milk
4 tbsp. freshly grated Romano cheese
Pinch of red pepper flakes
Pinch of freshly grated nutmeg, or one shake
   of dried
Salt/pepper to taste
2 cups pasta bows (farfalle)
Crusty bread (for cheese toast)
Paprika

If using fresh cauliflower, cut the leaves and central stalk away and discard. Divide cauliflower into florets.

Bring chicken stock to a boil. Add the cauliflower.
Simmer approximately 10 minutes till very soft.
Remove Cauliflower from broth and place in food processor.

Add the pasta bows to the chicken stock and simmer for 8 - 10 minutes just until al dente. Drain. Set pasta aside and pour stock over the cauliflower in food processor. Add cream or milk, red pepper and nutmeg. Blend until smooth, then press through a strainer.

Stir in cooked pasta. Reheat soup and stir in the Romano cheese.

Meanwhile: Make the cheese toast – cut bread into slices about ½ thick. Spread lightly with butter and sprinkle Romano cheese and paprika. Place on baking sheet and bake or broil until golden but not burned.

*Note: Garnish soup when serving with a sprig of Italian parsley in center.*

# Escarole Soup

*Serves 12*

*Another of my husband's favorite soups!*

1 lb. Italian sausage, casings removed
1 medium onion, chopped
2 cloves garlic, crushed or minced
1 – 28 oz. can whole tomatoes, cut in chunks.
1 – 46 oz. can chicken broth*
1 bunch escarole
1 cup – 4 oz. uncooked pasta**
1 – 6 oz. can cannelloni (white kidney beans)
1/8 cup grated Romano or Locatelli

*Homemade is great if you have it.
** Ditalini, bows, elbows, etc.

Brown loose sausage in Dutch oven pot, over medium heat, breaking it up into bite-size pieces with a spoon. Drain half of the fat off. Add onion and garlic and sauté until golden.

Stir in the tomatoes and liquid. Stir in the broth.
Bring to a boil.

Clean and coarsely chop the escarole. Add escarole to pot. Drain and add beans. Simmer uncovered about 15 minutes.

To serve: Cook pasta to al dente stage. Drain. Rinse. Place a large spoonful of cooked pasta in each soup bowl, ladle soup over. Pass freshly grated Romano or Locatelli cheese at the table to sprinkle over. Serve with salad and hot bread.

*Buon Appetito!*

# Italian Chicken Soup

*Serves 4-6*

*Just a little "twist" on my old-fashioned chicken soup recipe*
*to make it Italian! A form of Italian Wedding Soup.*

1 whole chicken
1 lb. ground beef
1 egg, beaten
Small amount of breadcrumbs
1 med. bunch of escaroles
3 stalks of celery, with leaf tops
1 medium onion, cut in half
4 carrots, cut in fourths
Salt/pepper/garlic powder and parsley to taste
1 lb. Ditalini pasta*
Grated Romano or Locatelli
*Use bows, elbow, etc. as well

Place chicken in large soup pot and cover with water. Bring to boil and continue to boil for about 4 hours or until meat leaves the bone. Remove chicken and strain broth.

Return meat from bones. Return broth and meat to stove, adding the onion, celery and carrots. Cover and simmer for 30 min.

While vegetables are cooking, mix ground beef, egg, salt, pepper, garlic powder, parsley and breadcrumbs together. Roll mixture into tiny meatballs. Add to the broth last 15 minutes of simmering. Add escarole last 10 minutes of simmering.

In a separate pan, cook the pasta to al dente.
Drain. Rinse with cold water. Serve in bowls with soup ladled over. Sprinkle with grated Romano or Locatelli. Enjoy!

# Italian Seafood Stew

*Serves 4*

*The fresh fish and vegetables makes this delicious
dish a healthy choice!*

1 tbsp. olive oil
1 onion, chopped
4 garlic cloves, chopped
1 green bell pepper, seeded and diced
1 ½ cups dry white wine
1 ¼ cups fish, chicken, or vegetable broth
1 can (32 oz.) chopped tomatoes
2 tbsp. tomato puree
1 tsp. dried oregano leaves
3 tbsp. fresh parsley, chopped
1 medium zucchini, sliced
½ cup fresh shelled or frozen peas
½ cup spinach leaves
½ lb. skinless cod fillet, cut into chunks 1 lb. combination of peeled or shelled mixed shellfish (shrimp, scallops, mussels, squid rings.)

Sauté the onion in the olive oil in a skillet till golden. Add the garlic, green pepper. Cook till garlic is golden.

Add wine, broth and tomatoes with their juice and season lightly with salt/pepper.

Simmer about 30 minutes to thicken. Stir in puree, oregano, parsley, and zucchini slices.

Simmer 10 minutes, adding a little water if too thick.

Stir peas, spinach, fish and shellfish into tomato mixture. Cover and simmer gently over medium heat until seafood is cooked – about 5 minutes.

Serve stew with a nice, crusty Italian bread and your choice of wine or beverage.

*Buon Appetito!*

# Jim's Cream of Crab Soup

*Makes 1 Quart*

*I wish you could have seen Jim the day he created this recipe. After all his tastings (to get it just right, of course), it isn't any wonder he came up just a little short of the quart!*

3 tbsp. butter or margarine
½ cup chopped green onion
1 cup chopped celery
2 tbsp. flour
¾ cup water
1 cup chicken broth
1 cups milk
1 pint half & half, optional Few drops hot sauce
   (Tabasco) or pinch of crushed red pepper
¼ cup dry Sherry or White Wine
12 oz. Lump Crabmeat
2 white potatoes, diced
1 can cream of mushroom soup
Salt/pepper to taste

In 2 –quart saucepan, melt butter or margarine. Sauté chopped onion and celery until just golden. Dissolve flour in one-half cup water and add to above. Then add chicken broth and diced potatoes. Bring to simmer and cook on low until potatoes are tender. DO NOT BOIL.

Next: Add crabmeat, milk, half & half, hot sauce, sherry or white wine and cream of mushroom soup.

Bring up to a simmer again without boiling. Serve immediately. Enjoy!

Note: You'll want to at least double this recipe, and add more liquid if too thick (water, milk, broth, your choice).

*Buon Appetito!*

# *Kathy's Chili*

*Serves 4*

*Everyone makes Chili different, and this is my version of
an old standby. Enjoy!*

1 lb. ground beef
1 to 2 tbsp. butter
1 small onion, diced
1 clove garlic
1 green bell pepper, diced
1 No. 2 can red kidney beans
1 large can tomatoes
1 can water
1 tsp. salt
¼ tsp. black pepper
2 tbsp. chili powder
Gravy Master or Kitchen Bouquet

Melt butter in heavy frying pan. Add onion and garlic. Sauté. Add meat; sauté till brown. Add remaining ingredients. Stir; cover.

Cook over low heat 20 – 25 minutes. Stir Occasionally. Add more water as it cooks if a thinner consistency is desired.

Note: Add more chili powder to taste as the chili cooks.

Serve as is or with cooked macaroni for "Chili-Mac," or with bowls of toppings such as sour cream, grated cheeses, chopped raw onion.

*Note: The green bell pepper in my Chili sets it apart and I also add a couple caps of "Gravy Master" or "Kitchen Bouquet" to darken the sauce, but this is optional.*

*I also have been known to "kick it up a notch" as Emeril Lagasse would say – by adding more (hot) chili powder or a little hot sauce, crushed red pepper flakes, hot peppers from my garden – or – some Emeril's "Essence"! Experiment – it's fun!*

# Lentil Soup

*Serves 4 to 6*

*One of my husband's favorite soups.*

1 lb. dry lentil beans
Water
2 – 3 cloves garlic, minced
Olive oil
1 pkg. ham hocks or leftover ham bone, or 4 to 6
strips of bacon*
1 cup (small can tomatoes)
1 tsp. dried oregano leaves
½ tsp. salt
¼ tsp. black pepper
¼ tsp. crushed red pepper flakes, optional
Freshly grated romano cheese
8 oz. Ditalini pasta (small tube shape)

*If using ham hocks or leftover ham bone, just sauté the garlic and add the tomatoes, etc. first – then add the meat or bone when you combine all with lentils.

Cook lentils for about 2 hours in water to cover in a dutch oven pot.

Meanwhile:
In small saucepan or skillet: Cut bacon into small pieces and sauté along with garlic in a little olive oil till garlic is golden. Add diced tomatoes along with juice from can to the saucepan. Add the oregano, salt and pepper. Simmer together on low for a few minutes and then combine with the lentils. Add a handful of the freshly grated Romano cheese. Stir and cook for approximately 30-45 min. more low heat.

To serve, cook Ditalini pasta to al dente stage. Drain. Rinse. Place a large spoonful of cooked paste in each soup bowl, ladle soup over. Pass freshly grated romano cheese at the table to sprinkle over.

*Buon Appetito!*

# Lobster Bisque Italiano

*Serves 6*

*At the request of my son Michael – I came up with this recipe for a friend of his who has a restaurant in Dewey Beach, Maryland called The Salad Factory who was looking for a good recipe for Lobster Bisque.*

1 - 2 lbs. fresh or frozen Lobster meat*
1 medium onion, chopped fine
1 small whole shallot, chopped fine
3 cloves garlic, minced
½ cup butter
¼ cup flour (Wondra works best)
2 cans 14 ½ oz. each chicken broth
½ cup dry or semi-dry white wine
2 cups milk or light cream
2 cups broth from cooking lobster
1 14 ½ oz. can tomatoes, diced small
Salt/White pepper to taste
Fresh Parsley, chopped fine
Crushed red pepper (optional)

* Or buy a lobster at your local grocery store and have them steam it for you

Cover lobster in water in pan and bring to boil. Boil approximately 8-10 minutes. Remove from heat and reserve liquid. Plunge lobster in cold water immediately to stop cooking.

Cut lobster in bite-sized pieces. Sauté the onion, shallot, and garlic in butter in skillet until just clear (2 -3 minutes)

Stir in flour, seasonings and 1 – 2 tbsp. parsley. Stir till smooth and slightly bubbling. Add chopped tomatoes.

Cook on low heat 10 min. Stir occasionally, adding more lobster broth if too thick until desired consistency. Smells "delicious" at this point!

Add milk or light cream sparingly and a tbsp. tomato paste for color, stir to right consistency.

That's it. So easy, so "delicious!" *Buon Appetito!*

# Minestrone

*Serves 6*

*A nice hearty soup served with a crusty Italian bread.*

1 ¼ cups navy beans*
¼ lb. salt pork or ham hocks
3 tbsp. olive oil
1 small onion, chopped
2 cloves garlic, chopped fine
2 stalks celery
2 carrots
1 or 2 medium potatoes
¼ head cabbage
1 tbsp. chopped parsley
½ cup frozen peas
¼ cup tomato paste
Salt/pepper to taste
Romano cheese, grated fine
Ditalini pasta (short cut macaroni)

*You may use canned navy beans if time is short. No need to wash.

Heat 6 cups water to boiling in a large pot. Wash beans. Add to water. Simmer 2 hours. Remove from heat. Set aside to soak 1 hour. Then: add salt pork or ham hocks to beans. Return to heat and simmer 1 hour stirring once or twice.

Meanwhile: Heat in skillet 3 tbsp. oil. Sauté the garlic and onion in the oil until lightly browned. Set aside.

Wash, pare and dice potatoes. Wash and cut into ½ inch pieces the carrots and celery. Set aside. Wash cabbage, remove coarse outer leaves, ad shred finely.

Add all vegetables and garlic/onion mixture to beans. Add chopped parsley, salt, pepper, tomato paste. Simmer 1 hour longer or till beans are tender. Add frozen peas about 10 minutes before beans are done.

Serve soup with paste cooked al dente. Sprinkle with grated Romano cheese.

# New England Boiled Dinner

*Serves 4 to 6 people*

*Also known as "Corned Beef and Cabbage." One of Jim's absolute favorite dinners.*

3 to 4 lb. corned beef brisket
6 whole peppercorns
1 clove garlic, peeled and crushed

Add later
1 medium head cabbage
6 white potatoes, peeled & quartered
3 carrots, peeled & quartered
salt/pepper

Put brisket into a deep pot on stove with the peppercorns and crushed garlic clove and enough water to cover the meat. Bring it just to the boiling point, remove the scum that forms and simmer until tender – about 3 to 4 hours.

About 1 hour before done, add the potatoes and carrots.
Add ¼ of the head of cabbage. Cook about ½ hour until potatoes, carrots and meat are fork tender.

Add the remainder of the cabbage, quartered. Add salt and pepper as desired. Cook 15 minutes longer until cabbage is just tender, not cooked away.

Remove meat. Slice into serving portions. Serve in bowls with the boiled dinner. I always add a pat of butter to my bowl which gives it that extra special touch! Enjoy!

# Old-Fashioned Beef Stew

*Serves 4 - 6*

*I have been making this hearty stew for my family since the children were able to hold a spoon!*
*It became a favorite early on, especially during the winter months.*

1 – 2 lbs. lean beef, cubed
2 tbsp. cooking/olive oil
½ tsp. salt
¼ tsp. black pepper
1 medium onion, diced
2 cloves garlic, pressed/minced
2 ½ cups boiling water
1 med. size canned tomatoes
1 tbsp. Worcestershire sauce
4 small potatoes
4 carrots
1 pkg. frozen green peas

Add cooking/olive oil to skillet.

Brown meat on all sides.
Add diced onion, garlic. Sauté.
Add boiling water, canned tomatoes*, salt, pepper, and Worcestershire sauce.

Cover. Simmer on low for approximately 2 hours or till meat is tender.

Add potatoes and carrots. Cook for 15 minutes.
Add peas and cook 15 to 20 minutes longer.

Enjoy!

* Cut tomatoes into quarters or smaller before adding. Note: This cooks well in a crock pot (slow cooker). But I still sauté the meat, onions and garlic in cooking or olive oil in a skillet first. Then I put all remaining ingredients in the crock pot at the same time and let it cook all day. You can thicken the stew during last 15 minutes of cooking by dissolving 1 or 2 tbsps. flour in ¼ cup water and adding.

# Old-Fashioned Chicken Soup

*Serves 4 to 6*

*"Just like Mom used to make!" This recipe is especially for my children - Carl, Tara and Michael, because I truly believe in the benefits of this soup when you have a cold or the flu! Remember…eat some of Mom's "Old Fashioned Chicken Soup!"*

1 whole chicken*
3 or 4 stalks of celery, with leaf tops
1 medium onion, cut in half
4 carrots, cut in fourths
Parsley (fresh is best)
Salt/pepper to taste

*Boneless chicken parts are ok too, but the bones do add more flavor – you just have to pick them out at the end of cooking

I served my family this soup so many times when they didn't feel well and it seemed to work wonders! Try it… you'll like it!

Wash chicken. Place in a large pot and cover with water. Bring to a boil and simmer over medium-high heat for 15 minutes to bring foam to top. Skim off foam. Add celery stalks, carrots, onion and a sprig of parsley. Cover tightly. Reduce heat to a simmer. Simmer 2 – 3 hours. Add water if it seems to evaporate along the way.

Once cooked, put a large colander over a clean pot and pour soup into colander, letting the broth drain through into the clean pot and holding back the chicken and vegetables to cool slightly.

When cool enough to touch, pick chicken off bones and add to broth. Retrieve as many carrots and pieces of celery as you can next from vegetables you set aside and add them to the broth. Add a little freshly chopped parsley. Place in refrigerator to cool.

Few hours later or next day: Skim off the fat that has settled on the surface of the broth and discard. Cook noodles of your choice and serve with the soup. I keep the noodles separate as they will become too soft if store in the broth.

# *Pasta Fagioli*

*Serves: 4 to 6*

*Another soup I raised my family on. And
every once in a while I get brave and serve it to company!
I serve a nice salad first, followed by the soup, a nice crusty bread and wine and...people love it!*

1 lb. dry navy beans*
2 – 3 cloves garlic, minced
Olive oil
1 pkg. ham hocks or leftover ham bone
1 cup (small can) tomatoes
1 tsp. dried oregano leaves*
½ tsp. salt
¼ tsp. black pepper
¼ tsp. crushed red pepper flakes,
optional
Freshly grated Romano cheese
8 oz. Ditalini pasta (small tube shape)

* You may use 3 cans navy beans instead if short on time. If using, you would begin recipe where you sauté the garlic, etc. and add 2 - 3 cans of water to the pot when you combine everything and then only about 45 min. cooking time is required.

Wash dry navy beans well and check for stones. Place in large dutch oven pot and cover with water. Bring to boil, then remove from heat and set aside to soak 1 hour covered.

Next: Return beans to burner and begin cooking again over medium heat.
Meanwhile:
In small saucepan or skillet: Sauté garlic in a little olive oil till golden. Dice the tomatoes and add along with juice from can to the saucepan. Add the oregano, salt and pepper. Simmer together on low until blended and nice aroma. (few minutes)

Next: Combine beans and tomato mixture with ham hocks or ham bone in the dutch oven. Add a handful of the freshly grated Romano cheese. Stir and cook on medium-low heat until beans are tender, adding more water as it cooks if too thick.

To serve: Cook Ditalini pasta to al dente stage. Drain. Rinse. Place a large spoonful of cooked paste in deep soup bowl, ladle soup over. Pass fresh grated Romano cheese at the table to sprinkle over the soup. *Buon Appetito!*

# Potato Soup

*Serves 4-6*

*I consider this a "comfort food" – really great in Autumn
when you're just starting to think about how
good "soup" will taste on those damp, chilly nights!*

1 tbsp. butter
1 medium onion, chopped fine
6 large potatoes, peeled and diced
Water
2 to 3 cups of milk or the combination
of milk and half & half
2 tbsp. butter
Salt/pepper to taste

Sauté the onions in the 1 tbsp. butter in a medium sauce pan over medium-high heat until softened. Add potatoes and just enough water to cook, about 1 cup.

Season lightly with salt. Bring to boil. Cover. Reduce heat to low. Simmer until potatoes are tender, about 15 minutes.

Add the milk or combo of milk and half & half, remaining butter, salt and pepper to taste.

Continue cooking over medium heat until hot; do not boil.

With a potato masher, mash some of the potatoes right in the pot to slightly thicken the soup.

Enjoy!

# Real New England Clam Chowder

*This recipe was given to us by Jim's Navy buddy Paul's mother,*
*Noel, from Worcester, Massachusetts. She is deceased now*
*but used to always make this when she knew we were*
*coming to visit for us to take home.*
*A real favorite of Jim's!*

½ stick of Oleo or Butter
1 small onion, cut up
4 cups cubed potatoes (or more)
3 cans clams
1 can Carnation evaporated
milk
Salt/pepper

In a dutch oven pot over low heat on stove, cook the onion in the oleo or butter to a golden yellow.

Add 4 cups of cubed potatoes (or more if you wish).
Add the broth of your canned clams (set clams aside).
Add just enough water to cover potatoes. Cook until potatoes are done (fork tender).

Then add the clams with the can of Carnation milk, salt and pepper. Never let it boil.

Enjoy!

*Note: When she sent it home to Virginia with us, she left out the milk for us to add when we got home to keep it from spoiling until we were to serve it.*

# *Roasted Garlic Soup*

*Serves 4 -6*

*A nice hearty soup served with a crusty Italian bread.*

2 large whole unpeeled garlic heads, roasted - plus 1 clove, minced

3 tbsp. olive oil

2 Bay leaves

1 tbsp. unsalted butter

2 cups minced onion

1 cup minced carrots

1 large potato (1 ¼ cups), peeled and cubed

4 cups chicken stock

½ cup dry white wine

1 tsp. salt

½ tsp. fresh ground pepper

¼ cup heavy cream

To roast the garlic:

Cut off top of heads to expose top of each. Place on aluminum foil. Drizzle with olive oil. Add bay leaves and fold to form a packet. Place packet in 350 degrees oven for 45 minutes. Cool slightly. Squeeze garlic into small bowl. Discard paper covering and bay leaf.

Make soup:

In pot, heat remaining olive oil, butter, onions. Cook over medium heat until onion are translucent (4 minutes). Add carrots and continue to cook 5 min. more. Add clove of minced garlic and cook for 2 min. Stir in potato, chicken stock, white wine, roasted garlic, salt/pepper.

Reduce heat to med – low and continue to cook for 35 min.

**Finishing**:

Blend/puree the soup in small batches till smooth. Return to saucepan over med. Heat and whisk in the heavy cream. Heat till warm. (Do not boil.) Serve and enjoy.

# Roman Spinach/Egg Soup

*Serves 4 - 6*

*This has become one of my granddaughter Jennifer's,
favorite soups!*

1 quart chicken broth, homemade* or bought
3 eggs, or cholesterol-free egg substitute
1 ½ tbsp. semolina or flour
1 ½ tbsp. grated Romano cheese
¼ cup minced fresh parsley
1 tbsp. minced fresh basil
2 tbsp. lemon juice
¼ tsp. pepper
¼ tsp. salt
8 cups fresh spinach washed, stems removed and chopped
<u>Variation</u>: Serve ladled over cooked noodles in soup bowl if desired.

*For homemade chicken broth, see broth in "Old Fashioned Chicken Soup recipe in this cookbook

Bring chicken broth just to boil in 4 quart Dutch oven pot over medium heat.

Beat together eggs or egg substitute, flour, grated cheese, parsley, basil, lemon juice, salt and pepper.

Set aside.

Chop spinach, removing and discarding stems. Add spinach to broth. Stir and simmer on low until spinach is cooked – about 10 minutes.

Slowly pour egg mixture into broth and spinach, whisking constantly so egg threads form. Simmer 2 – 3 minutes more until egg is cooked.

Serve immediately in bowls alone or atop cooked noodles. Garnish with lemon slices if desired. Pass more grated Romano cheese to sprinkle over.

*Buon Appetito!*

# Shrimp Chowder

*Serves 4 -6*

*This recipe is so easy and delicious!*

¾ cup margarine
¾ cup chopped onions
¾ cup flour
6 cups milk
1 ½ cups low-fat chicken broth
2 cups fresh or frozen corn*
1 lb. cooked, deveined shrimp
Salt/pepper to taste
Couple shakes of Emeril's Original Essence spice

*Can also use creamed corn

Note: Works well also if you substitute trans-fat-free margarine and whole wheat flour

Melt margarine in pan. Sauté onion till golden.

Add flour and a little milk and stir until smooth and bubbly. Add remaining milk. Continue cooking over medium heat, stirring until thickened.

Add chicken broth, corn, shrimp and seasonings.

Cover and cook over low heat just until heated through.

Serve with biscuits or rolls and/or a nice salad.

*Buon Appetito!*

# Spanish Black Bean Soup

*Serves approximately 8*

*Nice served by candlelight even to company.*
*Jim and I first had this soup in a restaurant in Tampa, Florida*
*years ago and we serve it in steps just their way.*

1 lb. dry Black beans
6 to 8 cups water
Ham hocks or leftover ham bone*
1 small onion, chopped
2 or 3 stalks celery with leaves
1 clove garlic, minced
Salt and pepper to taste
2 cups Uncle Ben's Long-Grain
white rice, cooked according to directions on box
*May use a couple strips bacon in place of ham hocks or ham bone if you don't have the other
**Optional – add some grated Romano cheese to the soup as it cooks or pass it at the table and sprinkle over.

Rinse beans well in colander under cold water. Check for stones. Drain.

Place on stove in large pot with the water. Bring beans to boiling, boil 2 minutes, and then shut off for an hour.

Add meat and return to heat and simmer with the chopped onion, celery, garlic, salt and pepper to taste for minimum of 3 hours, covered. Stir occasionally, adding water to replace any that cooks away.

Remove the celery to a blender with about one cup of the cooked beans. Puree together, then stir back into pot. Taste and correct seasoning.

Serve as follows: Place ½ cup cooked rice in each bowl, ladle soup over rice, then … pass the chopped onion to garnish top of soup – encourage the onion … it enhances the flavor of the soup! Serve with a good bread and your favorite wine. My original recipe!

My children would remember the first time I serve this soup to them – I turned the lights down low, put the candles on the table, etc. and they said – "You can't fool us – this soup is black!" But they tasted it and loved it. It remains a favorite of theirs to this day!

# Vegetable Soup, Italian-Style

*Serves 4-6*

*An old, hearty standby in our house. Great for those cold, snowy, wintry evenings.*

1 pound stewing beef
2 tbsp. olive oil
1 large onion, sliced or diced
2 cloves garlic, minced
1 large (1 lb. 12 oz.) can Italian
plum tomatoes
2 – 3 cups water
2 medium carrots, sliced or diced
3 celery sticks, sliced
3 large potatoes, peeled and diced
6 oz. green beans, sliced in bite-sized pieces
1 can white beans (Navy or other)
½ small head cabbage, sliced thinly
¾ cup green peas
2 tbsp. chopped Italian parsley
Salt/pepper
Small pasta shapes, cooked al dente
Romano cheese, freshly grated
Crushed red pepper, optional

Heat the olive oil in dutch oven pot. Add the onion and garlic and sauté until golden. Remove and set aside. Cut stewing beef into bite-sized cubes and sauté in same pot until brown. Add onions and garlic back, along with the carrots and celery and cook 2 – 3 minutes more until vegetables are softened.

Add the tomatoes, water, potatoes, green beans, white beans, salt and pepper to taste.

Cook 1 hour until the beef cubes are fork tender. Add the cabbage, green peas, Italian parsley and a handful of freshly grated Romano cheese. Cook additional 15 minutes.

To serve: Place a large spoonful of the small cooked pasta shapes in soup bowl, top with soup and pass more freshly grated Romano cheese and crushed red pepper (optional) to sprinkle over. ***Buon Appetito!***

Vegetables

# Artichoke Hearts au Gratin

*Serves 8*

*You may prepare the béchamel sauce the day before to get a jump-start on this recipe. This makes a wonderful accompaniment to dinner or great served as an appetizer before dinner.*

2 boxes frozen artichoke hearts or
2 cans artichoke hearts, drained
1 lemon, cut in half
1 sprig of thyme
1 tsp. whole peppercorns
1 small bay leaf
4 cups béchamel sauce (see recipe*)
1 tbsp. unsalted butter
Salt and fresh ground pepper to taste
4 slices Prosciutto, cut in half cross- wise

Béchamel Sauce
1 tablespoon minced onion
3 tablespoons unsalted butter
¼ cup all-purpose flour
3 cups milk
¼ tsp. salt
White pepper, to taste

**Prepare Béchamel Sauce**

Cook the onion in the butter over moderately low heat, Stirring, until it is softened.

Stir in the flour and cook the "roux" for 2 minutes, stirring constantly. Watch closely so it doesn't burn.

Add the milk, whisking vigorously until mixture is thick and smooth. Add the salt and white pepper. Simmer the sauce for 10-15 minutes, or until thickened to desired consistency. Strain the sauce through a fine sieve into a bowl. Cover the surface with a piece of buttered waxed paper to prevent skin from forming.

**Proceed**

If using frozen artichoke hearts…place in pot of water with the lemon cut in half, thyme, peppercorns, and bay leaf. Cover with lid and cook over medium heat until artichokes are tender when pierced with knife,
approximately 10 – 15 minutes. Drain.

Heat oven to 350 degrees. Grease glass gratin baking dish. Ladle in half of the béchamel sauce. Place artichoke hearts on top of the béchamel sauce. Season with salt and pepper to taste.

Place folded Prosciutto into each artichoke heart. Fill with mound of béchamel sauce. Bake 20-25 minutes till golden. Serve 2 or 3 hearts per person spooning some of the sauce over. Enjoy.

# *Artichokes, Served Whole*

*Serves 4*

*My family likes these served alongside a good old-fashioned spaghetti dinner.*

4 whole artichokes, washed
Butter, melted, for dipping

Note: Some people like to dip their cooked artichoke leaves in mayonnaise or béarnaise sauce instead of butter, simply whatever your preference.

Wash the artichokes and drain. Cut stems off to sit flat when cooking.
Cut the pointy tips off each leaf on each artichoke with sharp knife.

Place artichokes heads up in a deep dutch oven pot in about 1 inch water on stove. Bring water to boiling. Place lid on and cook over mediumlow heat approximately 45 minutes until a leaf pulls away easily from artichoke indicating they are done. Check occasionally to see if more water is needed while cooking. Drain.

Serve individually alongside each person's dinner, or – can be served first as an appetizer. Provide each person a warmer with melted butter. To eat, break the leaves away from the artichoke one at a time and dip in the melted butter and scrape the cooked artichoke pulp off each leaf by scraping with your teeth. Enjoy!

# Baked Tomato Halves, Italian-style

*Serves 6*

*Good also done quickly under the broiler.*

3 large tomatoes
1 ½ tsp. salt
1 tbsp. chopped parsley
1 tsp. chopped oregano leaves
Grated Romano cheese*
1 tbsp. butter or margarine

* We use Locatelli cheese

Wash tomatoes; remove stem end and cut in half.
Sprinkle tomatoes with salt, chopped parsley, chopped oregano, and grated Romano cheese.

Dot each half with butter.
Bake at 350 degrees for 30 minutes or till golden and tender.

# Best Baked Beans

*Serves 4 - 6*

*So easy and so good!*

2 large cans Pork 'n Beans
1 tsp. prepared mustard
4 rounded tbsp. brown sugar
4 tbsp. ketchup
1 small onion, chopped

Mix all ingredients together.

Pour into greased casserole.

Bake in preheated 350 degrees oven for approximately 20 – 30 minutes.

# Broccoli/Cauliflower Casserole

*Serves 6*

*Easy, popular side dish in our family. Yummy!*

2 pkgs. frozen broccoli
2 pkgs. frozen cauliflower
2 jars Cheez Whiz
2 containers dried onions
2 – 3 cans cream of mushroom soup

Thaw frozen broccoli & cauliflower according to pkg. directions.

Place in appropriate size buttered casserole. Stir in soup and Cheez Whiz. Crush dried onions and stir in. Bake approximately 30 – 35 minutes in a 325 degrees oven until bubbly.

Serve.

Note: May be prepared ahead of time and refrigerated until ready to bake.

# Broccoli Florentine

*Serves 4*

*A favorite of my husband, Jim's! Wonderful aroma fills the kitchen while it's cooking!*

1 lb. broccoli, fresh or frozen
1 tsp. salt
3 – 4 tbsp. olive oil
Pat of butter
2 – 3 cloves garlic, sliced

Par cook broccoli in salted water until just tender when pierced with fork. Drain and set aside.

Meanwhile, in a skillet, sauté garlic slices in the olive oil/butter combination until lightly golden brown – careful not to burn. Discard garlic.

Add drained broccoli to skillet. Sauté broccoli lightly, turning occasionally – careful again not to burn. Season with salt and pepper and serve.

# Chiles Rellenos

*Serves 4 to 6*

*These are great served alone or with a side of Mexican fried rice and refried beans.*

1 can (4 oz.) green chilies
4 to 6 pieces Monterey Jack cheese, each about
   2 x 1 x ½ inches
3 eggs, separated
2 tbsp. all-purpose flour
Cooking oil for frying

Sauce
½ onion, minced
1 clove garlic, minced
1 tbsp. cooking oil
1 can (1 lb. 12 oz.) whole tomatoes
1 jar (14 oz.) chicken stock
1 ½ tsp. salt
½ tsp. black pepper
1 tsp. oregano

In a skillet, sauté onion and garlic in oil. Blend tomatoes, chicken stock and seasonings in blender till smooth. Add to onion mixture and bring to boil. Simmer 5 min. Just before serving the rellenos put them into the sauce just long enough to heat through. Serve.

Preheat 1 ½ inches of cooking oil in frypan (electric) to 400 degrees.

Carefully remove seeds and ribs from chili peppers.

Beat egg whites until stiff with electric mixer.
Beat egg yolks lightly.
Fold egg yolks and flour lightly into beaten egg whites.

Stuff the green chilies with the slices of Monterey cheese.
Gently drop the stuffed chilies into egg mixture, one at a time.

Pick each one up with a spoon and place in preheated oil.
Fry until golden, turn and brown second side.
Drain on absorbent paper. Serve as is or with sauce.

# Brown Rice

*Serves 6*

*As simple as it gets and very good!*

1 cup long-grain white rice
3 beef boullion cubes
¼ cup onion, chopped
1 tsp. celery salt
¼ cup butter
2 ½ cups boiling water

Spread rice out on a flat pan.

Roast at 275 degrees, stirring occasionally, until golden brown.

Place rice in a 1 ½ quart casserole.
Dissolve boullion cubes in boiling water.
Add to the rice with all remaining ingredients.
Bake at 350 degrees for 30 minutes.

# Crunchy Broccoli Casserole

*Serves 6*

*Easy, popular side dish in our family. Kids like it!*

2 pkgs. frozen broccoli
1 can cream of mushroom soup
1 ½ tsp. table cream
1 cup grated cheddar cheese
4 tbsp. butter
1 cup Italian-style breadcrumbs
½ cup slivered almonds
Salt/pepper to taste

Cook broccoli according to pkg. directions until fork tender.
Drain – reserving ½ cup liquid.

Combine soup, table cream, reserved liquid, salt and pepper.
Pour over broccoli. Sprinkle with grated cheese, pats of butter and breadcrumbs.
Top with slivered almonds.

Bake approximately 30 – 35 minutes in a 325 degrees oven.

Note: May be prepared ahead of time and refrigerated until ready to bake.

# Eggs, Potatoes & Peppers

*Serves 4*

*An old "stand-by" Jim's mother taught me! Good quick meal when you're in a hurry or don't feel like a meat dish. Delicious! My kids loved it growing up. Jim and I still make it for ourselves.*

4 to 6 mediums to large potatoes*
4 eggs
2 to 3 green bell peppers**
Cooking oil or olive oil
Pat or two of butter
Salt/Pepper

* I use white Idaho-type potatoes
** You may use any kind of peppers —mild, hot, etc. — Jim likes hot banana peppers if cooking just for the two of us.

Cover the bottom of a non-stick skillet with the oil/butter. Heat to medium.

Slice the potatoes (peel on or off – your choice) in oval slices. Add to skillet. Remove stems and seeds from peppers. Slice them lengthwise. Add to skillet with potatoes. Raise heat to medium-high. Sauté until potatoes get crispy and basically cooked (fork tender).

Sprinkle with salt and pepper.

Crack the eggs over all one at a time, turning mixture with spatula all the time until all the egg is distributed and cooked.

Serve immediately and enjoy. Smells delicious. Is delicious! We serve this with the Italian tomato salad found in this book for an easy, economical and nourishing meal!

# Garlic Mashed Potatoes

*Serves 6 to 8people*

*Enjoy these in a restaurant? Very easy to make and "gourmet" delicious!*

Roasting the garlic
1 large head garlic
Salt
Olive oil, with or without basil added

Cooking the potatoes
6 to 8 potatoes
2 thinly sliced raw garlic cloves
Butter*
Salt/pepper*
Milk or half & half (warm if you wish) *

*Desired amounts for desired consistency & taste.

Preheat oven to 325 degrees. Cut off top third of large head of garlic. Put the head of garlic in a greased baking dish top of head up. Add a little water to dish. Drizzle olive oil over head.

Cover with lid or aluminum foil. Bake about 1 hour until garlic is soft and tender. Squeeze the garlic out of its paper shell and set aside in small bowl.

Next: Peel, rinse and cut into cubes the potatoes. Put potatoes in dutch oven pot. Cover by 1 inch with cold water. Add ¼ to ½ tsp. salt. Add the raw garlic slices.

Bring water to boil and cook potatoes/garlic about 15-20 min. until potatoes are tender. Drain water off. Immediately add to potatoes & garlic in same saucepan the milk (or Half & Half), butter, roasted garlic, salt & pepper (to taste) and mash either by hand or electric mixer. Serve & enjoy a real gourmet treat!

# Green Beans with Almonds

*Serves 6*

*These are a good accompaniment to just about any main meat dish.*

2 (10 oz.) packages frozen green beans
1/3 cup slivered blanched almonds
½ cup melted butter or margarine

Cook beans according to package directions.
Drain.

Sauté' almonds in butter in small skillet until golden.

Pour over hot, drained beans.
Enjoy!

# Roasted Pepper Strips

*Good side dish for roast beef and a delicious*

*addition to an antipasto tray, Italian sub sandwiches, pizza – you name it!*

3 green Bell peppers
1 Red sweet pepper
¼ cup olive oil
1 ½ tbsp. red wine vinegar
½ tsp. salt
¼ tsp. black pepper
1 clove garlic, quartered

Remove seeds from peppers and cut lengthwise into ¼ inch strips. Place in oblong baking dish. Mix remaining ingredients.

Pour over peppers. Let stand, turning occasionally, at least 1 hour.

Heat oven to 375 degrees. Bake peppers until crisp tender, about 25 minutes. Enjoy!

# Herbed Spinach Casserole

*Serves 6*

*Very good and great way to get your spinach!*
*Our kids used to love this cut in squares and eaten cold.*

1 (10 oz.) pkg. chopped spinach
1 cup cooked rice, white or brown
1 cup grated sharp cheese
¼ cup grated mozzarella cheese
2 eggs, slightly beaten
2 tbsp. melted butter
½ cup milk
2 tbsp. chopped onion
½ tsp. Worcestershire sauce
1 tsp. salt
¼ tsp. thyme

Cook and drain spinach. Cool. Mix with remaining ingredients and place in greased shallow baking dish (10 x 6 x 1 ½ inch).

Bake at 350 degrees for 25 – 30 minutes until just turning golden at the edges and on top.
Serve.

Note: Can be cut into squares and served that way too. I use fresh thyme from my herb garden.

# New Potatoes & Scallions

*Serves 4- 6 people*

*A little different "twist" on serving potatoes. Delicious!*

15 to 20 tiny redskin
new potatoes
Scallions
Butter
Salt/pepper

Wash the potatoes and put them in a dutch oven pot on the stove covered with water to which you have added a little salt.

Bring the water to boiling and boil the potatoes until done (fork tender) – about 20 minutes.

Drain the water off. Add desired amount of sliced scallions (green tops included), butter and salt and pepper. Turn potatoes with a large spoon to coat evenly with the butter/ scallion mixture. Serve as an accompaniment to any meat.

# Mexican Rice

*Serves 8*

*I raised my kids on this which I usually served alongside tacos.*

3 tbsp. cooking oil
Pat of butter
2 cups rice, white or brown
1 cup chopped onion
1 clove garlic, minced
2 (10 oz.) cans chicken broth
1 (8 oz.) can tomato sauce
½ green or red bell pepper, diced
½ tsp. salt
1/8 tsp. black pepper

Pour the oil in medium-sized saucepan.
Sauté the onion and garlic in the oil.
Add the rice and pat of butter and sauté the rice with the onion and garlic until rice is golden brown.

Add the chicken broth, tomato sauce, bell pepper, salt and pepper.
Cover and cook on low heat for approximately 20 minutes until liquid is absorbed and rice is cooked. Check occasionally to keep from burning once liquid is absorbed.
Serve.

# Potato Pancakes

*Serves 4*

*These are a good accompaniment to just about any main meat dish or serve alone as a meal in itself. My mother's were the best!*

1 egg
2 tbsp. flour
Milk
Salt
Pepper
Onion, finely chopped or onion-juice
Cooking oil, Crisco or other pat of butter
Serve with a dollop of sour cream, optional

Scrub and peel potatoes. Grate into cold water to keep from discoloring. Drain well.

Add the egg, well-beaten, the flour, and enough milk to make a stiff batter.
Season with salt, pepper and stir in the onions or onion-juice.

Heat about ½ inch cooking oil with a pat of butter in skillet.
Use a large spoonful of batter for each pancake and fry in the hot oil until browned and crisp on each side. Serve with meat of your choice or as a meal in itself. Enjoy!

# Old-Fashioned Scalloped Potatoes

*Serves 6 to 8*

*Just like my mother used to make!*

5 to 6 medium potatoes
1 medium onion, chopped (1/2 cup)
2 tablespoons flour
4 tbsp. butter
½ tsp. salt
¼ tsp. pepper
3 cups milk, more or less

Peel raw potatoes and cut into thin slices. Place in a buttered baking dish a layer of potatoes one inch deep. Season with part of the salt/pepper. Sprinkle a portion of the flour over, and a part of the butter cut into small pats.

Then add another layer of potatoes, flour, butter pats and seasonings. It is advisable not to have more than two or three layers, if possible, because of the difficulty cooking thoroughly.

Add milk until it can be seen between the potato slices, cover and Bake at 350 degrees - 400 degrees F until potatoes are fork tender-approximately 1 – 1 ½ hours. Remove cover the last 15 minutes to brown the top. Serve.

# Spinach Sautéed with Garlic

*Serves 4*

*Very easy, tasty way to serve spinach!*

1 lb. fresh spinach
2 – 3 tbsp. olive oil
1 tbsp. butter
6 cloves garlic, chopped fine
Salt
Fresh ground black pepper
2 – 3 tbsp. fresh grated Romano Cheese

Wash and dry spinach.

Sauté garlic in olive oil and butter over medium heat until just lightly golden, being careful not to burn the garlic.

Add the spinach and sauté just until wilted, about 2 to 3 minutes. Remove from heat. Serve.

Sprinkle with fresh grated Romano cheese and a little salt and pepper. Serve immediately

# *Old-Fashioned Mashed Potatoes*

*Serves 4 to 6 people*

*Nothing fancy, just down home good! I raised my family on these!*

5 to 6 medium-sized white potatoes
Milk*
Butter
Salt
Black pepper

*Warm the milk if you wish

Peel and rinse potatoes. Cut into large chunks.
Place potatoes in a medium saucepan. Cover with cold water.

Bring potatoes to a boil. Reduce heat. Simmer 15 – 20 minutes or until tender when pierced with a fork. Drain. Immediately add to potatoes in the saucepan desired amount of milk, butter, salt and black pepper. Add these a little at a time beating* the entire time until you reach desired consistency and taste. Serve immediately.

* I use an electric mixer, but some people still use the old-fashioned hand potato masher.

*Note: On Thanksgiving – for something a little more special – I peel and cook 2 – 3 turnips (either in with the potatoes or in another pot with water just as you do the potatoes). Mash them together. I got the idea from my friend, Ann Lavallee, in Massachusetts. Delicious*

# Ricotta Spinach Croquettes

*Serves 8*

*A versatile recipe that can be what you want it to be, appetizer, entrée
or accompaniment, leftovers are delicious!*

1 lb. ricotta cheese, well-drained
10 oz. pkg. frozen chopped spinach
1 large egg
1 tsp. salt
¼ tsp. black pepper
½ tsp. crushed oregano leaves
¼ tsp. garlic powder
¼ cup grated Romano cheese
Egg/water combination
1-2 large eggs
1 -2 tbsp. water

Italian or plain dry breadcrumbs
Olive oil

Drain the ricotta cheese well over cheesecloth (or paper towel works) in colander.

Cook spinach about 5 minutes per pkg. Drain well. Cool slightly.

Combine ricotta cheese, spinach, 1 egg, salt, pepper, oregano, garlic powder and Romano cheese in bowl.
Stir to blend well.

Cover and refrigerate at least 1 hour.

Pick up 1 rounded tablespoon of mixture at a time, shaping into thick 2-inch smooth rounds. Now flatten slightly.

Dip croquette into well-beaten egg/water combination. Drain well.

Coat with breadcrumbs. Let stand on waxed paper 10-15 minutes turning over in between.

Sauté 3 min. each side in ¼ inch medium hot oil till golden and crisp. Serve as you wish, ladled with your favorite Italian tomato/meat sauce* as a main dish or as an appetizer with bowl of sauce for dipping.

*See recipes in this book for spaghetti sauce/quick spaghetti sauce.

# Scalloped Potatoes With Cheese

*Serves 6 to 8*

*Savor the distinctive nutty, rich flavor of the Gruyere cheese!*

5 to 6 medium potatoes
1 medium onion, chopped (1/2 cup)
2 cloves garlic, minced
3 tablespoons olive oil
3 tablespoons all-purpose flour
½ tsp. salt
¼ tsp. pepper
3 to 4 cups milk
4 ounces Gruyere cheese, shredded* (1 cup)

*Your choice, i.e., Swiss, cheddar Gruyere, etc.

Preheat oven to 350 degrees F. Grease a 2-quart round casserole (with cover); set casserole aside.

Peel potatoes and thinly slice (5 – 6 cups). Rinse.
Place slices in colander to drain. Make sauce:
Place onion, garlic and olive oil in medium saucepan. Cook till onion and garlic is tender, not brown. Stir in flour, salt, pepper. Add milk all at once. Cook and stir over medium heat till thickened and bubbly. Remove from heat.

Layer half of the potatoes in prepared casserole.
Cover with half the sauce. Sprinkle with half the cheese. Repeat layering with the potatoes and sauce.

Bake, covered for 40 minutes. Uncover and bake an additional 20 - 25 minutes till potatoes are just tender. Sprinkle with remaining cheese.

Bake, uncovered, 5 minutes more. Let stand 10 minutes before serving.

# String Beans and Sauce

*Serves 6*

*Easy, hearty meal! Filling!*

1 lb. pork country ribs
1 lb. fresh green beans
1 tbsp. olive oil
2 cloves garlic, minced
1 tbsp. dried oregano
1 can (1 lb. 13 oz.) tomato sauce
1 can (15 oz.) tomato sauce
½ cup water
1 loaf crusty Italian/French bread

Wash the green beans, cut off ends and set aside.
Sauté the country ribs in a dutch oven pot in the olive oil till browned on all sides. Add garlic and sauté just until golden.

Slowly add all the tomato sauce, water and oregano. Add the green beans. Stir. Bring to boiling and simmer on medium-low heat, stirring occasionally, until meat is tender and beans are fork tender (approx. 1 hour). Serve in large soup bowls with bread for dipping in the sauce.
Enjoy!

# Veggies Casino

*Serves 6*

*These are a good accompaniment to just about any main meat dish.*

1 yellow squash
1 zucchini squash
3 Roma tomatoes
Coarse salt
Garlic powder
1 Green bell pepper
1 mild red pepper
Red onion
3 – 4 slices Crispy bacon, crumbled
Romano cheese

Grease an oblong baking dish with butter. Slice veggies lengthwise in 2-inch pieces. Place in buttered casserole. Sprinkle garlic powder and crumbled bacon over with coarse salt and Romano cheese. Top with 3 pats of butter.

Bake at 350 degrees for 10 minutes until butter is melted. Stir veggies. Sprinkle a little more Romano cheese over all and continue baking until veggies are cooked – approximately 15-20 minutes more.

# *Twice Baked Potatoes*

*Serves 4*

*A delicious side to grilled steak or other meats. My friend, Juanita, taught me how to make these.
They are a little more "special" than the average baked potato!*

2 baked potatoes, cut in half
1 egg
¼ cup milk
2 tbsp. butter
¼ cup finely chopped red or green pepper
2 tbsp. chopped onion or scallions
1 cup cheddar, grated
Salt/pepper to taste
Paprika
Sour cream (optional)

Season two potatoes with butter, salt and pepper.
Cut an "x" in each potato to aid in cooking.
Wrap each potato in aluminum foil. Bake at 400 degrees for approximately 45 min. – 1 hr. till fork tender.

Remove from oven. Unwrap. Cut each potato in half. Scoop out cooked potato leaving the skin intact.

Mash potatoes lightly with all remaining ingredients except the paprika. Mound potatoes back in skins.

Sprinkle with paprika. Bake potatoes again in 350 degrees oven for approximately 20 – 25 minutes until golden.

Serve along side a steak or other meat. Enjoy!

Optional: Serve with a dollop of sour cream.

# *Walnut-Sage Potatoes Au Gratin*

*Serves 8 to 10*

*Savor the distinctive nutty, rich flavor of the Gruyere cheese!*

5 to 6 medium potatoes
1 medium onion, chopped (1/2 cup)
2 cloves garlic, minced
3 tablespoons walnut oil*
3 tablespoons all-purpose flour
½ tsp. salt
¼ tsp. pepper
3 cups milk
3 tablespoons snipped fresh sage
4 ounces Gruyere cheese, shredded (1 cup)
1/3 cup broken walnut pieces

* If you can't find walnut oil, just use olive oil or regular cooking oil – will turn out fine.

Preheat oven to 350 degrees Fahrenheit. Grease a 2-quart round casserole (with cover); set casserole aside.

Peel potatoes and thinly slice (5 – 6 cups). Rinse. Place slices in colander to drain.

Make sauce: Place onion, garlic and walnut oil in medium saucepan. Cook till onion and garlic is tender, not brown. Stir in flour, salt, pepper. Add milk all at once. Cook and stir over medium heat till thickened and bubbly. Remove from heat; stir in snipped sage.

Layer half of the potatoes in prepared casserole. Cover with half the sauce. Sprinkle with half the cheese. Repeat layering with the potatoes and sauce.

Bake, covered for 40 minutes. Uncover and bake an additional 25 minutes till potatoes are just tender. Sprinkle with remaining cheese and nuts over top. Bake, uncovered, 5 minutes more. Let stand 10 minutes. If desired, garnish with fresh sage leaves.

# *Roasted Asparagus, Italian-Style*

*Serves 4-6*

*This is one of our family's most favorite dishes. It is made from just a few simple ingredients but makes a perfectly delicious dish for any meal!*

1-2 bunches fresh asparagus
¼ cup Italian breadcrumbs
¼ cup grated Romano cheese
(we like to use Locatelli)
Garlic Powder
Olive oil
1-2 tbsp. butter, melted

Preheat your oven to 350 degrees. Wash asparagus. Pat dry. Snap off ends at the bottom of each spear. (These are the tough ends you discard.)

Melt the butter. Pour in bottom of a 9 by 13-inch rectangle baking dish. Drizzle a little olive oil in bottom of pan as well. Layer asparagus spears side by side in baking pan.
Toss them with your hands coating them with the melted butter and olive oil.

Sprinkle the breadcrumbs, grated cheese, and garlic powder over the top of the spears.

Roast in the oven, covered with aluminum foil, approximately 25-30 minutes. The time it takes for the asparagus to barely reach fork tender. Do not roast too long as asparagus will turn mushy. Adjust roasting time according to thickness of the asparagus, thin take less time, thicker, longer. Remove the foil carefully when checking doneness, the steam coming out will be hot. If you like asparagus, you will love this!

*Buon Appetito!*

# Index

## Beverages, 37

## Fish & Seafood, 155

## Miscellaneous, 229

## Sandwiches, 291

## Soups & Stews, 309

## Vegetables, 332

*Cheers! Buon Appetito'*

# About the Author

Kathy Mugnolo currently resides in Warrenton, Virginia, a small town in the foothills of the Shenandoah Mountains. Kathy grew up in a small town in Pennsylvania, surrounded by farms and gardens. Her childhood memories are of her mother always in the kitchen cooking and baking and her father tending his large vegetable garden and orchard. She looks back now and realizes what she had as a child. Come winter, the shelves in the canning kitchen of their home were filled top to bottom with everything they would enjoy from their garden all winter long.

It wasn't until she was grown and married that she realized the joy that comes from creating and cooking a memorable meal for her family. Sharing what she cooked with others soon brought her to realize that she was actually sharing more than just the food she cooked but also an intimate expression of love and friendship. The Lithuanian-Ukranian influence of her mother's and the Italian influence of her mother-in-law's cooking led Kathy to create the tried-and-true, easy recipes you find in this cookbook. Her message to you is as Julia Child once said, "Cook by ear. Learn to cook! This is done simply by learning as you go."

Kathy's other accomplishments are serving as past president of her garden club, compiling two successful cookbooks for the club, and past president and current newsletter editor of her antique club. Kathy's new venture with her husband is volunteering at a Willing Warriors Retreat Center to work on their Beautification Project and help the chefs in the kitchen when needed to help prepare the gourmet meal they provide the Willing Warrior and their family on Sunday evenings during their stay at the Retreat.

Remember this old English proverb, "Nothing is invented and perfected at the same time. Don't be afraid to experiment a little with food and enjoy!

*Buon Appetito!*